Also by Robert W. Merry

Taking On the World: Joseph and Stewart Alsop—
Guardians of the American Century

SANDS OF EMPIRE

MISSIONARY ZEAL, AMERICAN FOREIGN POLICY, AND THE HAZARDS OF GLOBAL AMBITION

Robert W. Merry

SIMON & SCHUSTER

NEW YORK · LONDON · TORONTO · SYDNEY

SIMON & SCHUSTER
Rockefeller Center
1230 Avenue of the Americas
New York, NY 10020

SIMON & SCHUSTER and colophon are registered trademarks of
Simon & Schuster, Inc.

For information about special discounts for bulk purchases,
please contact Simon & Schuster Special Sales at
1-800-456-6798 or business@simonandschuster.com

DESIGNED BY PAUL DIPPOLITO

Manufactured in the United States of America

1   3   5   7   9   10   8   6   4   2

Library of Congress Cataloging-in-Publication Data
Merry, Robert W., date.
Sands of empire : missionary zeal, American foreign policy, and
the hazards of global ambition / Robert W. Merry
p.   cm.
Includes bibliographical references (p.   ) and index.
1. United States—Foreign relations—1989– 2. United States—Military
policy. 3. Intervention (International law) 4. Imperialism. I. Title.
E840.M466   2005
327.73'009—dc22   2005042580
ISBN-13: 978-0-7432-6668-0

To the Memory of Steve Neal

Husband, Father, Reporter, Historian, Friend

CONTENTS

The Ozymandias Syndrome

I met a traveler from an antique land
Who said: Two vast and trunkless legs of stone
Stand in the desert. Near them, on the sand,
Half sunk, a shattered visage lies, whose frown,
And wrinkled lip, and sneer of cold command,
Tell that its sculptor well those passions read
Which yet survive, stamped on these lifeless things,
The hand that mocked them, and the heart that fed;
And on the pedestal these words appear:
"My name is Ozymandias, king of kings:
Look on my works, ye Mighty, and despair!"
Nothing beside remains. Round the decay
Of that colossal wreck, boundless and bare,
The lone and level sands stretch far away.

—PERCY BYSSHE SHELLEY, "OZYMANDIAS"

I RECALL PRECISELY when Shelley's powerful poem first intruded into my consciousness as I sought out what would become the essential argument of this book. I was rereading the criticism that surged from intellectual circles in response to Francis Fukuyama's famous 1989 essay, "The End of History?" Fukuyama had caused a swirl of spirited debate by suggesting in *The National Interest* magazine that the West's coming Cold War victory marked the culmination of mankind's development—"the universalization of Western liberal democracy as the final form of human government." The particular essay before me was a knife thrust toward the heart by Irving Kristol, the neoconservative writer and thinker, who dismissed Fukuyama's thesis with the words, "I don't believe a word of it."

Kristol could not buy Fukuyama's concept of America and the West as the wave of the future because, he said, he didn't place any stock in waves of the future. Instead, he suggested that all such waves are temporary, receding ultimately into the undertow of history. Citing Aristotle, Kristol argued that "all forms of government—democracy, oligarchy, aristocracy, monarchy, tyranny—are inherently unstable . . . all political regimes are inherently transitional . . . the stability of all regimes is corrupted by the corrosive power of time."

That's when I thought of Ozymandias with his haughty sneer and conceit that his mighty empire represented some kind of historical culmination. I thought, "This is precisely what Kristol is talking about." "The End of History?" will be crushed by history, as Kristol and Aristotle and Shelley all teach us.

And yet the fundamental Fukuyama thesis—that America and the West represent a culminating universal culture that offers peace and happiness to the world's other peoples if they will simply embrace it—retains a powerful hold on the American consciousness. Indeed, it shapes and drives American foreign policy in the post–Cold War era. As President Bill Clinton's deputy secretary of state, Strobe Talbott, put it around the time of America's 1999 bombing campaign against Yugoslavia, U.S. foreign policy is "consciously intended to advance universal values"—with particular emphasis on the word *universal*. A few years later, as the American occupation of Iraq took on the appearance of a geopolitical trap, George W. Bush's national security adviser, Condoleezza Rice, wrote of spreading America's "vision of democracy and prosperity" throughout the Middle East and predicted that the people there would "fully join the progress of our times" if they just had "greater political and economic freedom and better, more modern education." Some weeks later the president himself echoed those sentiments, declaring that "freedom can be the future of every nation" and committing America to perhaps decades of struggle in behalf of this goal of freedom. He invoked God in saying that "we can be sure that the author of freedom is not indifferent to the fate of freedom."

As these sentiments propel America toward a level of global ambition unprecedented in the country's history, some powerful questions emerge: What is the intellectual etymology of these notions? How did they develop? And, perhaps most important, where are they leading us?

Those questions and the corollary search for answers form the basis of this book. I will seek to demonstrate that America's prevailing foreign policy outlook and its "End of History" conceit emanate from a certain strain of Western thinking that emerged over centuries of intellectual development. It goes by the name of the "Idea of Progress," and it is a distinctly Western concept. It is the notion that mankind has advanced over the centuries through quickening stages of development, from primitiveness and barbarism to enlightenment and civilization—and that mankind will continue to advance throughout the human experience on earth. "No single idea has been more important than, perhaps as important as, the idea of progress in Western civilization," writes Robert Nisbet, who produced a history of the concept in 1980.

The Idea of Progress has animated the thinking, to some degree and in some fashion, of nearly every significant Western philosopher since its first stirrings in the thirteenth century. But this regnant Western concept, as I shall seek to show, contains two internal contradictions that can complicate Western efforts to see the world as it truly is, and a particular corollary of the Idea tends to generate mischief in the realms of political and social activity. In short, the Idea of Progress, so powerful in Western thought and so thoroughly an unconscious bedrock of the American outlook in the post–Cold War era, is guiding America in directions that could prove troublesome for the country, perhaps even disastrous.

Standing contradictory to the Idea of Progress is another view of history that has emerged at various times in Western thought. It is sometimes called the "Idea of Decline," but this is misleading.

Just as the bicyclist knows that every incline along the road carries with it the prospect of a corollary descent, every cultural or societal decline can only happen following a corollary cultural or societal rise. Thus I prefer the term "Cycles of History" or the "Cyclical View of History." This is the idea that history is the story of various discrete cultures or civilizations that emerge, develop, reach maturity, and then inevitably decline. The two greatest twentieth-century proponents of this concept were Oswald Spengler and Arnold Toynbee, although others explored the notion of cultural decline and historical cycles both before and after these two: Jacob Burkhardt, Friedrich Nietzsche, Vilfredo Pareto, Georges Sorel, Fernand Braudel. In America, the Adams brothers, Henry and Brooks, offered New World versions of this cyclical outlook at the turn of the twentieth century. And Arthur M. Schlesinger Sr. pioneered a way of looking at his country's history based on political cycles "between public purpose and private interest," as his son, Arthur Schlesinger Jr., described it in his 1986 book, *The Cycles of American History*—a process of determinism in which each new phase flows out of the conditions and contradictions of the phase before it.

The Cyclical View of History, as applied to civilizations and cultures, carries with it certain underlying perceptions. First, cultures and civilizations are distinct, and so there can be no universal culture. No body of thought emanating from one culture can be imposed upon another, either peacefully or through force. Civilizational decline is an immutable rule that applies to the West just as it does to every other culture; indeed, both Spengler and Toynbee, in the early decades of the twentieth century, viewed the West as already in decline. Finally, the Cyclical View rejects utterly the Idea of Progress, particularly the notion that it applies to all mankind.

These two Western views of history—the Idea of Progress and the Cyclical View—emerged as subtexts in the profound debate that materialized in America following the West's Cold War victory in 1989. The fifty-year era of bipolar balance of power (or terror) was now over, and intellectuals naturally probed for answers as to what was going to replace it. Many theories and notions emerged, but the two with the greatest weight turned out to be tied to the two contrasting views of history.

The Idea of Progress lay at the heart of Fukuyama's End of History notions and also the related globalization thesis that captured the fancy of some journalists and thinkers about the same time. This is the notion that the integration of capital, technology, information, and peoples across national borders is creating a global convergence of politics, economics, and culture. According to this view, this powerful global integration will force the spread of free market capitalism throughout the world. That's because no other system can accommodate these new economic forces. And where free market capitalism thrives, the reasoning goes, Western democratic liberalism inevitably will take root.

Thus we see in both the End of History thesis and its globalization variant strong strains of the Progress idea—that mankind's development over centuries is reaching a kind of end point, defined as Western democratic liberalism and free market capitalism.

Standing athwart this outlook comes the Clash of Civilizations thesis put forth by Harvard Professor Samuel P. Huntington in his famous 1993 *Foreign Affairs* article and later in book form. Huntington argued that the twenty-first century will be shaped not by ideology or big-power maneuverings or inexorable waves of economic convergence but by the immutable force of culture. Cultural impulses, identities, outlooks, and animosities, he wrote, will drive geopolitical events into the future, often in ways that could be quite brutal and persistent.

In putting forth his thesis, Huntington rejected not only the End of History/globalization concept but also the Idea of Progress upon which it rests. Without embracing the full philosophical framework of either Spengler or Toynbee (whose fundamental political perspectives are actually very much at variance), Huntington accepts certain key elements of their Cyclical outlook. These include the inevitability of Western decline; indeed, like Spengler and Toynbee, he suspects this decline has already begun. He sees the various civilizations of history and their present-day remnants as unique and thus rejects the notion of a universal culture. And, instead of seeing America's urge to spread its values around the world as a recipe for global peace, he sees it as a likely spur to instability and bloodshed.

THE AIM OF THIS BOOK is twofold. First, I will seek to provide a historical prism through which to view and analyze the geopolitical events of our time, particularly America's struggle against the rise of Islamic fundamentalist terrorism directed at U.S. citizens and the West in general. I believe the debates surrounding those events and that struggle are discernible only through an understanding of the Idea of Progress as the antecedent of American foreign policy in the post-9/11 era. Likewise, the true nature of the choices facing the nation cannot be fully appreciated without a sense of the Cyclical View as applied to the post–Cold War world.

The fundamental debate at the root of events and American action in our time comes to this: Does America want to become a Crusader State promoting a universal culture and extolling presumed universal values that must be spread throughout the world in the righteous cause of peace? Or will any such missionary zeal inevitably collide with other world cultures and thus spread conflict and turmoil?

The book's second aim is to explore the future implications of the prevailing universalist outlook guiding American foreign policy in the post–Cold War era. President Bush and his top officials repeatedly disavow any interest in American empire or any other form of American aggrandizement as we send troops around the world. But, as American actions intensify the civilizational clash between the West and Islam (and, potentially, the West and other non-Western cultures as well), America is likely to find itself reaching for the tools of imperialism to bring stability to enflamed regions. At what point do events take over, dominating the proud superpower that set out to dominate the globe?

American presidents have embarked on nearly fifty foreign interventions since the fall of the Berlin Wall, compared to just sixteen during the entire forty-five years of the Cold War. These interventions certainly weren't executed in the name of empire; most often the underlying rationale focused on sentiments resembling Fukuyama's End of History thesis and the globalization outlook. And so it seems pertinent to ask just where these universalist sentiments are taking us.

Anti-imperialists and isolationists from Mark Twain to Robert Taft to Patrick Buchanan have warned that if America becomes overextended in a hostile world through imperial or hegemonic ambition, the resulting domestic stresses and strains could threaten the American republic itself. That is in fact what happened to the Roman republic in the latter decades of its nearly five-hundred-year existence, and in the end it couldn't survive those pressures. Could that really never happen to America?

As these questions suggest, America and the world stand at the threshold of a new era without precedent in world history. During most of human existence, contacts between civilizations were intermittent or nonexistent. Then came the modern era beginning around 1500, characterized by the West's dominance over other civilizations. Next came the Cold War, when the bipolar standoff between two rival superpowers froze in place the standing and position of other civilizations not directly involved in the great East-West confrontation. Now we find ourselves in a world with multiple civilizations in close contact with one another and possessing sufficient power and influence to challenge or threaten one another.

For a brief moment of history as this new era dawns, America stands as the lone superpower upon the globe, with the ability to influence the course of events that will give shape and direction to the new global era. This is an awesome role, and how America exercises that responsibility will affect the course of Western history for a century or more. That's why I believe the nation needs a full understanding of those choices as well as the philosophical underpinnings upon which they rest. Our foreign policy debates must lay out the choices open to us, along with the fundamental concepts that drive them.

So far, the universalist outlook that has guided America's

post–Cold War adventures in such places as Somalia, the Balkans, Haiti, and now the Middle East has been largely unchallenged. Though critics have emerged here and there in academic circles, their arguments have not seeped into the country's political dialogue with any particular force. I should like to see that change. That's why I put forth this book. And that's why I begin it with an exploration of that seminal Western notion that seems to have such a hold on the American consciousness, the Idea of Progress.

PART I

THE PRISM OF HISTORY

CHAPTER 1

The Idea of Progress

B ACK IN EARLY-EIGHTEENTH-CENTURY Paris, inside that city's famous intellectual *salons* that played a pivotal role in the development of modern Western thought, there emerged a social philosopher known as the Abbé Charles-Irénée Castel de Saint-Pierre. Neither his life nor his thought has come down to our own time with any significant degree of fame or familiarity. Amazon.com's used-book store offers for sale a single Saint-Pierre work, and it's in French. He is known in our own day, to the extent that he is known at all, chiefly to historians of philosophy and of the West's distinctive view of history.

But he deserves attention because he grafted onto an emerging Western idea a corollary notion of great force and serious potential for mischief. The emerging idea was the Idea of Progress: the thesis that mankind has advanced slowly but inexorably over the centuries from a state of cultural backwardness, blindness, and folly to ever more elevated stages of enlightenment and civilization—and that this human progression will continue indefinitely into the future. By the time Saint-Pierre began showing up at the Paris *salons* of the social luminaries of his day, the Idea of Progress was much in the minds and discussions of French intellectuals. But the focus had been almost exclusively on the development of human knowledge and scientific inquiry. One didn't need much proof, or any particular leap of faith, to see that man's knowledge and particularly his scientific understanding had expanded over time and that the fruits of scientific inquiry were cumulative—or that this cumulative expansion was likely to continue into the future. This reality had soared into the Western consciousness upon the wings of Descartes' mechanical theories and the breathtaking discoveries of Kepler, Leibniz, and Newton. Even confined to the pursuit of knowledge, this nascent Idea of Progress stirred excitement in many breasts during those days of intellectual exploration.

But the Abbé wasn't satisfied with this narrow view of the Idea of Progress. He wanted to see it applied to human nature, to man in society, to a whole new concept of social science. And he foresaw not just an ever greater human mastery over the mysteries of the physical universe, and not just greater human comfort as a result, but also inexorable progress toward social perfection, human happiness, and world peace. He foresaw nothing less than "a golden age," as historian J. B. Bury puts it, "a paradise on earth."

Saint-Pierre observed that the expansion of sea commerce was producing more wealth, which in turn was generating greater leisure—more time for writers to write and readers to read their thoughts. The art of printing was leading to a wider dissemination of new thinking, rendered all the more powerful because more and more books were written in the vernacular. The growing study of mathematics and physics was freeing his contemporaries from their stifling fealty to the authority of the ancients. All this, believed the Abbé, was accelerating the rate of progress and hastening the day when happiness and peace would reign on earth.

But the Abbé also saw other things that didn't generate much confidence that the earthly paradise he longed for was in immediate prospect. The problem was human nature—human tendencies toward crime and violence and all the other familiar sins of avarice, jealousy, envy, lying, pleasure seeking of all kinds. That essential nature of man seemed to be standing in the way of the kind of progress Saint-Pierre wanted to see.

But what if human nature could be changed? Or even improved? What if governmental approaches and structures and laws could actually transform peoples in favorable ways? Then that earthly paradise could be possible—and quite soon. That was the Abbé's insight: the malleability of human nature—or, as Bury expressed it, "the omnipotence of government and laws to mould the morals of peoples." It was a powerful idea.

Sadly for the Abbé, his idea didn't encounter a hospitable environment in his own time. He was viewed by others in the *salons* as a bit of a gadfly, an intellectual dilettante. His reputation wasn't helped by the fact that he had a tiresome habit of skipping promiscuously from an idea to hopelessly naive "projects" for applying that idea to the transformation of man and society. Thus, his buoyant notions didn't leave much of a mark on his contemporaries. He was a man ahead of his time.

But in later times he commanded considerable respect. Within just a couple of decades his ideas were embraced and hailed by the French Encyclopaedists, who tilled the soil in which grew the French Revolution. "His principles," says Bury, "are theirs. The . . . subordination of all knowledge to the goddess of utility; the deification of human reason; and the doctrine of Progress." And, most important, the idea that governments and laws can shape and mold human nature into cathedrals of civic rectitude and peace.

Today they should erect statues of the Abbé de Saint-Pierre in major cities throughout the West because his notions have become so dominant in Western thought that it is hardly possible to dispute them. Saint-Pierre grafted his thoughts onto the Idea of Progress at a time when the Idea was just emerging as a central Western concept of human development and history; today the Abbé's thoughts are viewed by many as indistinguishable from the Idea of Progress, which has become probably the single most animating concept in Western thought.

Many books, theses, tracts, articles, and dissertations have been written about the Idea, but we shall look at it through the prism of two twentieth-century volumes designed to give readers a survey history of the concept. One, J. B. Bury's *The Idea of Progress: An Inquiry into Its Growth and Origin,* was published in 1920. Bury, for many years a prominent professor at King's College, Cambridge, produced a compact little volume densely packed with intellectual history of particular significance to the story of Western civilization. The other book, by the noted American humanities scholar Robert Nisbet, was published in 1980 under the title *History of the Idea of Progress*. Nisbet traced many of the same threads of Western philosophy as Bury, profiled many of the same thinkers, and shared Bury's conviction that Western history is truly intelligible only to those who understand this powerful Idea of Progress. But Nisbet challenged Bury on a number of important interpretations of the Idea and its development, and thus his book and Bury's, taken together, present a kind of philosophical debate on the subject.

Their combined works also offer a doorway to hundreds of years of Western thinking. Nisbet considered the Idea to be probably the most important to emerge throughout Western civilization. Bury suggested in a 1903 Cambridge lecture that man could never really understand history "until [he] had grasped the idea of human development. This is the great transforming conception, which enables history to define her scope." Such rhapsodic musings are not uncommon among intellectuals. The American historian Charles A. Beard once wrote that the emergence of the Progress Idea constituted "a discovery as important as the human mind has ever made, with implications for mankind that almost transcend imagination."

Such scholarly enthusiasms pose a question: Why such a fuss over a concept that most moderns would view as simply obvious, even commonplace? After all, anyone could see that horse-drawn transportation gave way to steam, steam to the internal combustion device, and that to jet propulsion. You don't have to be a philosopher to comprehend that when the electric light replaced kerosene lanterns, that was progress. Or that progress lay at the heart of the evolution in thinking from Ptolemy to Copernicus to Newton to Einstein. The same for biological advances from Harvey's discovery of blood circulation to modern cancer research or the mapping of the human genome. Thus, on one level it would seem that progress is simply a fact of life involving the cumulative expansion of man's knowledge and scientific understanding.

But on another level the Idea of Progress poses fundamental

and even profound questions about humankind and society. Some wonder whether the development of the nuclear bomb or the prospect of human cloning actually constitutes progress. And in the cultural realm is it really true that today's popular culture is on a higher plane than, say, Mozart or Wordsworth or Tiepolo? Does Eminem represent progress? But the most fundamental and profound questions posed by the Idea of Progress focus on the intellectual uses to which the Idea can be put. It's one thing to talk about man's seemingly inexorable advances in scientific knowledge. It is something else entirely to suggest, as many have in the tradition of the Abbé de Saint-Pierre, that these advances actually are altering and improving the nature of man—"thus leading," as Nisbet puts it, "toward ever-greater perfection of human nature."

Progress and human nature. The relationship between the two has generated preoccupation and debate for centuries, and it lies at the heart of many profound questions facing America and the West today. To understand this debate and its relevance to our own time, we must trace the history and significance of the Idea of Progress, as illuminated by the works of Bury and Nisbet.

Nisbet (1913–1996) equates the Idea to the cultural health of the West. And he tends to see strains of it throughout history—in Greek and Roman thought, in medieval times, and in the Renaissance, as well as in the modern West. Bury (1861–1927) is more circumspect, more inclined to define the Idea narrowly, and more focused on the Idea's impact on Western views about the immutability or malleability of human nature. Their debate begins with questions surrounding the origins of the Progress Idea and the intellectual climate in which it emerged.

Bury posits the view that the Idea of Progress never really germinated in the intellectual gardens of ancient Greece or Rome. This may seem strange to moderns, he avers, because the Idea seems to us so simple and obvious. And yet it shouldn't be surprising because the ancients didn't have much recorded history at their backs, and the history they knew didn't reveal many profound changes in the human condition. Indeed, says Bury, the ancients generally believed that humanity was retrogressing as civilization became more sophisticated. "The old legend of a 'golden age' of simplicity, from which man had fallen away, was generally accepted as truth."

Besides, the ancients tended to venerate the world they saw around them and resist change as almost inevitably bad. "The theories of Plato," writes Bury, "are only the most illustrious example of the tendency characteristic of Greek philosophical thinkers to idealize the immutable as possessing a higher value than that which varies." Thus, the ancients' fundamental world outlook "excluded the apprehension of civilization as a progressive movement."

Nisbet studied the same epoch, read the same philosophers—and reached an opposite conclusion. "Is the idea of progress to be found in classical Greek and Roman thought?" he asks and answers with "an emphatic yes." Nisbet concedes that Bury's perception was the "conventional wisdom" among scholars, but he sees elements and hints of the Progress Idea ribboned throughout classical thinking, going all the way back to Hesiod, the Boeotian farmer-philosopher of the late eighth century B.C., and including later thinkers such as Protagoras, Plato, Lucretius, and Seneca.

The Bury-Nisbet debate serves to crystallize an important point about the Idea of Progress—namely, it isn't so important when the Idea actually emerged in the thinking of mankind or how it can be discerned; rather, what's crucial is how the Idea was interpreted and how it was used to fortify other outlooks and philosophical conclusions. On the matter of classical thought, it is clearly true that the Idea didn't serve as any significant underpinning in the philosophical thinking of the ancients; it is also true that ripples of thought akin to what we now call the Idea of Progress emerged in the works of numerous classical thinkers. Bury focused his attention on the former point, Nisbet on the latter.

But the crucial point is that, to the extent the Progress Idea did in fact emerge in classical thinking, it never took the form of utopian visions or flights of societal perfection. It never led to ideas about changing human nature, much less improving it. There emerged no dreamy notions of a new world of universal happiness and guaranteed peace. The ancients tended toward pessimism, the tragic sense of life, resignation with the inevitable whims of fate. The guiding concept for these people was called Moira, often translated as "fate" but meaning far more—the fixed order of things, a reality of the universe demanding resignation and acceptance. "It was this order," writes Bury in a passage that encapsulates the fundamentals of classical thinking, "which kept things in their places, assigned to each its proper sphere and function. . . . Human progress toward perfection—towards an ideal of omniscience, or an ideal of happiness, would have been a breaking down of the bars which divide the human from the divine. Human nature does not alter; it is fixed by Moira."

The Bury-Nisbet debate reasserts itself as the two scholars turn their focus to the medieval centuries. Bury, not surprisingly, sees no hint of the Idea of Progress during this era of religious preoccupation. Nisbet just as predictably begs to differ.

For Bury, the Idea of Progress couldn't get a foothold in the medieval era because it was trumped by the Idea of Providence, the view that history was simply the story of a small portion of the human race finding salvation and happiness in another world. This powerful concept preoccupied nearly all Christian fathers and the great religious thinkers throughout the medieval era—particularly the greatest of the early religious philosophers, St. Augustine of Hippo. As Bury sees it, this preoccupation left little room for any focus on human development in this world.

In Augustine's epochal *City of God,* for example, the Christian era represented the last period of history, the old age of humanity, which would endure only long enough to enable God to gather in the predestined number of saved people. In the meantime, the idea of human development was simply irrelevant. "So long as the doctrine of Providence was undisputedly in the ascendant," writes Bury, "a doctrine of Progress could not arise."

But Nisbet reads St. Augustine far differently—and finds fundamental seeds embedded in his text that would eventually grow into seedlings of the Progress Idea. He cites Augustine's vision of the unity of all mankind, the role of historical necessity, the image of progress as the slow unfolding of a design stretching back to the beginning of man's history and his confidence in a future that would encompass "the spiritual perfection of mankind . . . a golden age of happiness on earth."

In other words, Augustine's philosophy granted God's place as Creator and Master of this eventual Providence. But within that context He gave man plenty of leeway to fashion his destiny and make the most of life on earth. And so it wasn't surprising that Augustine thrilled at the beauty of nature and also man's creative urge to capture that beauty in sculpture, painting, and pottery. Or that he would express his exuberance at man's terrestrial journey with the words, "What wonderful—one might say stupefying—advances has human industry made in the arts of weaving and building, of agriculture and navigation."

Once again the Bury-Nisbet debate illustrates an important point about this persistent Western Idea of Progress. Bury is clearly correct in saying that the medieval mind never conceived, much less embraced, the Progress Idea as it later developed in European thought, whether in conjunction with Christianity or in entirely secular garb. At the same time, Nisbet has a point worth pondering—namely, that elements of Christian theology were later incorporated into the Progress Idea as it emerged in an increasingly secular culture. This is an observation of profound significance— that as Providence waned as a powerful idea holding the Western mind in thrall, it was replaced by its secular counterpart, Progress, which in various guises has manifested its own capacity to hold the Western mind in thrall.

Of particular significance is the Augustinian idea of the unity of all mankind, a fundamental tenet of Christian theology as well as of the Idea of Progress. As an important element of Christianity, it drove that religion toward its impulse of conversion and missionary zeal. As an important element of the Idea of Progress, it led inevitably toward impulses of humanitarianism and a desire to spread democracy around the world. Another element that crossed over was the idea of man's immanent journey toward perfection and a golden age of happiness on earth. It was probably inevitable that this concept of theology would, in a more secular age, find expression in utopian dreams, revolutionary prescriptions, socialist formulas, racialist theories, and democratic crusades. And it is important to note that most of these offshoots emanated from a conviction that progress could encompass the improvement or perfection of human nature.

But, long before this development unfolded, the Idea of Progress as a hallmark concept in Western thought had to emerge, and that took centuries of intellectual exploration. Through those centuries came the slow development of the scientific method, the tools of inquiry that gave zest and confidence to the Western pursuit of knowledge. Many philosophers and scholars contributed to this development, but for purposes of this narrative we shall look at three, beginning with Roger Bacon, the thirteenth-century English scientist, encyclopedist, alchemist, philosopher, and Franciscan monk who sought to build a bridge between theology and science. His life's aim was to reform higher education by introducing into the universities a program of secular inquiry based on a dimly perceived concept of the scientific method.

But his era—still in the Middle Ages, dominated by a powerful church protective of its orthodoxies—posed a danger to anyone bent on pursuing secular knowledge. Thus Bacon addressed his greatest work, *Opus Majus,* to Pope Clement IV and sought to assure the pontiff that the pursuit of science contained substantial ecclesiastical value. With clever ingenuity he presented a case that a true understanding of theology and Scripture was not harmed by, but rather enhanced by, the study of mathematics, astronomy, physics, and chemistry. And he got away with it.

What we see in Roger Bacon is a mind seeking to break away from the constrictions of ecclesiastical orthodoxy in order to pursue pure secular knowledge. Some scholars have suggested that in doing so he "announced the idea of Progress," as Bury puts it. Bury himself dismisses that notion on the ground that in most respects Bacon was a thorough product of his time, seeing the world in much the same light as St. Augustine. But in putting forth his manifesto for the pursuit of secular knowledge, Roger Bacon pointed to a new path of intellectual pursuit.

It took some three and a half centuries, but eventually his ideas reemerged in the thinking of another Bacon, Francis Bacon, the English philosopher and essayist, whose aim was nothing short of a "great renovation" of human knowledge. This renovation was possible, he pronounced, through the tools of experiment, what Bury terms "the direct interrogation of nature." Bury calls him "the first philosopher of the modern age," and it would not be altogether fanciful to call him the father of applied science. That's because he was truly the first to declare that the ultimate goal of scientific inquiry was "the endowment of human life with new inventions and riches."

Bacon's musings on history led him to the idea that there had been three great epochs in human history—antiquity before Greece and Rome; the era of Greece and Rome; and the modern era, which included the medieval epoch as well as his own time. This entire history was largely a wasteland, said Bacon, except for three exemplary eras—the era of ancient Greece, in which moral and political matters preoccupied the greatest minds; the era of ancient Rome, in which civic affairs were honed to a fine point; and his own era, which, armed with the power of experiment, was destined to disgorge all the secrets of nature within a few generations.

As an expression of the Idea of Progress, it was pretty rudimentary stuff. But it represented a great leap into a new realm of thinking: the idea that secular inquiry actually could lay bare the mysteries of the universe. And Bacon was revolutionary in his declaration that the value of science is in its utility to the human race and its capacity to improve man's comfort and happiness. This connection between scientific knowledge and man's fate was to become a foundation for all subsequent contributions to the development of the Idea of Progress.

It certainly served as foundation for the next major contributor to the rise of the Progress doctrine—René Descartes, the seventeenth-century French philosopher and mathematician famous for the observation "I think; therefore I am." That phrase has come down to us so many centuries later not just because it has a certain ring of obscure profundity, but because it so neatly encapsulates

Descartes' famous four rules for acquiring knowledge. First, doubt everything unless it can be "clearly and distinctly" seen as true; second, practice inductive reasoning, breaking a problem down into its smallest possible intellectual particles before moving to general conclusions; third, begin the reasoning process with the simplest elements that are the easiest to know, then move methodically to the more complex; and, fourth, reason with rigorous syllogistic logic.

The Cartesian philosophy posited two fundamental axioms— the supremacy of reason and the invariability of the laws of nature. And his analytical method was applicable to history as well as to physical knowledge. What's more, as Nisbet notes, Descartes insisted his method was available to any ordinary seeker of truth with the willingness and the discipline to follow his four rules. No longer was knowledge the preserve of scholars, scientists, archivists, and librarians. This was utterly revolutionary, a kind of declaration of independence of man in his pursuit of knowledge and mastery of the universe.

All this had a profound effect upon subsequent thinkers. Offering new tools for acquiring knowledge and a new freedom from the tethers of Christian orthodoxy, Cartesianism unleashed a virtual spree of intellectual ferment in Europe. It wasn't long before the Cartesian method was being applied to new realms of thinking, and the Idea of Progress took on a whole new coloration. This coloration has come down to us under the rubric of "humanism"—the idea that man is the measure of all things. As Bury notes, psychology, morals, and the structure of society now riveted the attention of the new thinkers instead of the larger "supra-human" inquiries (astronomy and physics, for example) that had preoccupied the minds of Descartes, Bacon, Newton, and Leibniz.

It was probably inevitable that this humanism would lead to a powerful new outlook about the potential of progress to mold and shape human nature. By the mid-eighteenth century, this outlook was generating waves of intellectual exuberance among the French Encyclopaedists whose great work exemplified the rationalist movement and paved the way for the transformation of the France of 1715 into the France of 1789. These men—Diderot, Baron d'Holbach, Helvétius, Voltaire, among others—harbored ultimate confidence that reason would triumph over prejudice, that knowledge would prevail over ignorance. For these thinkers, the big question wasn't whether the progressiveness of knowledge was a fundamental reality of history; it was whether this light of progressivism could spread its illumination beyond the world of scholars and reach all mankind. To fuel their optimism, they abandoned Descartes' rigors of inquiry and developed a quite handy a priori theory—namely, "the indefinite malleability of human nature by education and institutions," as Bury puts it.

Bury captures the power of this intellectual development when he writes, "This doctrine of the possibility of indefinitely moulding the characters of men by laws and institutions . . . laid a foundation on which the theory of the perfectibility of humanity could be raised. It marked, therefore, an important stage in the development of the doctrine of Progress."

It also ushered in a new era characterized by a growing interest in forging the desired worldly paradise through naked force if necessary—and increasingly it was seen as necessary. From "Progress as Freedom," to use Nisbet's label for such thinkers as Turgot, Condorcet, Adam Smith, and John Stuart Mill, we see the emergence of "Progress as Power." The man who most vividly personified this new development was Jean-Jacques Rousseau.

In one sense Rousseau's tough-minded outlook was anti-Progress because he utterly dismissed those who viewed history as a steady upward progression of mankind from a state of cultural backwardness to ever higher levels of civilization. He cast his mind back to man in his primitive state and conjured up an idyllic era of equality, peace, and happiness—a natural state of things, he believed, because of man's innate goodness and wisdom (the famous "noble savage"). But, said Rousseau, this idyllic state of man's existence had been killed, and man's nature warped, by what he called "combinations fatal to innocence and happiness." What were these combinations? Agriculture, metallurgy, private property, the pursuit of material things—and, eventually, class, nation, the political state. So the solution was simple: destroy those institutions and start over, recapturing that idyllic natural state in which all mankind can live in harmony and contentedness. In other words, human nature, being malleable, had been distorted by bad institutions; but, being malleable, it could be perfected by good institutions.

Rousseau was probably the first Western thinker to take the Idea of Progress and twist it into a doctrine of state control. "If it is good to know how to deal with men as they are," he wrote, "it is much better to make them what there is need that they should be. The most absolute authority is that which penetrates into a man's inmost being, and concerns itself no less with his will than his actions." This breathtaking manifesto is philosophy as Will to Power, bent on shaping men's intellectual and moral thoughts through coercion. Going far beyond those benign dreamers such as Saint-Pierre, who believed that institutional and governmental reforms would serve as a benign catalyst for human improvement, Rousseau saw that these improvements would have to be force-fed into the very thoughts and moral fiber of citizens. And how would this be done? "If you would have the general will accomplished," Rousseau wrote, "bring all the particular wills into conformity with it; in other words, as virtue is nothing more than this conformity of particular wills with the general will, establish the reign of virtue!"

The world has yet to see anything approaching a reign of virtue as envisioned by Rousseau. But, as it turned out, the Frenchman's theoretical reign of *virtue* wasn't far removed from the French Revolution's very real Reign of *Terror*. By cleverly turning the Idea of Progress on its head, Rousseau in many ways stirred thoughts and impulses that contributed to that flow of blood. But he wasn't alone. The intellectual ferment of French thinkers in the decades leading up to that chaotic time, whether Rousseauian Will to Power or more dreamy variants on the Idea of Progress, served as wellspring for that civic carnage.

But across the Channel and across the Atlantic, where the Anglo-Saxon mind was grappling with the Idea of Progress, the concept was seen in much more limited terms. The notion that institutional reforms could alter mankind and usher in a golden era of peace and happiness struck most British thinkers as dangerous nonsense. "The general tendency of British thought," writes Bury, "was to see salvation in the stability of existing institutions, and to regard change with suspicion." English thinkers generally agreed with John Locke that the appropriate function of government was not to refashion human nature or remake society, but to preserve order, protect life and property, and secure the conditions in which men might pursue their own legitimate purposes.

This rejection of the fiery French outlook is vividly reflected in the writings of Edmund Burke, the British statesman and philosopher. As he put it in his famous *Reflections on the Revolution in France*, the bloody events of the Terror were "the sad but instructive monuments of rash and ignorant counsel in time of profound peace"—in other words, the result of abstractionist thinking divorced from any real understanding of human nature. This skepticism of the French model also is seen in the work and thought of the American Founding Fathers, many of whom believed with Burke that human nature, far from malleable and in fact potentially harmful to society, needed to be checked. The principal difference between the American and French revolutions, as conservative writer Russell Kirk has noted, was that the American revolutionaries generally held a "biblical view of man and his bent toward sin," while the French revolutionaries generally opted for "an optimistic doctrine of human goodness." The American aim was to fashion a practical secular covenant "designed to restrain the human tendencies toward violence and fraud . . . [and] place checks upon will and appetite."

Most intellectuals among the Founders skipped over the thinking of the French philosophes and sought civic wisdom in the thought and history of the Roman republic, where the Idea of Progress was barely perceived at all. "Two thousand years later," writes Kirk, "the reputation of the Roman constitution remained so high that the framers of the American constitution would emulate the Roman model as best they could"—initiating the Roman checks and balances and separation of powers. Even the American presidency would be modeled somewhat on the Roman consular imperium, and the American Senate patterned after the Roman version. Thus did the American Anglo-Saxons deviate from the French abstractionists and fashion their governmental workings to fit humankind as it actually is—capable of great and noble acts but also capable of slipping into vice and treachery when unchecked. That bedrock outlook, based on the conscious rejection of the French view, was the genius of the American system, probably the greatest civic achievement in the history of the world.

But, as the American success story unfolded, various intellectuals, theorists, and utopian crackpots continued to toy with the Idea of Progress, seeking to mold it and shape it into some kind of ultimate prescription for paradise on earth. And an interesting new phenomenon emerged. After Western theorists had devoted centuries of intellectual effort to developing the Idea of Progress as an ongoing chain of improvement with no perceived end into the future, a new breed of "Progress as Power" thinkers began to declare their own visions as the final end point of this long progression.

Thus, notes Nisbet, did the great French intellectual Comte de Saint-Simon view his "ideal society" as "the final stage of a progression that began millennia earlier." Thus did Georg Wilhelm Friedrich Hegel, in putting forth his famous dialectic and wedding it to his profound devotion to the Prussian state, posit the view that Germany represented the fourth phase of historical development and "the ultimate result which the process of history is intended to accomplish"—an ultimate result rendered inevitable because "Europe is absolutely the end of history." And thus did Karl Marx, applying Hegel's dialectic to his vision of total economic equality, posit his belief, as Nisbet describes it, "in necessary, inexorable development toward a single, inevitable, golden end."

This development reveals one of the two great contradictions in the Idea of Progress—namely, that the original concept of endless progression ultimately leaves the Idea's adherents rather cold. To progress endlessly to the end of time, or to the termination of human life on earth, negates the idea that there is a point to the progression. Who can say that things are always getting better if the

Idea of Progress simply means a constant state of flux? What's to prevent this flux from taking a flight toward retrogression? No, said many latter-day adherents of the Idea, this powerful progression was taking humankind to a particular end point, to a destination that was going to reveal the final phase of human development. The idea of "the end of history," as Hegel so provocatively put it, turned out to be so powerful as to negate one of the central tenets of the Idea. And that negation in turn spawned the multitude of utopian notions of man's fate that modern Westerners know so well.

The other great contradiction centers on the concept that this Idea of Progress applies to all mankind—a legacy of the Augustinian heritage, as we have seen. And yet the actual progress that is the focus of this Idea has taken place almost exclusively within Western civilization. It is all about Western science, Western technics, Western methods of inquiry, Western philosophy, and, in the end, Western political and economic ideals. Nisbet offers a penetrating insight into all this when he notes that the Idea of Progress has always been essentially "Eurocentric." By the seventeenth and eighteenth centuries, he writes, "the spell of the idea of progress—and with it the Eurocentric view of the entire world—had grown to such proportions that little if anything in the world could be considered in its own right. Everything had to be seen through the West and its values." Implicit in this was the view that other cultures were inferior to the West, and hence universal progress required that these inferior cultures embrace the Western heritage.

This phenomenon is not particularly surprising. As many scholars have noted, each civilization and culture through history has tended to see the world through the prism of its own values, ideals, philosophy, and impulses of ethnicity and religion. But what then does this say about the concept, developed through centuries of Western thought, that the Idea of Progress is universal in its import, applicable to all mankind? If Western ideas, developed via the intellectual progress of which Western minds are so proud, clash with those of other cultures, what does that say about the universality of the Idea of Progress? A corollary question, to be explored later in this volume, concerns whether this contradiction leads inevitably to a kind of Western hubris in global relations.

Notwithstanding these contradictions, the Idea of Progress, in various guises and varying degrees of intensity, has essentially conquered the consciousness of European civilization, becoming the animating concept of the secular West. It is embraced almost unconsciously by people who could hardly articulate the concept and who know nothing of its long, agonizing emergence. It is assumed as a given among intellectuals toiling in the academic groves of the West. It serves as the foundation of modern American liberalism. As Nisbet points out, it represents in many ways the secularization of major elements of Christian theology, which may be one reason why it is embraced by some with almost religious fervor.

In his book, though, Nisbet saw the beginnings of a serious decline in the Idea of Progress in the twentieth century. Skepticism about the Idea, once confined to a small segment of intellectuals, he writes, "has grown and spread to not merely the large majority of intellectuals in this final quarter of the century, but to many millions of other people in the West." He goes so far as to suggest that, when the identity of the twentieth century is established by historians, a major element of that identity will be not faith in the Idea but its abandonment. Nisbet identifies five fundamental premises of the Idea—belief in the value of the past; conviction of the nobility and even superiority of Western civilization; acceptance of the value of economic and technological growth; faith in reason as the only source of knowledge; and belief in the intrinsic worth of life on earth. "Each of these premises," he writes, "has been severely challenged by doubt and disillusionment, even outright hostility, in the twentieth century."

But the professor was writing in the very late 1970s, when America appeared at a low point in the Cold War and faced its greatest economic crisis since the Great Depression. Within a decade, Ronald Reagan had restored economic growth to its traditional place in the dialectic of politics and America had engineered the utter collapse of the Soviet Union. The result was a kind of popular resurgence in the Idea of Progress and a desire by politicians to embrace it as much as possible as a guide to policy making, particularly in the realm of international relations. And so the question facing America today, in the very dangerous post–Cold War era, is not whether the Idea of Progress is declining as a guiding tenet of thought (although in certain respects this is indisputably true), but whether it is being embraced in ways that impede the country's ability to see the world as it really is.

CHAPTER 2

Cycles of History

I N THE SUMMER AND FALL of 1911, an obscure German
intellectual named Oswald Spengler, living modestly in Munich on an inheritance, watched with growing horror as his
country nearly stumbled into war with France in what was known
as the Second Moroccan Crisis. As it happened, Germany backed
down when Britain threw her support behind France, and war was
avoided. But the cost to Germany was international humiliation.
The episode left an indelible mark on the consciousness of young
Spengler, who concluded that war between Germany and the
French-British alliance had become inevitable. What's more, this
war was likely to be a clash of epic proportions with profound consequences for Western civilization.

Spengler set out to write a book predicting this impending conflagration and exploring the underlying essence of the West's two
antagonistic cultural entities—Great Britain, the trade empire of
liberal democratic capitalism, perceived by many Germans as a
decadent civilization; and Germany, a rising socialistic empire
widely viewed in Spengler's country as representing a more hallowed Prussian *Kultur.*

But then he wandered into a bookstore and happened upon
Otto Seeck's *Geschichte des Untergangs der antiken Welt—The History
of the Decline of the Ancient World.* In a flash he had a vision for a
much wider book—an exploration of the rise and fall of world civilizations, including the West, which he viewed as culturally spent
and sterile. History, he would argue, was not a story of the slow, in-

exorable progress of mankind from backwardness to ever greater enlightenment, but rather the story of a number of discrete world civilizations that had emerged, developed, matured, and then declined. And the West, the civilization Spengler revered, was now heading into a long twilight of decline.

He plunged into the project, continuing even as the war he had predicted turned into blood-soaked reality. With electricity out much of the time, he wrote by candlelight. In winter he placed his chair atop a table to capture what little warmth there was in his apartment. By early 1917 he had completed the first volume, but a wartime shortage of paper and publishers' skepticism thwarted publication. Finally in April 1918 the Viennese house of Wilhelm Braumueller brought out the first volume of *Der Untergang des Abendlandes—The Decline of the West*. Anticipating little interest and tepid sales, Braumueller printed just fifteen hundred copies.

The book hit the German consciousness like a boulder tossed upon an anthill. As one scholar wrote a few years later, "Never had a thick philosophical work had such a success—and in all reading circles, learned and uneducated, serious and snobbish." Within eight years sales had hit a hundred thousand, and the book had been translated into numerous languages. As H. Stuart Hughes wrote in his *Oswald Spengler: A Critical Estimate*, the year following publication became the "Spengler year," while the man became "the philosopher of the hour."

Readers were beguiled and intrigued by this new thinker's sheer audacity. He didn't paint with little brushstrokes but attacked the whole canvas with wide swings of his arms, casting aside whole strands of Western philosophy. And he plunged right at the heart of conventional thinking when he rejected the Idea of Progress. What's more, Spengler's bold flight of historical analysis inspired an English intellectual with a far different political outlook to undertake a competing effort to elucidate the cycles of history and the rise and fall of civilizations. Arnold Toynbee's multivolume *A Study of History* began appearing in 1934, and while he came at his mission from an entirely different perspective he reached remarkably similar conclusions about the Cycles of History, the Idea of

Progress, and what he considered the fallacy of Eurocentrism. Others subsequently probed the same territory, coming to similar conclusions. But the story of the emergence of the Cyclical View of History in the twentieth century must begin with Oswald Spengler.

He was born in 1880 at the northern region of the Harz Mountains. His father, an austere and distant patriarch, was a mining engineer and later a postal official in the town of Halle. Oswald attended a classical high school and went on to study mathematics and the physical sciences at universities in Berlin, Munich, and Halle. He completed his doctoral thesis in mathematics at Halle and then experienced perhaps the greatest disappointment of his early life. He failed his oral exams on the ground that he quoted insufficiently from the specialized literature. Though he passed six months later, the misstep barred him from that rarefied life of the German university professor, and he resigned himself to a career as teacher in the *Realgymnasium* (high school) system. But after a few years he gave up teaching and moved to Munich, where he read, studied, and wrote occasional short articles. Aside from intermittent visits to Italy, he remained in Munich the rest of his life.

Although *The Decline of the West* was a commercial success and a conversational sensation, conventional historians attacked it immediately. Subsequent critics have never really seemed to know how to respond to it. The scholarly world, suggests H. Stuart Hughes, writing some three decades after the book appeared, "has been embarrassed to know what to do about it." Though based on prodigious reading and substantial knowledge, the book is not considered respectable scholarship. "It is too metaphysical," writes Hughes, "too dogmatic—in all respects, too extreme. Yet there it sits—a massive stumbling-block in the path of true knowledge." And it attracts new adherents and intrigues new intellectual explorers every generation.

As John Farrenkopf points out in his *Prophet of Decline: Spengler on World History and Politics,* the book stirred serious interest on the part of numerous men of ideas as well as men of action in post–World War II America. They included George Kennan, Henry Kissinger, Paul Nitze, Louis Halle, Hans J. Morgenthau, and Reinhold Niebuhr. Kennan read Spengler in the original language, with the aid of a dictionary, during a stay in Germany in his youth. Kissinger's undergraduate thesis at Harvard focused on Spengler, as well as on Toynbee and Immanuel Kant. Nitze left Wall Street as a young man to study *Decline* at Harvard, while Halle reported receiving poor grades there because of his preoccupation with the book. And yet, as Farrenkopf notes, Spengler's "place in modern international theory has received relatively little attention . . . [and] his challenging ideas have not been reformulated into a theoretical stance on international relations." Probably, he suggests, this is because his pessimism is just a little too ominous for any but the most theoretical musings.

We shall attempt to elucidate Spengler's thesis by breaking it down into its component parts, beginning with his rejection of the idea that history becomes discernible through a kind of natural science approach, a search for root causes explaining unfolding events. No, says Spengler, history can be understood only through an appreciation of the mystery of destiny, which is "the essence and kernel of all history" and is "unapproachable through the cognition-forms which the *Critique of Pure Reason* [of Kant] investigates." Hence, Spengler rejects the aim of studying the past through scientific methods and opts instead for an analytical framework focused on a rigorous pursuit of historical analogy.

Second, Spengler rejects the notion of a unified mankind whose exploits on earth can be traced through historical inquiry. "'Mankind,'" he writes, "has no aim, no idea, no plan, any more than the family of butterflies or orchids. 'Mankind' is a zoological expression." He posits instead his thesis of distinct living cultures. "I see . . . the drama of *a number* of mighty Cultures, each springing with primitive strength from the soil of a mother-region to which it remains firmly bound throughout its whole life-cycle; each stamping its material, its mankind, in *its own* image; each having *its own* idea, *its own* passions, *its own* life, will and feeling, *its own* death."

Third, if "mankind" is a meaningless abstraction and history is the story of the rise and fall of distinct cultures, then it is simply fatuous to suggest that the West holds center stage in world history. Spengler dismisses this Eurocentric view as the "Ptolemaic system of history" and puts forth instead his own "Copernican discovery in the historical sphere," which gives no special position to the classical or the Western culture as against any other of the great cultures. Those others, he writes, are "separate worlds of dynamic being which . . . count for just as much in the general picture of history" as the classical or Western experience and in some ways surpass them in "spiritual greatness and soaring power."

At this point the Spengler outlook turns a bit mystical as he pictures the great cultures as essentially organic entities whose phases of emergence, development, and decline are remarkably similar from culture to culture, not unlike the phases of human life. "Cultures are organisms," he writes. "If we disentangle their shapes we may find the primitive Culture-form that underlies all individual Cultures and is reflected in their various manifestations." That's why, says Spengler, the pursuit of historical analogy is so critical to understanding the Cycles of History: by studying the patterns of past cultures we can better understand our own, including its current stage of development and its state of cultural health or decline.

And how do these cultures emerge? They are born, says Spengler in his mystical way, when a people in a particular region rather suddenly develops a distinctive way of looking at the world. This world outlook is entirely new and fresh, unencumbered by influences from other cultures. And as this new culture emerges it develops a sense of its own mortality, which stirs powerful longings for fulfillment, which in turn unleash a passion for creative expression, new methods of inquiry, new modes of knowledge—all conforming to the distinctive "soul" of the new culture. Indeed, Spengler goes so far as to apply a rather dogmatic existentialism to all this, arguing that there isn't any universal knowledge at all but merely the distinctive bodies of thought emanating from the distinctive cultures.

This passion for creative expression and new strains of culture knowledge runs on for centuries, generally a thousand years or more unless interrupted by external forces. But eventually it peters out as the culture passes beyond the autumn of its existence. And then a new phase begins, the civilizational phase, characterized by the deterioration of the folk traditions and innocent enthusiasms of the culture. Its essence, once of the soil and spread throughout the "mother-region" in town, village, and city, now becomes the domain of a few rich and powerful "world-cities," which twist and distort the culture concepts of old and replace them with cynicism, cosmopolitanism, irony, and a money culture. "To the world-city," writes Spengler, "belongs not a folk but a mob. Its uncomprehending hostility to all the traditions representative of the Culture (nobility, church, privileges, dynasties, convention in art and limits of knowledge in science), the keen and cold intelligence that confounds the wisdom of the peasant, the new-fashioned naturalism that in relation to all matters of sex and society goes back far to quite primitive instincts and conditions, the reappearance of the *panem et circenses* in the form of wage-disputes and sports stadia—all these things betoken the definite closing down of the Culture and the opening of a quite new phase of human existence—anti-provincial, late, futureless, but quite inevitable."

Thus, Spengler draws a sharp distinction between culture and civilization. The former is the phase of creative energy, the "soul" of the countryside; the latter is a time of material preoccupation, the "intellect" of the city. As biographer Hughes elaborates, "So long as the culture phase lasts, the leading figures in a society manifest a sure sense of artistic 'style' and personal 'form.' Indeed, the breakdown of style and form most clearly marks the transition from culture to civilization."

But what most clearly mark the civilizational phase are two inevitable developments: Caesarism and empire. Spengler's historical analogies suggest that the transition from culture to civilization unleashes a kind of Will to Power. This impulse manifests itself internally in a drive to consolidate power within the civilization. It manifests itself externally in a drive to assert dominance over other peoples. "Imperialism," writes Spengler, "is Civilization unadulterated." This Spenglerian perception poses profound questions about the fate of our own Western civilization. But an understanding of that connection requires an exploration into Spengler's historical analogies as they apply to the great cultures of world history.

He identifies eight such cultures—Western, Greco-Roman, Indian, Babylonian, Chinese, Egyptian, Arabian, and Mexican. He applies in-depth analysis to three—Western, Greco-Roman, and Arabian—and gives each a descriptive label: the Western culture is "Faustian," he says, while the classical is "Apollinian" and the Arabian is "Magian." Each of the great cultures was utterly distinctive in its worldview, its philosophical underpinning, its approach to artistic expression, its science and technics, even its mathematics.

And each culture possessed its own concept of space, which provided its prime symbols of perception, shaped its identity, and guided its every thought. The Egyptian soul, for example, saw itself as moving down a narrow and inexorably prescribed "life-path" to come at the end before the judges of the dead. That was its "destiny-idea," says Spengler, and the entire "form-language" of the culture illustrates this one theme. Thus, the pyramids of the Fourth Dynasty are a rhythmically ordered sequence of spaces— passages, halls, arcaded courts, and pillared rooms that grow ever narrower and narrower. The Egyptians' reliefs and paintings appear as rows that lead the beholder in a definite direction. "For the Egyptian," writes Spengler, "the depth-experience which governed his world-form was so emphatically directional that he comprehended space more or less as a continuous process of actualization."

Or take the Chinese prime symbol, similar to the Egyptian in that it is guided by the intensely directional principle of the Tao. But whereas the Egyptian treads a path prescribed with inexorable necessity, the Chinese wanders through his world, conducted to his ancestral tomb not by ravines of stone but by friendly nature herself. "Nowhere else has the landscape become so genuinely the material of the architecture," writes Spengler. "The temple is not a self-contained building but a layout, in which hills, water, trees, flowers and stones in definite forms and dispositions are just as important as gates, walls, bridges and houses." He adds that this culture is the only one in which "the art of gardening is a grand religious art." Similarly, Chinese paintings take the beholder from detail to detail, "a sequence of space-elements through which the eye is to wander from one to the next."

The classical, or Apollinian, culture had a far different prime symbol, best described as "body and form"—that which was small, circumscribed, clearly delineated, and anchored. Think of the Parthenon. Apollinian architecture, writes Spengler, is characterized by a firm footing and a socket. "The Doric column bores into the ground, the vessels are always thought of from below upward . . . [and] the legs are disproportionately emphasized." This emphasis on body led classical man to adopt sculpture as his quintessential art form and polytheism—"the plurality of separate bodies"—as his religious framework. As H. Stuart Hughes puts it, "The free-standing nude statue, with its harmonious contours and untroubled gaze, symbolized in visible form the classical attitude of personal detachment and serene acceptance of an inscrutable destiny."

To Magian man, the prime symbol is the cavern, into which light shines through and does battle with the darkness. Architecturally, this is characterized by the early Magian churches with their heavy walls that shut in the cavern and their utilitarian windows that offered no artistic expression besides bringing the light without to the darkness within. This constant clash defines the Magian spirit, preoccupied as it is with the "persistent and unresolved struggles" between good and evil. In these struggles, the concept of individual wills, says Spengler, "is simply meaningless, for 'will' and 'thought' in man are not prime, but already effects of the deity upon him." And this brings us to a fundamental difference between the Magian and Faustian cultures: "In the Magian world . . . the separation of politics and religion is theoretically impossible and nonsensical, whereas in the Faustian Culture the battle of Church and State is inherent in the very conceptions—logical, necessary, unending."

As for the Western or Faustian culture, Spengler writes that, if the guiding form concept of classical man was body and magnitude, the West's guiding form concept was nothing less than "pure, imperceptible, unlimited space." In other words, "the Faustian strove through all sensuous barriers toward infinity." Infinity as a concept was utterly alien to classical thinkers, whose mathematical orientation was geometry (form and proportion) and who had no conception of negative numbers or even zero. But Western man, says Spengler, pushed aside Euclidian formulations and moved to entirely new mathematical approaches that incorporated the great new Faustian idea. "In place of the sensuous element of concrete lines and planes . . . there emerged the abstract, spatial, un-Classical element of the point . . . [and] variable relation-values between positions in space." This led inevitably to Western calculus and Western physics, modes of thought and inquiry inconceivable in any other culture.

A similar distinction is seen in architecture. While the Ionic hovers, the Gothic soars. It was no accident that Western man invented the flying buttress, enabling him to construct cathedrals reflecting his relentless drive toward space. Or that he developed the window as architecture: "In it can be felt the will to emerge from the interior into the boundless."

And just as Classical architecture led to sculpture as the premier Apollinian art form, Western architecture led inexorably to music. From around 1500 to about 1800, writes Spengler, as Faustian man grappled with his "will to spatial transcendence," instrumental music emerged as the West's ruling art form. But first Western man had to transform the art of painting, which went through its own "decisive epochal turn" in the sixteenth century. Using light and shadow to burst through space and time, Western painters brought dimension to their work, and the background as symbol of the infinite conquered the sense-perceptible foreground. Thus was "the depth-experience of the Faustian soul . . . captured in the kinesis of a picture." This artistic expression reached its fullest flowering with the Dutch masters, particularly Rembrandt. And it is significant that, as the Dutch Baroque painting reached culmination, the West's cultural momentum was picked up by the soaring new expression of Baroque music.

Western science, writes Spengler, reflected this same drive toward infinity. It wasn't accidental that the telescope was a Western invention or that human flight first occurred in the West. Likewise with drama, particularly tragedy, the West developed a penetrating "biographical" approach, as opposed to the Greeks' "anecdotal" outlook. One deals with the entirety of a life, the other with a single moment. Asks Spengler, "What relation . . . has the entire *inward* past of Oedipus or Orestes to the shattering event that suddenly meets him on his way?" On the other hand, "there is not the smallest trait in the past existence of Othello—that masterpiece of psychological analysis—that has not some bearing on the catastrophe." Western artistic expression probed deeply into the psychology of life and ultimately found its way to a preoccupation with the individual—the dawning of that personality idea that later was to create the sacrament of contrition and personal absolution.

"If, in fine," writes Spengler, "we look at the whole picture—the expansion of the Copernican world into that aspect of stellar space that we possess today; the development of Columbus's discovery into a worldwide command of the earth's surface by the West; the perspective of oil-painting and the theatre; the passion of our Civilization for swift transit, the conquest of the air, the exploration of the Polar regions and the climbing of almost impossible mountain-peaks—we see, emerging everywhere, the prime symbol of the Faustian soul, Limitless Space. And those specially Western creations of the soul-myth called 'Will,' 'Force' and 'Deed' must be regarded as derivatives of this prime symbol."

But, says Spengler, all that yearning and probing and exploration and artistic expression were now finished in the West, which had passed into its civilizational phase. Signs of this, he writes, were evident in the new pseudo-artistic expression that no longer celebrated the West's fundamental cultural ideas but rather assaulted them; in the rise of impersonal world-cities whose cosmopolitanism flooded the folk traditions of old; in the preoccupation with the money culture; in declining birthrates and the rise of a new type of woman "who belongs to herself," as Ibsen put it; and finally in the death struggle that had emerged between the democratic state of England with its ethic of success and the socialist state of Germany with its ethic of duty.

Spengler harbored no doubt that Germany would win this struggle and emerge as "the last nation of the West," spawning ground for that future Caesar who would lead the West to its final civilizational glory of world dominance. It was all written in the historical analogies he had studied so carefully. But he was wrong about that death struggle, and he died too soon in 1936 to see his native land crushed by the awesome force of the Anglo-Saxon world with its focus on liberal democracy, free markets, and control of the individual over his own destiny. Thereafter, it was America, not Germany, that would become the last nation of the West, that would define the West and determine its fate in its enveloping civilizational phase.

BEFORE ANY OF THAT came to pass, though, Spengler would have a profound impact on a brilliant mind that reflected important elements of Anglo-Saxon thought in the early twentieth century. Arnold Toynbee, writes Arthur Herman in his *The Idea of Decline in Western History,* was one of the first Englishmen to buy a copy of *The Decline of the West* when it appeared in London bookstores. Herman reports that Toynbee, then a young academic, was both exhilarated and dismayed by this provocative new book—exhilarated by its "firefly flashes of historical insight"; dismayed to think that a German had stolen a march on his own ambition to produce a definitive tome on the cycles of history.

In the end, Toynbee concluded that Spengler's philosophy was flawed in most of its particulars, though largely correct in its view of history as the rise and fall of civilizations. Thus Spengler served mainly to spur Toynbee on to one of the grand feats of twentieth-century Anglo-Saxon scholarship. To understand Toynbee's work it is necessary to understand the political and intellectual milieu from which he emerged.

If Spengler revered Western culture as a glorious tribute to the

Faustian spirit, Toynbee rather despised the West. "I am conscious of having a certain 'down' on Western civilization and have often tried to think out why I have it," he wrote to a friend in 1930. "Partly it is the feeling that the Ancient World is the real home of the human spirit, and that what came after is rather a pity—like dog Latin."

Toynbee came from the genteel society of British intellectuals and academics who, in the wake of the Industrial Revolution and the First World War, found themselves wallowing in a kind of civic pessimism. There was little doubt among these people that the West was in crisis. The only question was what could be done about it. Some sought a new social order in Marxism and its various offshoots. Others turned to certain strains of "vitalism bordering on fascism," as Herman puts it. Still others bought into Spengler's civilizational Will to Power. But for Toynbee and his intellectual soul mates of the interwar period, none of these resonated. They sought a future based on humanitarian impulse and soft values such as tolerance, compassion, and compromise.

In seeking Toynbee's intellectual antecedents, a good place to start is Matthew Arnold, whose 1869 *Culture and Anarchy* predicted a cultural disaster born of the Industrial Revolution and the resulting emergence of "mechanical and material civilization." This in turn, predicted Arnold, would spawn a growing middle class, which would accumulate decisive social and political power but would lack any sense of culture or refinement. The result would be cultural decay, brought on by the rise of what he famously called "philistines." They would rule Britain by their energy, he predicted, but would "deteriorate it by their low ideas and want of culture."

Ironically, this intellectual snobbism led directly to British neoliberalism. Herman notes that Arnold's cultural pessimism was augmented by the decline of religious belief at Britain's leading universities. The Calvinist conscience, deprived of the traditional outlets for fighting sin, sought new areas of moral endeavor. "One of these," he writes, "was the 'discovery' of urban industrial poverty, which threw into severe disrepute British liberalism's central tenet, that human progress involved the unfettering of the forces of economic growth and production throughout society."

One of the greatest of these discoverers was Toynbee's own uncle, Arnold Toynbee Sr., a teacher at Balliol College, Oxford, who posited a classic critique of the Industrial Revolution as the systematic exploitation of the working classes by bourgeois capitalist barons. The older Toynbee became the leader of a group of British idealists who believed that the day of the free market was over and must be replaced by a new future based on a morality more elevated than self-seeking individualism and crass property rights. As Herman notes, the idealists also rejected the classic economic model of the autonomous individual, whose personal rights were sacrosanct and whose rational self-interest would fuel civilizational progress. They argued for a "moral model"—also a statist model—in which the individual would choose goals and ends to the benefit of society generally—an approach, they assumed, that would have to be forced upon businessmen and industrialists.

These intellectuals also developed a strong hostility to the British Empire, a perceived impediment to this new order of peace and harmony. Benjamin Kidd, in his *Principles of Western Civilisation* (1902), argued that the assertive, manly Brits who built the empire had enhanced science, freedom, and affluence throughout Britain. But now, he argued, those traits stood in the way of further development toward social responsibility and duty. Others argued that nationalism and the nation-state also had to give way to these softer sentiments so that the new vision could materialize.

Into this intellectual milieu emerged the brilliant, idealistic younger Toynbee. He was born in London in 1889 at the twilight of the Victorian era, one of the world's rare golden ages. His family tree, Whittaker Chambers once wrote in *Time* magazine, noting his famous uncle, "was an exfoliation of the eager 19th Century British mind." Toynbee's father was a social worker, his mother one of the first British women to receive a college degree. Wrote Chambers: "The Golden Age shed its westering light over young Toynbee in the guise of a thorough classical training at Balliol, the most intellectual of Oxford's colleges." Touring Crete in

1912, he studied the ruins of the Minoan civilization, the first great sea power of the Middle Sea. Then one day he came upon the ruins of a Venetian doge's palace, testament to the once mighty Venetian sea power that also had held sway over much of the Mediterranean in more recent times. A flash of insight hit him: if those great civilizations were mortal, wasn't the British Empire also destined to fade? Instantly he became an adherent of the Cyclical View of History.

Toynbee devoted the next ten years to his study of civilizations, consuming books on China, Japan, pre-Columbian America, Russia, and Eastern Europe, as well as anthropology and ethnology. He produced three volumes of *A Study of History,* which were published to enthusiastic reviews in 1934. Three more arrived by 1939, with subsequent volumes emerging in the 1950s. In 1947 a scholar named D. C. Somervell squeezed the first six volumes into a single abridged edition, which became an instant bestseller. In place of Spengler's undisciplined and at times mystical flights of analysis, Toynbee brought to his task scholarly rigor and an expanse of knowledge that was truly comprehensive. *A Study of History,* wrote Chambers in *Time,* "was the most provocative work of historical theory written in England since Karl Marx's *Capital.*"

Toynbee identifies twenty-one civilizations of world history, of which he says only five had survived to our own time—Western; Orthodox Christian; Islamic; Hindu; and Far Eastern (China, Korea, Japan). All civilizations, argues Toynbee, are born of adversity and the challenges it poses. It may be the challenge of the sea, as in the Minoan and Hellenic civilizations. It may be the challenge of a hostile physical environment, such as the Nile delta before it was tamed by the Egyptians or the exuberant tropical forests converging upon the Mayans. It may be the challenge of hostile peoples, such as the Moors pushing through Spain and into France in the eighth century.

Whatever the challenge, a successful response breeds civilization, led by a "creative minority" that assesses the challenge and marshals the resources to fight it. The masses, inspired by this development and grateful to the creative minority, accept its leader-

ship. But every response to a challenge brings with it new challenges. The Athenians, for example, responded to overpopulation
on a thin soil by becoming a naval power and commercial empire.
But that spawned new challenges related to the empire's dealings
with its vassals and with Sparta.

This process of response-and-challenge never ends and thus
stands as an ongoing threat to the health and durability of the civilization. That's because ongoing success tends to breed a complacent conviction on the part of the creative minority that its past
success will breed future success. History shows that the inventors
and beneficiaries of any given military innovation, for example,
tend to then rest on their oars, allowing the next innovation to
come from their enemies. Flexibility of intellect and action tends
to decline as the forms of governance, culture, and habit begin to
freeze up. In short, as Chambers put it, "the creative minority
ceases to be creative."

This gives rise to the internal proletariat, generally "a social element or group that is 'in' but not 'of' any given society." It breaks
away from the leadership of the creative minority, posing a challenge that is met when the creative minority becomes a dominant
minority that rules by force. This sets in motion a time of crisis—
internal struggles and foreign wars—that abates only when one
nation emerges triumphant through the chaos to become a "universal state." Rome became one such universal state after it triumphed over Carthage and Macedonia.

The universal state is one of history's great paradoxes. Although
it appears powerful, it is in fact a manifestation of progressive decline. This decline is reflected in a "schism in the body social,"
which in reality masks a more fundamental "schism in the soul" of
the decaying civilization. This is seen in the vulgarity and barbarism in manners and art, in a "general confusion of tongues" as
language loses its coherence and distinctiveness, in the "syncretism of religion"—the fusion of rites, cults, and faiths that is the
"outward manifestation of that inward sense of promiscuity which
arises from the schism in the soul in an age of social disintegration."

This degenerative process proceeds as the manners of the proletariat become more libertine while those of the dominant minority become more harsh and vulgar. But ultimately they come together into what Chambers described as "one indiscriminate vulgarity." This was, in Toynbee's view, the state of the West at the time of his writing. But he took some small comfort in the fact that no universal state had yet been imposed, despite an attempt by Napoleon and two by Germany. There was still some measure of hope.

His hope was based on the historical record that such a state of decline almost inevitably breeds a savior, appearing as a figure either *of* or *from* the disintegrating society. But many of them fail. There are the saviors of the sword, bent on maintaining the universal state. All their efforts prove ephemeral. There are the saviors of the "time machine," focused on returning the society to healthier times of old or fashioning new visions of the future. But these inevitably resort to the sword and suffer the swordsman's fate. There is the "philosopher masked by a king"—Plato's famous remedy—who ultimately fails because of the incompatibility between the detachment of the philosopher and the coercive methods of the king. And finally there is "the God incarnate in a Man." For the West, this savior has already been identified, and he is Jesus of Nazareth, who "alone conquers death."

And so Toynbee sees societal salvation through the same medium that had been viewed as the medium of personal salvation throughout Western history—namely, Christianity. For Chambers, who abandoned communism and espionage when he found religion, this gave Toynbee's work "one hopeful meaning"—namely: "Under God, man, being the equal of his fate, is the measure of his own aspiration."

For H. Stuart Hughes, the Spengler biographer, this poses a contradiction. Toynbee rejected much of Spengler because he found him "unilluminatingly dogmatic," and yet in his religiosity, says Hughes, the Englishman "displays a greater dogmatism than Spengler himself." That's because as a Christian believer he had to hold up his religion and its ethics as the final truth. And thus was it necessary for him to suggest that the West was fundamentally different from all other civilizations. "The Christian historian," writes Hughes, "can scarcely grant that a civilization which has the unique distinction of serving as the vehicle of the true Church can suffer the fate of its predecessors." But that also gave Toynbee his popularity with much of his reading public, adds Hughes, for "he has come to represent for his admirers not so much an analyst of the past as an inspiring prophet and moral teacher for the future."

Beyond that, Toynbee rejects "the illusion of progress," in which historians "dispose their periods in a single series end to end, like the sections of a bamboo stem between joint and joint." And he adds his considerable voice to the idea that the West is merely one of many civilizations that have run their course in history. Thus, he dismisses "the misconception of 'the unity of history'—involving the assumption that there is only one river of civilization, our own, and that all others are either tributary to it or else lost in the desert sands."

The cultures of non-Western peoples, says Toynbee, are durable and ongoing and certainly not susceptible to being superseded by the West. "While the economic and political maps have now been Westernized," he writes, "the cultural map remains substantially what it was before our Western Society started on its career of economic and political conquest."

TOGETHER, SPENGLER AND TOYNBEE offer a significant counterweight to the Idea of Progress. One needn't embrace Spengler's mystical "destiny" or Toynbee's ultimate religiosity to find elements of their thinking that are relevant to today's momentous decisions affecting the course of world history. The two fundamental and opposing views of history emanating from Western thought—Progress and the Cyclical View—are intertwined in the foreign policy debates occupying American politics with growing intensity in the post-9/11 era. For if progress is indeed inexorable and universal, that suggests a particular way of looking at civic decision making in our own country and our own time, particularly in the realm of foreign relations. On the other hand, if progress is an illusion and strictly a Western concept in any event; if the force of culture lingers powerfully in other peoples of other civilizations around the world; if history is indeed cyclical—then that suggests entirely different ways of looking at our national choices and our national destiny. The debates riveting the American people in the post–September 11 era can best be seen and understood through the prism of these two competing Western concepts of history.

CHAPTER 3

Globalization and the End of History

I N 1910, A STARRY-EYED BRITISH economist named Norman Angell published a book called *The Great Illusion,* positing the notion that war among the industrial nations had become essentially obsolete. "How," he asked, "can modern life, with its overpowering proportion of industrial activities and its infinitesimal proportion of military, keep alive the instincts associated with war as against those developed by peace?" The book was an instant smash, translated into eleven languages and stirring something of a cult following throughout Europe. "By impressive examples and incontrovertible argument," wrote Barbara Tuchman in her narrative history *The Guns of August,* "Angell showed that in the present financial and economic interdependence of nations, the victor would suffer equally with the vanquished; therefore war had become unprofitable; therefore no nation would be so foolish as to start one."

At major universities throughout Britain, study groups of Angell acolytes sprang up. Viscount Esher, friend and confidant of the king, traveled widely to spread the gospel that "new economic factors clearly prove the inanity of aggressive wars." Such wars, he suggested, would spread "commercial disaster, financial ruin and individual suffering" on such a scale that the very thought of them would unleash powerful "restraining influences." Thus, as he told one military audience, the interlacing of nations had rendered war "every day more difficult and improbable."

In recounting all this, Tuchman barely conceals her contempt for Angell and Esher, which seems understandable given the carnage unleashed upon the European continent just four years after Angell's volume began its massive flow through bookstores. And yet there's something remarkably durable about the Angell thesis. In 1930, a year when the memory of World War I's rivers of blood must have been vivid in European minds, the king of England gave him a knighthood. Three years later he won the Nobel Peace Prize for his earnest agitations for world tranquillity. And in 1999, nearly ninety years after *The Great Illusion* appeared, a prominent *New York Times* columnist, Thomas L. Friedman, pronounced Angell's thesis to be "actually right," although he leavened his endorsement with a bow to Thucydides' observations about the causes of war.

All this poses a question: to what can we attribute the durability of Angell's discredited thesis and its reemergence after nearly a century filled with global conflict? The answer lies in the convergence of two developments of significance to Western thought—one distant and occurring over centuries, the other recent and bursting forth with stunning rapidity. The recent development was the West's Cold War victory over the Soviet Union in 1989 after nearly a half century of eyeball-to-eyeball confrontation. The distant development was the emergence of that seminal Western concept, the Idea of Progress.

This convergence is reflected in two publishing events of deep significance in America's recent intellectual life. One was the 1989 publication, in an obscure scholarly journal called *The National Interest,* of that essay by Francis Fukuyama entitled "The End of History?" Fukuyama, then a functionary on the State Department's planning staff but now a prominent academic, posited the notion that the West's coming Cold War victory represented "the end point of mankind's ideological evolution and the universalization of Western liberal democracy as the final form of human government." Borrowing from Hegel, he said this represented "the end of history" in that the ideological struggles of the ages had reached absolute finality, with profound benefit to the cause of world peace. It was a bombshell article, stirring debates that still reverberate among academics and intellectuals.

The other publishing event was the 1999 publication of Thomas Friedman's *The Lexus and the Olive Tree,* an analysis and celebration of what he called "the new era of globalization," characterized by the triumph of Western-style democratic capitalism and by greater prospects for global tranquillity than ever before in history. Friedman's book was widely reviewed, generated abundant favorable comment, and spent several months on the *New York Times* bestseller list. One reviewer called it "[perhaps] the first indispensable book of the new millennium."

These two efforts to explain the post–Cold War world reflect a fundamental reality of current Western thinking—namely, that the Idea of Progress remains for many the central underlying philosophical precept and the wellspring for much of what we see today in the way of perceptions, outlooks, predictions, and convictions. Both "The End of History?" and *The Lexus and the Olive Tree* are distillations of the Idea of Progress, applied to the post–Cold War world. And both embrace the mischievous corollary and the two great contradictions of the Progress concept. The mischievous corollary suggests that progress can alter fundamental human nature. The contradictions are, first, the notion that this inexorable progress can actually stop at a perceived end point of history; and, second, the persistent underlying idea of Eurocentrism, the perceived superiority and universality of Western ideas and ideals.

FRANCIS FUKUYAMA, the son of a Congregational minister and religion professor, grew up in a middle-class housing development on Manhattan's Lower East Side. At Cornell, he majored in classics and lived at a residence called Telluride House, a haven for philosophy students who enjoyed sitting around and discussing the great thinkers. After Cornell it was on to Yale, where he did graduate work in comparative literature, and then to Paris to further his literary studies. But he became alienated from what he considered the postmodern nihilism of the prominent scholars there, and he redirected his focus toward the tangible world of geopolitics. Three years later he had a Ph.D. from Harvard in political science, with a specialty in Middle Eastern and Soviet politics.

Upon getting the doctorate he joined the RAND Corporation in Santa Monica, where he spent several years writing papers of informed speculation on the fine points and likely implications of Soviet foreign and military policy. Then in early 1989, just before he was to join the State Department's planning staff, he delivered a lecture at the University of Chicago that sought to place the day's geopolitical events in a broad perspective. Owen Harries, editor of *The National Interest* (just four years old at the time, with a circulation of 5,600), read the speech and considered it precisely the kind of attention-grabbing analysis he wanted. Running to ten thousand words and appearing in the summer issue, it instantly thrust Fukuyama into the role of intellectual celebrity.

Fukuyama's embrace of the Idea of Progress is manifest in his provocative title, in his declaration that Western democratic capitalism represents the final destination point of human civic development, and in his belief in the universality of Western political ideals. But more fundamental is his reliance on the philosophy and dialectic of Hegel, the great nineteenth-century German philosopher.

Penetrating Hegel and his thinking is not an easy task. Irving Kristol, the neoconservative intellectual, calls Hegel "the most unreadable of our great philosophers." But more than anyone else Hegel established the history of philosophy as an important area of study. Robert Nisbet calls him "without question the preeminent philosopher of the nineteenth century." Kristol calls him "along with Kant the greatest philosopher of modernity." Aiming to develop a field of philosophy that would integrate the thinking of all his great philosophic predecessors, he posited the notion that these predecessors represented so many states of mind, each signifying a particular stage in the development of the human spirit toward ever greater levels of maturity.

Thus he was crucial to the development of the Idea of Progress. "In no philosopher or scientist of the nineteenth century," writes

Nisbet, "did the idea of progress . . . have greater weight than in Hegel's thought. There is scarcely a work in Hegel's voluminous writings that is not in some fashion or degree built around the idea of becoming, of growth and progress." In his essay replying to the Fukuyama article, Kristol offers a penetrating analysis of Hegel and his significance to Fukuyama's End of History thesis. On one level, he writes, Hegel's outlook was rather conventional in that he viewed history as an evolution from the more simple to the more complex and from the more naive to the more sophisticated. "All this," he writes, "was familiar to the eighteenth century under the rubric of Progress."

But Hegel went further, suggesting that this evolution represented a destiny determined by an inner logic—"an inner dialectic, to be more precise"—of which the historical actors were themselves ignorant. Thus, it was left to Hegel to reveal this whole inner dialectic and this destiny. "From a metaphysical point of view," writes Kristol, "this accession of self-consciousness by a German professor represented an achievement of the universe itself, of which humanity is the thinking self-conscious vehicle." In other words, before Hegel came upon the scene the various philosophers hammered away at their various bits of thinking, not knowing how they all fit together. But now they had the benefit of Hegel's dialectic showing how these fragments fit together and showing further how they would continue to develop into the future. Thus the history of philosophy now could be regarded as a kind of cultural evolution "whose inner dialectic," writes Kristol, "aimed always at increments of enlightenment—an evolution which we, from the privileged heights of modernity, can comprehend as never before."

This was breathtaking. And soon it wasn't just the history of philosophy that came under the spell of the Hegelian dialectic, but history itself. As Kristol points out, the idea that history is a human autobiography in which events gradually and inexorably mature into modernity serves as the underpinning for nearly all of today's historical inquiry, which assumes, he writes, "that we have the intellectual authority to understand the past as the past failed to understand itself." And this heady, self-congratulatory thinking inevitably captured Western politics as well. "After Hegel," writes Kristol, "all politics too becomes neo-Hegelian." Hegel saw the modern constitutional state and its liberal social order as the end point and the final purpose of history. But he realized that this end point resided largely in the realm of theory and that, in the practical world, the evolution was ongoing. "Now," writes Kristol, "Mr. Fukuyama arrives to tell us that, after almost two centuries, the job has been done and that the United States of America is the incarnation we have all been waiting for."

Viewing the Fukuyama thesis through such a prism, it is easy to see why he stirred such interest and controversy. In his essay, Fukuyama identifies Hegel as "the first philosopher to speak the language of modern social science." That's because he pioneered the idea of man as the product of his concrete historical and social environment and not, as earlier natural right theorists had suggested, a collection of more or less fixed "natural" attributes. This is precisely where Hegel embraced the concept of the malleability of human nature. And this is where Fukuyama did likewise.

As Fukuyama sees it, this perception of human nature is fundamental to the inescapable modern view of mankind. He writes: "The notion that mankind has progressed through a series of primitive states of consciousness on his path to the present, and that these stages corresponded to concrete forms of social organization . . . [culminating in] democratic-egalitarian societies, has become inseparable from the modern understanding of man." In other words, we're all Hegelians now.

Fukuyama moves from his Hegelian analysis to the question of whether the modern world harbors any fundamental "contradictions" that cannot be resolved in the context of what he calls the "universal homogenous state" of liberal democracy. The End of History, after all, represents a state of human development in which no such contradictions can emerge because we have reached "the common ideological heritage of mankind." But to make his point he runs through the possibilities.

First, communism. Fukuyama wrote prior to the profound

events of 1989 that marked the end of the Cold War—the massive exodus of East bloc citizens through Hungary and into Austria in late summer; the Soviet loss of nerve in the face of this display of defiance; the consequent disintegration of the Soviets' Eastern European empire; and the dramatic demolition of the Berlin Wall and the reunification of Germany. Thus he was prescient in seeing that Soviet communism was disintegrating and that it posed no serious alternative to Western democracy. "The Soviet Union could in no way be described as a liberal or democratic country," writes Fukuyama. "But at the end of history it is not necessary that all societies become successful liberal societies, merely that they end their ideological pretensions of representing different and higher forms of human society."

Next he looked at the "Asian alternatives," with similar results. The Fascism of Imperial Japan had been smashed, and postwar Japan had created a consumer culture "that has become both a symbol and an underpinning of the universal homogenous state." In other Asian societies economic liberalism was ushering in varying degrees of political liberalism. And even China had abandoned the strictures of Marxism-Leninism in an effort to foster growing prosperity. China was a long way from accepting the Hegelian formula, Fukuyama suggested. "Yet the pull of the liberal idea continues to be very strong as economic power devolves and the economy becomes more open to the outside world."

Fukuyama notes the speculation of some that the Soviet disintegration could usher in a threatening wave of Russian nationalism. He dismisses this as "curious" on the ground that it assumes unrealistically that the evolution of the Russian consciousness had "stood still" during the Soviet interregnum. Similarly, he dismisses the idea that nationalism or ethnic zeal could emerge from any quarter to pose a serious threat to the universal homogenous state.

As for Islamic fundamentalism, he concedes that Islam has indeed offered a theocratic state as a political alternative to Western liberalism. "But," he adds, "the doctrine has little appeal for non-Muslims, and it is hard to believe that the movement will take on any universal significance."

So there it is, the triumph of Western democratic capitalism. The death of Marxism-Leninism, writes Fukuyama, will usher in the growing "Common Marketization" of international relations and a sharp decline in the likelihood of large-scale conflict between states. Oh, sure, he adds, there would be holdout adherents of this dying ideology in places such as Pyongyang and Cambridge, Massachusetts, but the ideological battle had been waged and won. And, sure, there will be ongoing struggles among those peoples who had not yet reached the End of History, such as Palestinians, Kurds, Sikhs, and Irish Catholics. Moreover, states residing at the End of History may find themselves having to put down peoples whose consciousness had not yet evolved to history's end point. "But large-scale conflict must involve large states still caught in the grip of history, and they are what appear to be passing from the scene."

Fukuyama concedes that this new era could be a "very sad time" in some respects. What's missing is any sense of principle or idealism that is larger than the individual, something to believe in and to die for, any ideological struggle calling for daring, courage, imagination, and idealism. No, in their place will be mere economic calculation, endless technical advancement, a drive to satisfy sophisticated consumer demands. "In the post-historical period," concludes Fukuyama, "there will be neither art nor philosophy, just the perpetual caretaking of the museum of human history."

The response to all this was quick and powerful. *Chicago Tribune* columnist Stephen Chapman first called attention to the thesis. Then George Will took it up in his *Newsweek* column. *Time* ran a story, along with a photo of Fukuyama. By autumn of 1989 the thesis had been discussed in just about every major U.S. publication. In September the story hit the London papers, and a month later it was discussed in France's *Le Monde*. Reprints were translated into nearly a dozen languages. A Washington newsstand dealer, according to the *New York Times Magazine*, reported that the little quarterly journal containing Fukuyama's article was "outselling everything, even the pornography." And many of those writing

about the thesis used the same words of flattery to describe it—
"bold," "important," "stimulating," even "brilliant."

But many critics attacked it. *Time* writer Strobe Talbott called it
"pernicious nonsense." Christopher Hitchens, the prominent
British writer based in Washington, dismissed it with the words,
"At last, self-congratulation raised to the status of philosophy."
Columnist Charles Krauthammer suggested Fukuyama had entirely missed a fundamental reality of mankind, namely, man's ongoing struggle with evil. "Hence conflict, hence history," he wrote.

Irving Kristol's words, "I don't believe a word of it," capped a
pungent critique in *The National Interest* itself. In dismissing this
particular "wave of the future" and expressing his general skepticism of all such perceived waves, Kristol suggested they are no
more than "mirages provoked by a neo-Hegelian fever of the political imagination." And in arguing that all forms of government are
inherently unstable, he added that he assumed that even the
American democracy was "at risk" precisely because of its particular brand of democracy with all of its inherent "problematics," including the longing for community and spirituality, a growing
distrust of technology, the confusion of liberty with license, "and
many others besides."

Similarly, Harvard's Samuel P. Huntington argued that the End
of History overemphasized "the predictability of history and the
permanence of the moment." Current trends may or may not continue, he writes, but past experience would indicate that they are
unlikely to do so. "Indeed," he suggests, "in the benign atmo-
sphere of the moment, it is sobering to speculate on the possible
future horrors that social analysts are now failing to predict."
(Note that he wrote well before September 11, 2001.)

More important, Huntington zeroes in on Fukuyama's seeming
obliviousness to the "weakness and irrationality of human nature." He writes that Endists (his term for Fukuyama and his adherents) tend to assume that human beings will operate in ways that
are rational. Sure, says Huntington, human beings are at times rational, generous, creative, and wise, but they also can be stupid,
selfish, cruel, and sinful. "The struggle that is history began with

the eating of the forbidden fruit and is rooted in human nature." Therefore, while there may be total defeats in history, there are no final solutions. "So long as human beings exist, there is no exit from the traumas of history."

Putting the debate into its most stark perspective, Huntington suggests that dreamy attitudinizings about eras of natural peacefulness can be worse than merely wrongheaded; they can be dangerous. "To hope for the benign end of history is human," he concludes. "To expect it to happen is unrealistic. To plan on it happening is disastrous."

THE END OF HISTORY reappeared in a new guise a decade later when Thomas Friedman's *The Lexus and the Olive Tree* appeared in 1999 to declare the triumph of globalization. There wasn't anything particularly new about the book's underlying concept. Intellectuals and academics had been touting the emergence of this new era for years. But Friedman popularized the concept by explaining it in everyday terms and seeking a synthesis between the juggernaut of economic development and the imperatives of cultural preservation. Indeed, that was the symbolism of the Lexus and the Olive Tree. Friedman had been riding a Japanese train one day in 1992, speeding through the countryside at 180 miles per hour and pondering the Lexus factory he had just visited where three hundred luxury cars were being produced every day with 310 robots and just sixty-six human beings. Reading the *International Herald Tribune,* he encountered a story about a territorial interpretation by the U.S. State Department that had angered both Arabs and Israelis in the disputed lands of the West Bank.

There he was, experiencing the very latest in economic and technological advancement while reading about people who were still arguing over who owned which olive tree. It occurred to him that this was indeed the great conflict of the post–Cold War era. The Lexus represented "all the burgeoning global markets, financial institutions and computer technologies with which we pursue higher living standards today." The Olive Tree represented "everything that roots us, anchors us, identifies us and locates us in this world—whether it be belonging to a family, a community, a tribe, a nation, a religion."

Friedman avers that "olive trees are important." But he clearly accepts the idea that a lot of olive trees are going to be destroyed by the crushing force of globalization, and while he wants to preserve as many as possible his heart is with the Lexus. Globalization, he writes, "involves the inexorable integration of markets, nation-states and technologies to a degree never witnessed before—in a way that is enabling individuals, corporations and nation-states to reach around the world farther, faster, deeper and cheaper than ever before." The globalization culture is "homogenizing" and consists largely of the spread of Americanization on a global scale—"from Big Macs to iMacs to Mickey Mouse." Globalization's defining technologies—computerization, miniaturization, digitization, satellite communications, fiber optics, and the Internet—are fostering the era's defining perspective, which is "integration," symbolized by the World Wide Web, "which unites everyone."

And ultimately, suggests Friedman, nearly everyone will join this great new era, and pockets of resistance will fall away, because it is essentially about finding a better life, as symbolized by a woman he once encountered on the streets of Hanoi who took a bathroom scale to the sidewalk to offer people a chance to get weighed for a small fee. "That lady and her scale," he writes, "embody a fundamental truth about globalization. . . . And it is this: globalization emerges from below, from street level, from people's very souls and from their very deepest aspirations." Ultimately, it is about "the basic human desire for a better life—a life with more choices as to what to eat, what to wear, where to live, where to travel, how to work, what to read, what to write and what to learn. It starts with a lady in Hanoi, crouched on the sidewalk, offering up a bathroom scale as her ticket to the Fast World."

Thomas Friedman is a reporter of rare ability and one of the most influential journalists of his generation. Born in 1953 and reared in Minneapolis, he grew up in a middle-class family and developed an early passion for the history and politics of the Middle East. He pursued that passion in undergraduate studies at Brandeis University and at St. Antony's College, Oxford. After schooling he joined United Press International and got himself assigned to Beirut, where he covered Lebanon's fiery civil war. Later he moved up to the *New York Times,* served as bureau chief in both Beirut and Jerusalem, and won Pulitzer Prizes for his reporting in both capitals. His first book, *From Beirut to Jerusalem,* won a National Book Award in 1988. Transferred to Washington, he covered the State Department and international economics before landing the coveted *Times* foreign affairs column in late 1994. In 2002 he won a third Pulitzer for his op-ed analytics.

In his current job Friedman travels the world in search of stories and the meaning behind events, and he is a master at collecting, collating, and synthesizing information, as attested by *The Lexus and the Olive Tree.* The book pulls together fragments from an interview here, a dinner conversation there, a factory briefing elsewhere, a government report somewhere else, a story told by a friend—all strung together into a chatty and charming analytical structure. Like his columns, though, the book has a certain preachy quality, and it manifests elements of naïveté when it comes to human nature and the forces of history.

Friedman identifies the "three democratizations" that he says are the engines of globalization. The first is the democratization of technology, which "is enabling more and more people, with more and more home computers, modems, cellular phones, cable systems and Internet connections, to reach farther and farther, into more and more countries, faster and faster, deeper and deeper, cheaper and cheaper than ever before in history."

The second is the democratization of finance, which encompassed a number of important financial developments: the emergence of junk bonds, or high-risk but potentially high-yield instruments; the lending revolution that "securitized" the international debt market, allowing mutual funds, pension funds, and individuals to buy a piece of foreign countries' debts; the democratization of investing, with more and more Americans owning

401(k) pension accounts and participating in defined contribution retirement programs; and the emergence of floating exchange rates, which encouraged more and more countries to open up their capital markets to foreign investors. Thus, writes Friedman, we have gone from a world in which a few bankers held the sovereign debts of a few countries to a world in which millions of individuals, through pension funds and mutual funds, hold the sovereign debts of many countries.

The third is the democratization of information. "Thanks to satellite dishes, the Internet and television," writes Friedman, "we can now see through, hear through and look through almost every conceivable wall." This is most vividly seen in the emergence of global multichannel television, which has destroyed the ability of governments to isolate their people or keep them in the dark about life in the rest of the world.

These three democratizations are fueling the juggernaut of globalization, which in turn is giving just two choices to countries, companies, and individuals. They can embrace this awesome force and join the Fast World, or they can resist it and get crushed. Indulging his propensity to create clever phrases of illustration, he concocts a disease he calls Microchip Immune Deficiency Syndrome, or MIDS, which afflicts "any bloated, overweight, sclerotic system in the post–Cold War era." It is contracted by countries and companies that fail to inoculate themselves against changes brought about by the microchip and the three democratizations. The symptoms include "a consistent inability to increase productivity, wages, living standards, knowledge use and competitiveness, and [an inability] to respond to the challenges of the Fast World."

To ward off the disease, countries need to don the "Golden Straitjacket," which means free market capitalism of the Thatcher or Reagan variety, including privatization, free trade, relatively open borders, anti-monopoly policies, an ongoing assault on government bureaucracy and bloat, and deregulation of commerce, industry, and finance. Countries that put on the Golden Straitjacket will thrive in the Era of Globalization, says Friedman; countries that don't will fail. And that's why, he predicts, more and more countries ultimately will come around and join the Fast World. In this amazing new era, countries can simply choose prosperity over stagnation.

But of course this Fast World generates an inevitable backlash. As Friedman points out, nearly every country that has donned the Golden Straitjacket has spawned at least one populist party or major political candidate bent on fighting the onslaught of globalization. "They offer various protectionist, populist solutions which they claim will produce the same standards of living, without having to either run so fast, trade so far or open the borders so wide."

Perhaps more important is what Friedman calls the Super-Empowered Angry Man, which is another word for terrorist. Friedman's point in creating such a term is to convey not just the anger spawned by "Americanization-globalization," but also the new tools available to these angry men in the era of globalization—cell phones, Internet communications, handheld Blackberries, jet travel, the fungibility of money, easy passage across national borders. Friedman cites Ramzi Yousef, a mastermind of the first World Trade Center bombing in 1993, whom he describes as having "a high degree of motivation or depravity." We won't be able to tame such people with social programs based on compassion. "The only defense," writes Friedman, "is to isolate that hard core from the much larger society around them. The only way to do that is by making sure that as much of that society as possible has a stake in the globalization system."

And that's where America comes in. We are not only the world's role model for "globally integrated free-market capitalism," says Friedman (writing, of course, before September 11, 2001), but we also have a responsibility to support, foster, and sustain globalization worldwide. Fortunately, he adds, most peoples and nations around the globe, except for those Super-Empowered Angry Men, accept American might as the linchpin of world stability. Still, we might have to get rough from time to time. "The hidden hand of the market will never work without a hidden fist," Friedman writes, adding that the relative peace of recent years stemmed in large part from "the presence of American power and America's willingness to use that power against those who would threaten the system of globalization."

And, in the Friedman view, by protecting this globalized system, America will be fostering global peace as well. He posits what he calls the "Golden Arches Theory of Conflict Prevention," which notes that no two countries with a McDonald's franchise had fought a war against each other since each got its McDonald's. "I'm not kidding. It's uncanny," he writes with apparent wonderment.

Friedman concedes that America may be a bit reluctant to assume this role of global enforcer and regulator. Americans at the time of Friedman's writing were in the "odd position" of being responsible for nearly all of world stability while not being particularly willing to die for anything. But American reluctance, if it extends too far, "can threaten the stability of the whole system," and so America must play the role of its destiny—"the ultimate tolerable hegemon."

To support his admonition, Friedman quotes an academic named Paul Schroeder, who once posed to Friedman the view that periods of peace often flowered in history when a "tolerable hegemon" emerged to enforce the norms and rules of the era. Schroeder cited the so-called Vienna system of nineteenth-century Europe that was dominated by Britain and Russia, and the later Bismarckian period in the same century when Germany played the dominant role. As Friedman puts it in his characteristic breezy idiom, "Attention Kmart shoppers: Without America on duty, there will be no America Online."

AN ASSESSMENT OF THE Friedman formulation might well begin with this idea of the benign hegemon and the Schroeder analogies. The so-called Vienna system lasted all of thirty-three years, the later Bismarckian period for less than two decades. And yet Friedman seems to be saying, echoing Fukuyama, that this grand new era of globalization represents a kind of culmination in man's development—or at the very least a long era of relative world peace fueled by the powerful economic forces of our time, regulated and enforced benignly by the one great nation, America, which Friedman views as "a spiritual value and a role model" for all the world.

This is naive stuff. Friedman is deft in identifying and analyzing the global economic forces of our time, and they are indeed every bit as powerful as he suggests. But when it comes to placing these forces into a context of history and human nature, his musings lack analytical rigor. This is particularly true when he discusses globalization's inevitable impact on culture. "A healthy global society is one that can balance the Lexus and the olive tree all the time," he admonishes, adding that America stands as the premier role model here. But when discussing how America itself can maintain this balance, he suggests that "we can do this by supporting our public schools, paying our taxes, understanding that the government is not the enemy and always making sure we're still getting to know our neighbors over the fence and not over the Web."

Political analysis as exhortation is not serious political analysis. And this particular exhortation reflects the underlying naïveté of Friedman's thinking, for it seems to be inserted precisely to fill the gap in his analysis. That gap is human nature and historical forces. The impulses of human nature go far beyond the material comforts and options that so preoccupy Friedman; it isn't simply a matter of being free to decide what to eat, what to wear, what to buy, where to go, and what to read. Indeed, many societies come to regard such things as destructive of the verities of life. There are deep human motivations that go beyond mere material matters and reach to religious identity, national identity, cultural identity, ethnic identity—all bundled up into individual identity. And many of the cultural and national and ethnic impulses of non-Western peoples flow from their nature, developed over centuries and reflecting fundamental elements of identity.

But Friedman clearly sees human nature as malleable, subject to the powerful material forces he writes about so pungently. When he suggests, for example, that America should handle the Super-

Empowered Angry Man by inundating his society with American-ization-globalization and thus isolating him, he is falling into the trap of the mischievous corollary of the Idea of Progress—the notion that we can change human nature to fit our own concepts of the good society. We may find that what we're really facing is the Super-Empowered Angry Nation or the Super-Empowered Angry Culture. Certainly, world events since Friedman's book first appeared would suggest as much.

Friedman seeks to pay obeisance to the importance of culture with his olive tree metaphor, but ultimately he gives it short shrift. His answer is for other peoples around the world to simply be more like America, whose growing multiethnic character he extols. Thus Friedman slips into one of the two great contradictions of the Idea of Progress—Eurocentrism; in this case more of an extreme Americentrism. He seems to understand the potential dangers in this when he quotes historian Ronald Steel as saying, "It was never the Soviet Union but the United States itself that is the true revolutionary power. . . . The cultural messages we transmit through Hollywood and McDonald's go out across the world to capture and also undermine other societies. . . . We are not content merely to subdue others: We insist that they be like us. And of course for their own good. . . . The world must be democratic. It must be capitalistic. It must be tied into the subversive messages of the World Wide Web. No wonder many feel threatened by what we represent."

And yet Steel's critical portrayal of the American outlook pretty much captures the Friedman outlook as well. He expresses utter confidence that the world has no choice but to adopt the American model. But what if he is wrong? What if major areas of the world simply refuse? Then Friedman's grand vision of peace could turn out to be as ephemeral as that of his great precursor, Norman Angell.

Another great threat to globalization is globalization itself. As we have seen, Irving Kristol perceptively cites Aristotle in arguing that all forms of government are inherently unstable and inherently transitional. History tells us that what is true of forms of government can be equally true of economic systems. Sometimes they collapse, and almost never is the collapse predicted. If the U.S. economy should somehow slip into a deflationary spiral, as it almost did a short period back and as the Japanese economy actually did a decade ago, that single development would do in Friedman's globalization system like a bullet to the head.

In putting forth his broad geo-economic thesis, Friedman wisely avoids any grandiose notions about the end of history or the culmination of human development (although he comes close to the latter), and thus he largely avoids the controversy that greeted Fukuyama's essay ten years earlier. But the two views of America's post–Cold War destiny sprout from the same soil. It is the soil of the Idea of Progress. And such was their ultimate influence that their views seeped inexorably into the American consciousness, guiding the thinking and debates that surrounded the country's geopolitical actions. But even before 9/11 it was clear to some that history hadn't ended with the fall of the Berlin Wall and that globalization would not define the future of the world.

CHAPTER 4

The Clash of Civilizations

I N THE SUMMER OF 1993, the elite internationalist journal *Foreign Affairs* brought forth a nine-thousand-word essay by Harvard political scientist Samuel P. Huntington called "The Clash of Civilizations?" The piece was similar to the Fukuyama treatise in just one small respect: the title of each ended in a question mark. That's because the two scholars had sought to penetrate the future shape of global events following the West's Cold War triumph, and both felt a need to hedge their predictions with an interrogative construction. Beyond that, these two efforts to portray the post–Cold War world could not have been more different. It wasn't simply that they represented two distinct visions of the future; they also reflected two contradictory views of history and humankind.

If Fukuyama's Hegelian discourse emanated from the Idea of Progress, Huntington's outlook emerged directly from the Cyclical View of History. Its essence was that post–Cold War conflicts and alignments would be shaped not by ideology or big-power maneuverings or economic convergence but by the immutable force of culture. "The principal conflicts of global politics will occur between nations and groups of different civilizations," he wrote. "The fault lines between civilizations will be the battle lines of the future." He observed that political boundaries were being redrawn increasingly to coincide with ethnic, religious, and civilizational impulses. And he predicted that civilizational conflicts stemming from this surge in cultural identity were likely to be highly intense, difficult to adjudicate, and potentially very bloody. "Differences among civilizations are not only real; they are basic," he wrote. "Over the centuries . . . [these] differences have generated the most prolonged and the most violent conflicts."

The Huntington thesis was a direct thrust against Fukuyama's earlier End of History thesis and would stand as a counterargument to Thomas Friedman's later globalization enthusiasms. It also served as an ongoing assault on the many manifestations of this optimistic outlook that emerged throughout the 1990s in various books, scholarly journals, and op-ed musings. As Robert D. Kaplan, a leading analyst of the geopolitical terrain and a Huntington enthusiast, put it in *The Atlantic Monthly,* "Neoconservatives assumed that democratic elections and the unleashing of market forces would improve life everywhere. Liberals assumed that power politics and huge defense budgets were relics of the past. . . . A new transnational elite was emerging, composed of prominent academics and business leaders who believed that the world was on the verge of creating a truly global culture." And then along comes Sam Huntington to declare this to be utter nonsense.

Like Spengler and Toynbee, Huntington rejects what he calls the "linear . . . nature of history" that is a bedrock of the Idea of Progress. He argues that the West is in decline, which would be impossible under the rubric of Progress. He sees the lingering cultures of the world as powerfully distinct and protective of their own identities, which assaults the idea that Western progress would or could apply to all mankind. His vision of ongoing world strife based on cultural impulse counters the notion that mankind, under Western auspices, is reaching a kind of end point of history. And he explicitly rejects the view that America or the West represents a universal culture that will be embraced by peoples everywhere. Thus it becomes clear that his tradition of historiography is not the Idea of Progress but the Cycles of History.

Huntington's *Foreign Affairs* piece hit America's intellectual consciousness with a rare force. For many, it was not a welcome intrusion into the post–Cold War discourse, and yet its cogency and internal logic demanded attention. It could not be ignored. The magazine's managing editor at the time, Fareed Zakaria (later editor of *Newsweek International*), called it "the most famous article that *Foreign Affairs* has published in decades, the most celebrated, the most widely quoted, reprinted." It was translated into twenty-six languages and served as topic of discussion for academic conferences throughout the world. Huntington himself was invited to discuss his views in more than twenty countries on five continents.

Three years after his article appeared, Huntington expanded the thesis into a book, removed the question mark, and bolstered the title: *The Clash of Civilizations and the Remaking of World Order*. It quickly became a national bestseller, was translated into twenty-four languages, and was, according to University of Washington political scientist Joel Migdal, "the most widely read book in the social sciences in the 1990s." The book took the theme in some new directions and explored in greater detail the implications of its fundamental insight. "Clashes of civilizations are the greatest threat to world peace," he wrote, "and an international order based on civilizations is the surest safeguard against world war."

Both book and article won praise as being "provocative," "imaginative," and "bold." But the thesis itself ultimately was rejected by most academics and other intellectuals. Some said it underestimates the ongoing importance of nation-states. Others said culture doesn't shape geopolitics because geopolitics trumps culture. Still others suggested it overestimates the cohesiveness of civilizations. Some of the attacks betrayed a certain political emotion. "Dubious propositions," wrote political scientist and former diplomat Jeane J. Kirkpatrick. "Misconceived, curiously ignorant . . . and a disastrous guide to thinking about international affairs and national policy," wrote William Pfaff in the *International Herald Tribune*. A "threat to peace and human well-being," wrote Thomas R. DeGregori in the *Houston Chronicle*.

TO UNDERSTAND THE HUNTINGTON thesis and its provenance it is necessary first to understand the man and his work. He has earned for himself a place among the preeminent political scientists of his generation and a reputation as one of the most penetrating big-picture thinkers in his field. From his academic redoubt as Harvard's Albert J. Weatherhead III University Professor and director of the university's John M. Olin Institute for Strategic Studies, he has produced what many consider seminal works in three of the four sub-disciplines of political science. All have reflected his well-known zest for controversy. As a young man he missed tenure at Harvard because of the ruckus he kicked up with his first book. Then a few years later, after the offending thesis became widely embraced, he was ceremoniously invited back. That seems to be a Huntington pattern: his analyses have generated waves of intellectual disparagement but slowly gained acceptance as more and more scholars penetrated his deeper insights.

He was born in 1927 and grew up in New York City amid middle-class surroundings and a family tradition of literary and publishing pursuits. His father was an editor for hotel industry publications. His mother wrote poetry and short stories. His maternal grandfather had been a crusading journalist and a founder of the muck-raking, turn-of-the-century *McClure's* magazine. Something of a prodigy, young Samuel was graduated from Peter Stuyvesant High School at sixteen and blitzed through Yale in two and a half years. After a stint in the army he took a master's degree at the University of Chicago and then headed for Harvard, where in 1951 he received his Ph.D. and began his teaching career.

He was a conventional anti-communist liberal who believed in collective bargaining, the minimum wage, Social Security, and government intervention into the domestic economy. "FDR was God," he recalls, reminiscing some years back in a series of conversations with the author. "And the New Deal was accepted wisdom."

But his political outlook shifted in subtle ways with the emergence of McCarthyism in the early 1950s. He deplored Senator Joseph McCarthy's communist-hunting crusade and bullying tactics. But he perceived that the liberal response, however eloquent, wasn't particularly effective. Many liberals, he felt, undermined their own position by adamantly refusing to acknowledge the threat of Soviet espionage at a time when most Americans knew the threat was real. "I concluded," he says, "that it was the conservatives who were providing a more effective response—particularly conservative institutions such as the army and the Senate." Questioning some of the implicit liberal assumptions that had guided his thinking up to that time, he came to regard human nature as unchanging, conflict as inevitable, evil as a part of life, and institutions as crucial in fostering societal stability.

These assumptions formed the bedrock for much of Huntington's subsequent scholarship, which focused largely on authority and stability. Influenced by the thinking of Reinhold Niebuhr, the twentieth-century Protestant theologian who viewed sound societal institutions as necessary to keep the reality of human wickedness in check, he developed a new interest in the writings of Edmund Burke and the American Founding Fathers. In a provocative 1957 article in the *American Political Science Review* entitled "Conservatism As an Ideology," he identifies Burke as representing most of the major components of the conservative creed: society is the natural, organic product of slow historical growth, and existing institutions embody the wisdom of previous generations; man is a creature of instinct and emotion as well as reason, and evil resides in human nature rather than in any particular societal institutions; the community is superior to the individual, and the rights of men derive from civic responsibility; except in an ultimate moral sense, men are unequal, and society always consists of a variety of classes, orders, and groups; and settled schemes of government based on human experience are always superior to abstract experimentation.

Thus, writes Huntington, conservatism differs from every other ideology (except radicalism) in that it lacks any "substantive ideal"—a vision of the perfect society. "No political philosopher," he writes, "has ever described a conservative utopia." On the contrary, true conservatism is situational, arising when a fundamental challenge is directed at established institutions. "The essence of conservatism is the passionate affirmation of the value of existing institutions." Burke's conservatism, for example, would stir him to defend the English constitution of his day first against the Crown's effort to aggrandize itself over Parliament and later against the democrats' resolve to broaden the people's control over Parliament.

The relevance of all this to his own time, writes Huntington, was that America's liberal institutions were under mortal threat from Soviet communism, and the greatest bulwark against that threat was the contingent of society that had the most at stake— America's liberals. "This defense," he writes, "requires American liberals to lay aside their liberal ideology and to accept the values of conservatism for the duration of the threat." He asks whether a liberal is any less liberal if he adjusts his thinking in order to defend the most liberal institutions in the world. His answer: "Conservatism does not ask ultimate questions and hence does not give final answers. But it does remind men of the institutional prerequisites of social order."

American liberals of 1957 pretty much ignored this admonition. But they reacted with fury the same year when he published *The Soldier and the State,* a penetrating study of the military culture and its role in civil-military relations. The book was attacked as a glorification of militarism, and its final passage extolling the culture of West Point was cited as a major reason for rejection when Harvard's Government Department met to determine the young professor's fate. When tenure was denied he took up teaching duties at Columbia, where he had four productive years before accepting the invitation to return to Cambridge.

That final passage was indeed provocative, proclaiming that West Point was "a gray island in a many colored sea, a bit of Sparta in the midst of Babylon." He wondered whether the military values of loyalty, duty, restraint, and dedication were the ones America needed most, then answered: "Today America can learn more from West Point than West Point from America." It was easy to see how that final passage would stir the passions of Harvard's liberal academic cadres. But the overall thesis was more subtle and more worthy than many critics would acknowledge.

The fundamental question of civil-military relations, argues Huntington, involves finding balance between the need to protect a society's security and the imperative of maintaining the essential ideologies and institutions of the society. A military reflecting the prevailing civilian mores probably won't succeed as a security institution, while a military entirely isolated from those mores could ultimately threaten its own nation. But in America, protected by a rare birthright of geography and circumstance, this delicate trade-off didn't pose much of a challenge through most of the nation's history. There wasn't much of an external threat to worry about.

In the world of nuclear warheads and intercontinental missiles, all that changed. Whereas in earlier decades Americans could afford to tailor their military to fit their liberal democratic values, the new imperatives of technology and the Cold War required Americans to think more about how to tailor civilian society to meet the nation's security threat. Yet many elements of American society continued to deride the military as reactionary and to judge the officer corps on the basis of civilian values. This undermines military professionalism, which contributes more to a sound military-civil balance than many civilian institutions. That's because the military is inherently conservative—accepting existing institutions, desiring balance in power relationships, espousing limited goals based on tradition and the lessons of history. Huntington's book extolled these traits as a national asset in a difficult time. Notwithstanding the controversy it generated when published, *The Soldier and the State* remains in print nearly fifty years later and is regarded as the premier theoretical treatise on its subject.

The same pattern can be seen in Huntington's subsequent works, including the 1968 *Political Order in Changing Societies*, which turned on its head the then conventional wisdom about Third World political development. At a time when many academics saw great promise in democratization efforts around the world, Huntington saw "political decay." He argued that levels of citizen participation and the development of political institutions needed to go hand in hand, or the result was likely to be chaos and revolution. The book begins with an intensely provocative statement of reality that would send his colleagues into intellectual tumult but eventually become accepted wisdom: "The most important political distinction among countries concerns not their form of government but their degree of government. The differences between democracy and dictatorship are less than the differences between those countries whose politics embodies consensus, community, legitimacy, organization, effectiveness, stability, and those countries whose politics is deficient in these qualities." In other words, the degree of democracy is less important than the degree of stability because democracy cannot emerge in unstable environments.

Predictably, the book was attacked as an apologia for anti-democratic dictators clinging to power for selfish ends and as a rationale for slowing down democratic movements in under-developed countries. But now it is widely embraced, and the academic world generally acknowledges that there is a logic to political development just as there is in economic development. Fareed Zakaria of *Newsweek* calls *Political Order in Changing Societies* "one of the three or four most influential books ever written in the field of comparative politics."

In 1981, after a stint on President Jimmy Carter's National Security Council, Huntington produced a book called *American Politics: The Promise of Disharmony*, a far-reaching exploration of the implications of America's traditional skepticism toward government. This skepticism, he argues, serves to limit government but also leads to intermittent times of anti-government fervor—or "creedal passion"—that stem from the country's inherent inability to fulfill the high ideals upon which it was based. In other words, the ongoing "disharmony" between America's liberal tradition and the realities of governance contributed to the anti-government sentiments of the Revolutionary, Jacksonian, and Progressive periods, as well as the fervent cultural revolts of the 1960s.

While this should be understood as a natural and even healthy element of the American experience, writes Huntington, it also poses a challenge and a danger. That's because these periods of creedal passion tend to diminish the authority of fundamental American institutions. "The American political system, which is so superbly designed to prevent and to rectify abuses of authority," he writes, "is very poorly equipped to reverse the erosion of authority."

What we see in Huntington's body of work is an intellect that focuses laserlike on human nature as it really is and not on dreamy ideas about the ideal society or how proper arrangements can transform mankind and spawn peace and happiness. From the beginning of his career, Huntington eschewed the more far-reaching elements of the Idea of Progress and pursued reasoning more in keeping with the American Founding Fathers and thinkers such as Burke and Niebuhr. Not surprisingly, this outlook also served as the foundation of his thinking when he sat down to put forth his stark vision of the Clash of Civilizations.

HE BEGINS THE BOOK with a number of anecdotes involving national flags, including a 1994 episode in Los Angeles when seventy thousand people marched beneath "a sea of Mexican flags" to protest the Proposition 187 referendum that would deny many state benefits to illegal immigrants and their children. When critics disparaged the use of another country's flag, protesters responded two weeks later by marching with the American flag—upside down. These flag displays, says Huntington, helped ensure a wide-margin victory for the referendum (which later was struck down by the judiciary).

"In the post–Cold War world," writes Huntington, "flags count and so do other symbols of cultural identity, including crosses, crescents, and even head coverings, because culture counts, and cultural identity is what is most meaningful to most people." He quotes the Venetian nationalist demagogue in Michael Dibdin's novel *Dead Lagoon:* "There can be no true friends without true enemies. Unless we hate what we are not, we cannot love what we are. These are the old truths we are painfully rediscovering after a century and more of sentimental cant. Those who deny them deny their family, their heritage, their culture, their birthright, their very selves!" Huntington adds, "The unfortunate truth in these old truths cannot be ignored by statesmen and scholars. For peoples seeking identity and reinventing ethnicity, enemies are essential, and the potentially most dangerous enmities occur across the fault lines between the world's major civilizations."

The salient elements of the Clash thesis are these:

The West is in decline. True, the West still dominates geopolitics and certainly international economics, says Huntington, and will continue to do so for a long time. But a broad historical perspective indicates a downward trend, manifest in the shrunken proportion of the earth's land and population under Western domination and also in the West's diminishing ability to hold sway over other regions. As the West attempts to assert its values and protect its interests in the face of this decline, non-Western societies will face a choice as to whether they want to emulate the West or build up their own economic and military power as a counterweight. "A central axis of post–Cold War world politics is thus the interaction of Western power and culture with the power and culture of non-Western civilizations."

Global politics is now multipolar and multicivilizational. This is unprecedented in world history. For most of recorded time, contacts between civilizations were intermittent or nonexistent. Then at the dawn of the modern era around A.D. 1500, global politics focused on two dimensions: a multipolar system within the West; and Western conquest or domination of other peoples outside the West. That lasted nearly four hundred years. Then came the bipolar Cold War period, which served to thwart the civilizational expression of non-Western societies. With the coming of the post–Cold War era, all that changed. Now we have seven or eight major civilizations, with the leading countries of the world nearly all coming from different ones. "Power is shifting from the long predominant West to non-Western civilizations," writes Huntington. Economic power, for example, is building in East Asia, and military power and political influence are starting to follow. India appears on the threshold of an economic takeoff, and the population surge among Muslims has spurred an "Islamic resurgence."

Thus, non-Western civilizations no longer are the objects simply of Western power and Western history. Increasingly they are becoming the movers and shapers of their own history—and to a growing extent of Western history as well. What's more, the period of intracivilizational strife within the West has come to an end. Those battles, dominating Western history for centuries, focused on political ideologies, the peculiar preoccupation of the West. Huntington points out that all the great ideologies of the twentieth century—liberalism, socialism, anarchism, Marxism, communism, social democracy, conservatism, and so on—were products of the West. "No other civilization has generated a significant political ideology." But the West has generated no major religion, and the pivotal Westphalian separation of religion and international politics was an idiosyncratic Western concept. So now, as the West recedes and the ideologies that typified late-Western civilization recede with it, those political ideologies will be supplanted by the religious and cultural elements of other civilizations. "The intracivilizational clash of political ideas spawned by the West," writes Huntington, "is being supplanted by an intercivilizational clash of culture and religion."

The West is unique, not universal. As noted above, Huntington dismisses "the widespread and parochial conceit that the European civilization of the West is now the universal civilization of the world." Invoking the two great Cycles of History intellectuals of the twentieth century, he notes approvingly that Oswald Spengler denounced "the myopic view of history prevailing in the West with its neat division into . . . phases relevant only to the West." He endorses Spengler's rejection of this "Ptolemaic approach to history" and embraces his Copernican vision of "the drama of a number of mighty cultures." Huntington also praises Arnold Toynbee's later castigation of the "parochialism and impertinence" of the West manifest in its "egocentric illusions" about Western superiority and the inevitability of progress. "Like Spengler," he writes, Toynbee "had no use for the assumption of the unity of history."

Clearly, Samuel Huntington has no use for it either. Displaying his brutally cold-eyed regard for history, he writes, "The West won the world not by the superiority of its ideas or values or religion (to which few members of other civilizations were converted) but rather by its superiority in applying organized violence. Westerners often forget this fact; non-Westerners never do."

Huntington's rejection of the "universal culture" concept constitutes what is probably the sharpest edge of his thesis. Although his prose never lacks for piquancy and directness, he seldom displays the dismissive tone that seeps into his writing on this subject. He notes that some of the most ardent proponents of Western universalism are "intellectual migrants to the West," such as V. S. Naipaul and Fouad Ajami, "for whom the concept provides a highly satisfying answer to the central question: Who am I?" He adds: "'White man's nigger,' however, is the term one Arab intellectual applied to these migrants, and the idea of a universal civilization finds little support in other civilizations." In dismissing the "naïve arrogance" of those who suggest non-Westerners will become "Westernized" by acquiring highly branded Western products, he asks: "What, indeed, does it tell the world about the West when Westerners identify their civilization with fizzy liquids, faded pants, and fatty foods?"

Huntington also rejects the notion, put forth by many in the globalization camp, that, as non-Western countries modernize their societies, they will inevitably become Westernized. Some will, but most won't, he says. Approvingly he quotes French intellectual Fernand Braudel's comment that it would be "almost childish" to think that modernization or the "triumph of *civilization* in the singular" would lead to the end of the plurality of historic cultures developed over centuries. No, says Huntington, modernization is more likely to strengthen non-Western cultures and thus reduce the relative power of the West. "In fundamental ways, the world is becoming more modern and less Western."

At this point it is necessary to puncture the widespread misinterpretation of the Clash thesis that dogged Huntington in the months and years after publication of his article and book. Many commentators criticized him for predicting a dark winter of unavoidable global conflict and glorifying cultural conflict in such a way as to make it a self-fulfilling prophecy. One stark example was Thomas Friedman in his *The Lexus and the Olive Tree,* which characterizes the Huntington thesis as suggesting that "with the Cold War over, we won't have the Soviets to kick around any more, so we will naturally go back to kicking the Hindus and Muslims around and them kicking us around." This betrays a fundamental lack of understanding of Huntington's thesis.

In truth, Huntington's book seeks to elucidate the forces unleashed upon the globe at the close of the Cold War so that the reality of those forces might inform policy makers bent on crafting a relatively peaceful world. Further elements of his thesis reflect this hope and hopefulness:

Global stability will depend upon civilizational "core states." Huntington believes that civilizational coalescence will center on certain core states—America for the West; Russia for the Orthodox civilization; China for the Sinic; India for the Hindu. Unfortunately, Islam has no core state, which is likely to be problematic in the future because core states must shoulder the burden of ensuring world stability. "The core states of civilizations," he writes, "are sources of order within civilizations and, through negotiations with other core states, between civilizations."

But the core states can also breed instability. Writing before 9/11, Huntington suggested the dangerous clashes of the future are likely to arise from "the interaction of Western arrogance, Islamic intolerance, and Sinic assertiveness." And the central problem in the relations between the West and other civilizations is the "discordance between the West's—particularly America's—efforts to promote a universal Western culture and its declining ability to do so." A wiser course, he suggests, would be for America and the West to acknowledge the distinctiveness of other civilizations and to foster relations with their core states.

Civilizations, says Huntington, are like extended families, a kinship, in which the core states act as the older members of the family, providing their kin with both support and discipline. What's more, the exercise of influence by core states is "tempered and moderated" by the common culture they share with their kindred countries. That's because it is the cultural commonality of civilizations that legitimates the leadership and the order-imposing role of the core state for both member states and for external powers. If this legitimacy is challenged, the result is likely to be instability or chaos; if it is recognized, then prospects for negotiation and discipline are bolstered.

Thus, for Huntington the post–Cold War era is likely to be more peaceful if the globe can become a "spheres-of-influence world" in which acknowledged core states play a leading role in both dominating and representing their particular spheres. "Where core states exist," he writes, ". . . they are the central elements of the new international order based on civilizations." World stability, he adds, will emerge "on the basis of civilizations or not at all."

The West is threatened not just from without but from within. "The central issue for the West," writes Huntington, "is whether, quite apart from any external challenges, it is capable of stopping and reversing the internal processes of decay." He bluntly links this decay with the fervent multiculturalism that has become so voguish among intellectuals in recent decades. He notes that for more than two centuries the American national identity has been defined culturally by the heritage of Western civilization and politically by the principles of what he calls "the American Creed"—liberty, democracy, individualism, equality before the law, constitutionalism, private property. In recent decades, both components of the American identity have come under "concentrated and sustained onslaught from a small but influential number of intellectuals and publicists." These are people who have attacked America's identification with Western civilization, rejected the idea of a common American culture, and "promoted racial, ethnic, and other subnational cultural identities and groupings."

In an era of civilizational conflict, it is more important than ever that the West appreciate its heritage and understand its identity. But this is all in serious erosion at present. "The contrast with the past is striking," writes Huntington, noting that the Founding Fathers saw diversity as a reality and a problem. That's why they adoped *e pluribus unum* as the national motto. Through most of our history this unity was considered a fundamental national goal, but in recent decades many national leaders have "assiduously promoted the diversity rather than the unity of the people they govern."

This is likely to be exacerbated, says Huntington, by current immigration patterns. He sees the West as facing a major challenge from "immigrants from other civilizations who reject assimilation and continue to adhere to and to propagate the values, customs, and cultures of their home societies." If assimilation fails, then America likely will become what he calls a "cleft country"—one in which large groupings belong to different civilizations, a circumstance that historically results in "potentials for internal strife and disunion."

Here's where we come to the crux of Huntington's thesis as it applies to how America and the West should think and operate in the era of civilizational competition and strife. "The preservation of the United States and the West requires the renewal of Western identity," he writes. "The security of the world requires acceptance of global multiculturality." What we're seeing in the United States, however, is just the opposite. The domestic multiculturalists want to make America like the world, while the global monoculturalists want to make the world like America. But a multicultural America is impossible, says Huntington, "because a non-Western America is not American." And a multicultural world is unavoidable "because global empire is impossible." The central point is that domestic multiculturalism and global universalism both deny the uniqueness of Western culture. And both threaten to destabilize the West as well as the world.

SAM HUNTINGTON'S Clash of Civilizations thesis emanates from the Cyclical View of History, just as Francis Fukuyama's End of History treatise and Thomas Friedman's globalization framework stem from the Idea of Progress. These are the two great Western views of history bequeathed to our time by our intellectual forebears. And they have been guiding America's foreign policy debates, however subtly or silently, since the end of the Cold War. If Western ideas and ideals, particularly as seen in the American system, represent the end point of history and the fruit of long centuries of human progress, then it's axiomatic that these ideas and ideals should be spread around the world. That's the best way to bring the peoples of the various civilizations together and ensure peace and happiness throughout the globe. The Abbé de Saint-Pierre would be proud.

But if history is the story of distinct civilizations, each with its own identity, cultural impulse, and sense of destiny, and if those things are deep in the consciousness of each civilization, then any drive to impose one civilization's values upon another is likely to end in disaster. In the geopolitical debates that have reverberated in America since the fall of the Berlin Wall, the participants have generally been in one camp or the other. When President Bill Clinton, in the 1990s, eschewed American involvement in blood-soaked Bosnia because he had read in Robert D. Kaplan's *Balkan Ghosts* that the animosities there were deeply embedded in cultural consciousness and hence intractable, he was buying into the Cycles of History outlook. When he reversed course and took his country into that crucible of enmity and wrath, he had crossed over to the Idea of Progress.

And the ideological struggle between these two competing philosophical perceptions of man in history is going to increase in intensity as America seeks its way in a post–Cold War world thrown into turmoil by the bloody assault on Americans by Islamic fundamentalists on September 11, 2001. But here's a question: Which of these two competing views of history best explains those fateful events? The Idea of Progress or the Cycles of History? Francis Fukuyama and Thomas Friedman or Samuel Huntington?

Friedman moved quickly in the wake of the attacks to provide his own answer. In a column published within days of the carnage he approvingly quoted Israeli foreign minister Shimon Peres as declaring, "This is not a clash of civilizations." The columnist himself drew a distinction between God-worshipping Muslims and the real enemy, whom he identified as people who pray to "the God of hate." This distinction, however flimsy, was necessary to Friedman because without it he would find himself hard pressed to preserve his paradigm of globalization. But if the problem is simply a contingent of hate worshippers who happen to be Muslims, then maybe it would still be possible to Americanize the Middle East. Maybe he could still preserve his conviction that American culture is the universal culture and will be embraced eventually and inevitably by people everywhere around the globe.

Huntington, on the other hand, largely fell silent following September 11, leaving his thesis to speak for itself. But even before that historic day he had answered Friedman's "God of hate" formulation in *The Clash of Civilizations and the Remaking of World Order.* "Some Westerners," he wrote, ". . . have argued that the West does not have problems with Islam but only with violent Islamist extremists. Fourteen hundred years of history demonstrate otherwise."

CHAPTER 5

Isolation and Intervention

ON JUNE 20, 1917, former President Theodore Roosevelt traveled with his family to New York harbor to see sons Archibald and Theodore Jr. off to war in a steel-hulled steamer called *Chicago*. As the two young men mingled with family and friends prior to departure, their father performed his usual ritual of fluttering about, issuing his characteristic pronunciamentos followed by his staccato guffaws. But some in the party became visibly uncomfortable when this father of four combat-trained sons suggested, with apparent grim elation, that one might very well be wounded or possibly even killed in the righteous cause of patriotism.

Sometime later the elder Roosevelt wrote to a friend, "how glad I would be if I could see Ted, Kermit, Archie, Quentin and Dick [a close family friend] all coming permanently home in a bunch, shy, say, three arms and two legs, evenly distributed among them!" As TR biographer Kathleen Dalton wrote in revealing this passage, "He was deadly serious."

From the perspective of twenty-first-century America, one feels compelled to wonder what this man possibly could have been thinking to toss off such casual grimness about his own offspring at such a moment or to set to paper such morbid thoughts. The answer is that he was a man who found glory in giving utter devotion to something far greater than himself and his family. That something was the United States of America, the greatest nation on earth, for which his ambition was boundless. This ambition manifested itself for the citizen in the splendor of personal sacrifice; for the country, in the credo of imperialism.

In his heart, Roosevelt thrilled to the idea of American empire on the British model, with American boys spreading national power to whatever corners of the world were still available for colonization. His outlook, very audacious, contained a kind of Will to Power expansionism of the kind that Spengler later would identify as representative of the civilizational phase of Western history. But there was also a strain of the Idea of Progress in liberal interventionist garb, based on the view, popularized in Britain by the famed poet Rudyard Kipling, that the extension of Anglo-Saxon power would actually benefit backward peoples around the world.

Roosevelt's imperialist impulse represented one of the five strains of foreign policy thinking that emerged in the United States after the country had consolidated its power across the breadth of the North American continent. In point of fact, imperialism of the stripe that Roosevelt favored—a kind of Will to Power variety based on the idea that America should expand its power and influence wherever it could do so—didn't survive his own presidency, as fundamental realities and new thinking converged to make clear the limits to this bold concept. But elements of it lingered in the foreign policy debates and actions of America throughout the twentieth century and into the twenty-first. And today, as America struggles with the forces of the post–Cold War world, it is stirring once again.

Besides the TR vision of American expansionism on the British model of his day, the other strains are: liberal or humanitarian interventionism, based on the view that American power should be exercised throughout the world on behalf of all mankind; conservative isolationism, based on the conviction that America is pristine and the world corrupt, and hence maintaining America's purity requires that it stay out of the evil world; liberal isolationism, which begins with the assumption that the world is pure while America is not, and hence American forays into the world are likely to generate evil results; and conservative interventionism, based on the conviction that America must play a major role in the world but only in behalf of vital national interests and the interests of Western civilization.

Throughout the century that unfolded after the great imperialist year of 1898, these strains battled for primacy as the guiding influence of American foreign policy. It began with the idea of empire, the natural extension of the Manifest Destiny concept that had spurred the Anglo-Saxon ascendancy in North America during the preceding century.

Even before 1898, America was flexing muscles it didn't have in behalf of its imperialist ambition. In 1895, with a navy that Kipling considered "as unprotected as a jellyfish," the country audaciously thrust a sword of belligerence at Great Britain, then involved in a dispute with Venezuela over the jungle border between that country and British Guiana. When President Grover Cleveland decided to intervene on the side of Venezuela, Theodore Roosevelt declared, "I rather hope that the fight will come soon. The clamor of the peace faction has convinced me that this country needs war." As it happened, the crisis passed without conflict.

But Britain resolved never again to slip into geopolitical controversy with this rising Anglo-Saxon power across the sea. As Joseph Chamberlain, the prominent British politician of the era, put it, "I refuse to speak or think of the United States as a foreign nation. They are our flesh and blood. . . . Our past is theirs. Their future is ours. . . . Their forefathers sleep in our churchyards." And for America's prevailing Anglo-Saxon elite, nurtured on large doses of Anglophilia dispensed at places such as Groton School and Harvard and Yale, the feeling was mutual.

In the meantime, William McKinley assumed the presidency in 1897 amid promises to avoid foreign entanglement. "We want no wars of conquest," he declared. "We must avoid the temptation of territorial aggression." Yet a clamor was rising throughout the land for American military action to terminate Spain's four-hundred-year Cuban presence, which had taken on a harsh brutality in response to widespread insurrection within the island colony. When McKinley hesitated, Roosevelt dismissed him contemptuously as being "as soft as a chocolate éclair." But when an explosion sank the U.S. battleship *Maine* in Havana harbor, the president could hesitate no longer. Though the ship's presence there was in itself a provocation and there was never any solid evidence that Spain sabotaged it, the incident inflamed America and led to a war that Spanish officials were nearly desperate to avoid.

For good reason. As it turned out, America destroyed Spain's Atlantic and Pacific fleets within four months, then moved quickly to extract Puerto Rico, Guam, and the Philippines from Spanish dominion. For good measure the country then acquired Hawaii. As the *Washington Post* proclaimed after Commodore George Dewey's liquidation of Spain's Pacific fleet in Manila Bay, "The guns of Dewey at Manila have changed the destiny of the United States. . . . An imperial policy!"

The American people cheered this new American empire. And Roosevelt himself, a hero to the nation after word spread of his bold charge up "San Juan Hill," came to personify it. Across the sea Rudyard Kipling added his voice of encouragement and admonition:

> Take up the White Man's burden,
> Send forth the best ye breed—
> Go, bind your sons to exile,
> To serve your captives' need.

The poet sent a copy to Roosevelt, who pronounced it "rather poor poetry, but good sense." Many others, though, castigated this new imperial policy. "The fruits of imperialism, be they bitter or sweet," declared William Jennings Bryan, Democratic presidential candidate against McKinley two years earlier, "must be left to the subjects of monarchy. . . . It is the voice of the serpent, not the voice of God, that bids us eat." Mark Twain, who devoted his considerable voice to the anti-imperialist cause, added, "We cannot maintain an empire in the Orient and maintain a republic in America."

But an empire in the Orient was what America had acquired, and most Americans embraced it as a manifestation of American destiny. "It is in vain that men talk of keeping free of entanglements," wrote Brooks Adams, scion of the famous political family and a leading intellectual of his day. "Nations must float with the tide. Whither the exchanges flow, they must follow; and they will follow as long as their vitality endures."

Intellectuals may talk in such terms of stark determinism, but statesmen must speak in a loftier language. That language was provided by John Hay, secretary of state to President McKinley—and later to Roosevelt after an assassin's bullet propelled TR to the White House in 1901. In 1899 Hay declared an "Open Door" policy in China, where dynastic disintegration and societal chaos were inviting the great powers to carve out spheres of interest. The British, concerned that this activity would diminish their hard-won influence in the region, invited America to make such a declaration as a way of establishing a kind of equality among imperialists. Thus, Hay's famous Open Door Notes declared China's territorial integrity to be inviolable and equal treatment for all imperial powers to be a requirement of doing business there. Under the policy, the powers could retain their respective spheres of interest, but China would keep control of its trade, and custom duties and port fees would be levied equally to all.

It was an audacious move from a country that had just emerged upon the international scene. But it worked, and it established a kind of backup strategy for American imperialism. As Andrew J. Bacevich points out in his 2002 book, *American Empire: The Realities and Consequences of U.S. Diplomacy,* Hay's Open Door formula "provided the benefits of empire without its burdens." As a formula for noncolonial imperialism, it proved useful during the Roosevelt presidency and later when the limits of colonial imperialism became clear.

In her biography, *Theodore Roosevelt: A Strenuous Life,* Kathleen Dalton portrays Roosevelt as "a transitional internationalist figure between the diplomacy of imperialism and the generation ready to create a League of Nations to forestall war." It would be naive to suggest that Roosevelt himself changed his outlook to any significant extent during his presidency. And the later maneuverings of his great foreign policy friend and ally, Massachusetts Senator Henry Cabot Lodge, would suggest otherwise. But his Oval Office tenure was marked by a subtle transition from colonial imperialism to a more commercial variety.

On the colonial side, Roosevelt prosecuted the Philippine-American War aimed at subduing the insurrectionists who hated American overlordship as much as the Spanish kind. He supervised affairs in Puerto Rico and Cuba. He created a powerful two-ocean navy befitting a nation with geopolitical ambition, and he sent his "Great White Fleet" around the world to announce that ambition to the rest of the world. He engineered the independence of Panama and the U.S. acquisition of the Canal Zone in order to build that potent symbol of imperialism, the Panama Canal. Decades later in the 1970s, when America's control of the canal became a domestic political issue, Senator S. I. Hayakawa of California generated widespread mirth when he declared, "We stole it fair and square." Beneath his effort at ironic humor, however, was the underlying reality that America acquired its canal according to the rules of the game that prevailed at the time.

But even within those rules the game could get nasty, and that's what America experienced in the Philippines, where the insurrectionist forces waged a brutal guerrilla war. When Roosevelt resumed the anti-insurgency effort following a McKinley decision to wind it down, the result was the death of four thousand Americans, along with 200,000 Filipinos. American tactics predictably turned oppressive as General "Howling Jack" Smith created "reconcentration camps" to separate civilians from guerrillas and then ordered his men to kill any Filipinos over age ten who ventured outside the camps. There were reports of American torture and other atrocities of the kind that invariably arise in such guerrilla wars, and the anti-imperialists naturally seized upon them as fodder for political attacks. "We have debauched America's honor and blackened her face before the world," declared Mark Twain.

An astute politician, Roosevelt could see the limits of his vision. The "impetuous imperialist," says Dalton, "was calming down." Though he would press for as much foreign expansion as he could, she writes, "he finally recognized that Americans had no patience for doing the slow work of imposing colonial rule on unwilling subjects." He turned his attention more to aggressive diplomacy such as his mediation effort to resolve the Russo-Japanese War, for which he eventually won the Nobel Peace Prize.

As the American fervor for colonial imperialism waned, a new strain of internationalism emerged. It was liberal interventionism, and it burst upon the scene at the behest of President Woodrow Wilson, who won reelection in 1916 on the slogan that he "kept us out of war." He then promptly began maneuvering America into war.

He was a man whose makeup contained large quantities of both sanctimony and arrogance—a potentially problematic combination in a politician. He craved the affection of a few friends—but only a few, for he could not expect from many the kind of fraternal devotion he demanded. "Should a friend disagree with him," writes Richard M. Watt in *The Kings Depart: The Tragedy of Germany: Versailles and the German Revolution,* "Wilson instantly concluded the man was now a mortal enemy." Watt tells the story of Wilson's friendship, during his years as Princeton University president, with Professor John Grier Hibben. They were inseparable, took tea together nearly every day, consulted each other on everything. But Hibben felt constrained by conscience to oppose a particular campus initiative put forth by Wilson. On a subsequent evening when Hibben and his wife appeared at the Wilson residence, the president shut the door in their faces. Some time later he ceased speaking to Hibben forever.

Such was Wilson's brilliance, says Watt, and his ability to articulate the progressive agenda, that his "objectionable personal characteristics" were successfully masked to most Americans. But when he ventured to take America into the world under the ensign of liberal interventionism, those traits began to emerge into public view.

It began on January 22, 1917. As Europe agonized through the bloody stalemate of the First World War, Wilson urgently requested permission to address the U.S. Senate on a matter of grave international interest. Four hours later the president strode through an expectant chamber to the Senate podium. Within minutes his intention was clear: the creation of a new American foreign policy, placing the country at the center of world events by entering the European conflict as a peacemaker.

Wilson's speech was packed with audacity, and not just because he was calling for a level of foreign involvement few Americans wanted. What was most breathtaking was his claim to speak for a higher moral authority applicable to all peoples throughout the world. "I hope and believe," he declared, "that I am in effect speaking for liberals and friends of humanity in every nation. I would fain believe that I am speaking for the silent mass of mankind everywhere."

In expounding this vision of America's role in the world, Wilson was saying that military excursions abroad are justified by a rationale that goes beyond a country's vital interests. The humanitarian needs of a foreign country or region could alone justify—and in some instances even mandate—American action. Thus, Wilson approached the formulation of foreign policy with a zeal born of his moralistic turn of mind. But he also possessed political guile and an iron will. By building up U.S. armed forces and manipulating the issue of neutrality rights, he managed to nudge America into the European war. But his real aim was more lofty: to move America to center stage in international relations so that it could act on behalf of humanity.

Wilson biographer August Heckscher notes that Wilson had developed a sense of national "honor" that he equated with America's commitment to the rights of all peoples. Inevitably, writes Heckscher, "it was a vague concept . . . not necessarily identical with the basic interests of the [American] people." And after the war this vague idealism led Wilson to foster and champion the League of Nations. As Heckscher points out, Wilson's League was first and foremost an instrument of international good works: "Fair treatment for labor, protection of nationalities and of religious minorities, elimination of racial and gender discrimination—all were to be brought toward fruition." And American power was to be committed to all such lofty goals whenever and wherever possible.

There was an implicit bow here to the Idea of Progress, although the connection was less overt than would be seen in later strains of liberal interventionism. Wilson left no doubt that his aim was nothing less than a quantum improvement in the human condition, building on the progress of the past and moving mankind to ever higher plateaus of development.

A year after his January 1917 speech in the Senate, with America now in the war, Wilson addressed a joint session of Congress and elaborated on his vision. "What we demand in this war," he declared, "is nothing peculiar to ourselves. It is that the world be made fit and safe to live in. . . . All the peoples of the world are in effect partners in this interest." He then enunciated his famous "Fourteen Points"—the basis, he promised, for the coming peace. "Almost everywhere the 'Fourteen Points' were hailed with vast enthusiasm," writes Richard Watt, "for they were superb propaganda. Their brevity allowed them to be reprinted on placard-size posters. Their simplicity made it easy to translate them into foreign languages. Their freedom from self-interest made them morally unassailable."

The success of the Fourteen Points prompted Wilson to conclude he was on a roll. So he put forward an additional "Four Principles" and then "Five Particulars." The most famous of these was the principle that peoples should be free to form their own nations on the basis of "self-determination." Watt points out that this bore an ominous warning to the enemy states, particularly the Austro-Hungarians. "Self-determination," he writes, "implied the freeing of the Czechs, the Slovaks, the Hungarians and the Croats, among many others." But even the allied states found this gave them the willies. Britain was not pleased to see its new ally encouraging the rebellious Irish in their push for self-determination.

At the 1919 Paris peace conference, the brutal realities of the diplomatic world bent and shredded most of Wilson's Fourteen Points, not to mention his Four Principles and Five Particulars. Indeed, Wilson's entire participation in the war and its aftermath had been a disaster. He manipulated neutrality principles by declaring American neutrality but actually favoring Britain over Germany in ways that forced Germany into a corner. When Germany inevitably responded by expanding its submarine attacks on merchant ships, Wilson declared this to be a provocation for American entry into the war. But he took pains to assure Germany that any peace settlement would be based on his evenhanded Fourteen Points. Then, after the beleaguered Germans accepted an armistice based on that assurance, Wilson proved impotent in his efforts to influence the Versailles outcome, which ultimately brutalized German sovereignty.

Wilson found himself forced to compromise again and again, something distasteful to a man of such moral fervor. On one issue he would not compromise—the League of Nations. In fact, every other principle was reluctantly abandoned in trade for the sake of protecting and preserving his hallowed League. Upon returning home, however, his success was attacked by a coalition of two groups—the Rooseveltian imperialists led by Henry Cabot Lodge and an emergent group of conservative isolationists fed up with the brutalities and ambiguities of foreign adventures. It was Lodge who led the attack from his commanding height as chairman of the Senate Foreign Relations Committee.

His driving vision was the same as his friend Theodore Roosevelt's—the ascendancy of America. He and his allies, as Patrick J. Buchanan notes in his *A Republic, Not an Empire: Reclaiming America's Destiny,* "were unmoved by some gauzy vision of a world without war or altruistic idea of what was best for mankind. They made decisions based on what would enhance U.S. power and glory." Thus, adds Buchanan, they were imperialists, not globalists; unilateralists, not multilateralists. And so, for Lodge and others of his stripe, Wilson's League of Nations was viewed as an abomination. "I must think of the United States first," he declared on the Senate floor on August 12, 1919, "and when I think of the United States first, I am thinking of what is best for the world, for if the United States fails the best hopes of mankind fail with it." His devotion to country was indivisible, Lodge said: "I have loved but one flag, and I cannot share that devotion and give affection to the mongrel banner invented for a league."

Notwithstanding his strong language, there is evidence that Lodge was willing to compromise on the issue. But Wilson, true to his temperament of sanctimony, was not. And so Lodge carried the day, sending Wilson's liberal interventionism into political eclipse. But Lodge's own brand of unilateral interventionism went into eclipse as well, forced there by a growing national weariness with misbegotten international adventures. And thus emerged the powerful new wave of conservative isolationism. It began with the simple aim of getting the country back to "normalcy" after Wilson's foreign policy idealism had dissolved into disillusionment. But it grew in intensity and force, reaching such a pitch by 1935 that Congress passed the Neutrality Act of Senator Gerald Nye of North Dakota, a rustic progressive and fiery opponent of U.S. arms manufacturers, or "merchants of death," as he called them.

Nye's legislation sought to place America on the sidelines of any international conflicts, and to that end it required the president to maintain a list of all foreign wars and prohibited American vessels from carrying arms to or for belligerents in those wars. Nye had plenty of allies in Congress, including crusty William Borah of Idaho, the fiery populist Hiram Johnson of California, the colorful Arthur Vandenberg of Michigan, and Montana's Burton K. Wheeler. A few years later they were joined by a rising star from Ohio named Robert A. Taft, who ultimately emerged as the preeminent conservative isolationist of his day.

Taft viewed American democracy as a delicately balanced system inherently threatened by the kind of internationalist adventurism personified by Wilson. America is a pristine experiment in self-government, he believed, operating in an evil world of power struggles and treachery. The best protection against contamination was to keep it removed from the evil world. "We should be prepared to defend our own shores," declared Taft, "but we should not undertake to defend the ideals of democracy in foreign countries." Besides, internationalism would only lead to militarism, which would then lead to more foreign entanglements, which would in turn lead to further erosion of the American system. "War is a vain policy, except a war fought at home to establish or preserve the freedom of a nation," Taft declared in the fall of 1940, as Britain faced the threat of a German invasion. "If the English Channel is our frontier, and this is our war," he argued, prophetically, "then we will have to defend it for years to come." By then, tumultuous new forces had swept across Europe and the Far East, and they threatened to draw America into the vortex of World War II. But the American people were not interested; conservative isolationism still carried the day.

In late June of 1940, as Buchanan points out, with France conquered and Britain forced out of continental Europe, an American poll found that 86 percent of Americans opposed going to war against Germany and Italy; only 5 percent wanted to fight. Americans, writes Buchanan, "did not believe Hitler was a threat to the United States." And, as the U.S. presidential election campaign gained intensity, with President Franklin Roosevelt seeking an unprecedented third term, the political rhetoric was noteworthy for its one-sided focus on keeping America out of war. Buchanan calls the campaign "among the most dishonest ever held," with Roosevelt and his Republican opponent, Wendell Willkie, competing for the title of most fervent antiwar politician. Meanwhile, both secretly wanted America in the war, and after the election they would work together toward that end.

Ultimately that war did come, and the first casualty was conservative isolationism, which since the morning of December 7, 1941, has rested as quietly in political oblivion as the battleship *Arizona* has rested on the floor of Pearl Harbor. And through the turmoil of World War II and its aftermath there emerged a powerful new doctrine—conservative interventionism. In many ways this interventionist outlook resembled that noncolonial imperialism that first became evident during the presidency of Theodore Roosevelt. The concept underlying John Hay's Open Door policy, for example, became a fundamental part of it. Andrew Bacevich calls the system fostered by this doctrine "global openness"—a drive to remove barriers that inhibit the movement of goods, capital, ideas, and peoples across national borders. The ultimate goal, he says, is "an open and integrated international order based on the principles of democratic capitalism, with the United States as the ultimate guarantor of order and enforcer of norms."

For many decades, though, this new doctrine was limited in its application by geopolitical circumstance and by certain habits of mind inherent in the doctrine's leading adherents. Conservative interventionism was the outlook of America's old Northeast elite that had had a heavy hand in the country's foreign policy for generations. For members of this elite, which was largely Anglo-Saxon, many principles of conservative interventionism were learned at home during the formative years and at institutions such as the Groton School. Postwar columnist and Groton graduate Stewart Alsop once wrote that in his five years at Groton he received five years of English history and no formal American history at all. In these lessons, the British Empire of old represented a force for good in the world. And America's "special relationship" with Britain was the cornerstone of American foreign policy.

Another Grotonian and child of the old elite was Franklin Roosevelt, arguably the twentieth century's greatest exponent of conservative interventionism. Roosevelt operated entirely in the realm of global realpolitik. Though always willing in his crafty way to dress up his policies in the language of Wilsonian idealism, his thinking was driven first and foremost by a concept found at the heart of the old British system, the balance of power. He always sought to ensure, moreover, that America's foreign policy was intertwined with Britain's.

A brutal realist, Roosevelt eschewed humanitarian impulses as a basis for foreign policy decisions—or domestic politics. Though he shared Wilson's internationalist outlook in general, he unceremoniously abandoned his support for the League of Nations when that proved necessary to secure the 1932 Democratic nomination. Later as president, when the Japanese invaded China and brutalized its civilian population, he stood by impassively. It would never have occurred to him, even in the face of the "rape of

Nanking," to send American servicemen into conflict merely to save the lives of history's hapless victims. But when Great Britain became mortally threatened after the fall of France in 1940, he nearly became apoplectic with worry and concern, and then he began to put a mighty squeeze on Japan as a way of forcing America into the global conflict.

As long as conservative isolationism dominated American public opinion, as it did right up to Pearl Harbor, little could be done overtly. "I am almost literally walking on eggs," Roosevelt wrote to a foreign official, explaining his precarious perch between his own powerful convictions and the public's aversion to war. "I am at the moment saying nothing, seeing nothing, and hearing nothing." But that was not quite true. His stealth and wiles were applied in every way possible to help Britain and to nudge his country to war: He passed diplomatic secrets to friendly reporters to help the cause. He maneuvered Japan into a position of near desperation in the effort to force a confrontation. And, as Robert Shogan writes in his book *Hard Bargain,* he almost certainly violated Gerald Nye's Neutrality Act by making destroyers available to Britain—an action that in another time and political climate could very well have been impeachable. As Shogan puts it, FDR didn't hesitate "to twist the law, flout the Constitution, hoodwink the public, and distort the political process."

In the end, Roosevelt, like Wilson before him, got his wish. But where Wilson had hoped to salve the wounds of the world, Roosevelt hoped to save Great Britain and lead America into a global role of fostering world stability with balance-of-power diplomacy and geopolitical force (together, of course, with the British). Roosevelt's dream was to establish a postwar Anglo-American alliance that would pick up where the British Empire had been fading out, a kind of noncolonial, benign imperialism.

He never would have seen his dream come to life even had he lived beyond the spring of 1945. With the emergence of the Cold War and Britain's precipitous postwar decline during the presidency of Harry S Truman, it became clear that nothing approaching an equal partnership was possible. On February 22, 1947, the

British ambassador to Washington, Lord Inverchapel, walked into the office of the new secretary of state, George Marshall, with an ominous message: His Majesty's government, facing financial collapse at home, could no longer afford to protect Greece and Turkey from the Soviet-backed insurgencies threatening those countries. Britain was pulling out and relinquishing responsibility within thirty days.

Roosevelt's American philosophical heirs quickly concluded that America would have to become the successor force to the old empire. Thus followed the U.S. commitment to Greece and Turkey, the Marshall Plan, the Berlin Airlift, and the resolve to thwart communist insurgencies that threatened any Western global interests. The architects of these epic policies had emerged at the war's end and had names such as Acheson, Bohlen, Kennan, McCloy, Lovett, Harriman, Forrestal, and Nitze. They fashioned conservative interventionism into a forceful doctrine to meet the challenge of the Cold War. Like Franklin Roosevelt, they had attended Groton or similar prep schools and then top Ivy League universities at a time when those institutions were all hotbeds of Anglophilia. Like Roosevelt, they were Anglophiles. And like Roosevelt, they believed global stability required a balance of power throughout the world, with America ensuring the balance.

It was an audacious doctrine, and it led to the projection of American power into the corners of the globe. But there were limits. The use or threat of force was reserved for three purposes: first, to protect America's vital interests, as in the Cuban Missile Crisis and Ronald Reagan's Central American initiatives in the 1980s; second, to save Western civilization from the threat of Soviet expansionism, as in the formation of NATO, the Berlin Airlift, and the forty-year presence of a large American land army on the European continent; and third, to maintain that world balance of power by thwarting communist expansion wherever Western global interests were threatened, as in Korea and Vietnam.

Yet even this prudent approach had its dangers, and they emerged in force during the Vietnam effort. It was during the agony of this Southeast Asian entrapment that a new doctrine emerged—liberal isolationism, which viewed the war as "immoral" and hence America as a treacherous country spreading its poison into pure and helpless corners of the world. This sentiment first emerged with the student antiwar movement, which vilified the U.S. as an immoral country waging an immoral war. The slogans, flag burnings, and chants were only the symbols of a deeper presumption: America lacked moral standing in the world. No foreign policy doctrine of any consequence had ever put forward such a view.

Liberal isolationism soon spread beyond student protesters as journalists, academics, and politicians, anguished over the killing in Southeast Asia, echoed the sentiment that America had forfeited its moral authority. *New York Times* columnist Anthony Lewis, outraged at President Nixon's 1972 bombing raids on North Vietnam, bemoaned a country veering "toward the eternal damnation that the Nazis earned Germany." Or, as 1972 Democratic presidential nominee George McGovern put it, electing him president would ensure that "there will be no more Asian children running ablaze from bombed-out schools."

The image was disturbing to any American, of course, and designed to be—but certainly no more than the images that could have been invoked a generation earlier when America incinerated 200,000 men, women, and children in the fire bombings at Hamburg and Dresden. The difference was that in the earlier episode, the vast majority of Americans believed these were the actions of a righteous nation, however horrific such actions may have been. In the post-Vietnam period, revelations of American overseas abuses—particularly those committed by the CIA—only bolstered liberal isolationism and ensured that it became the fundamental foreign policy outlook of the Democratic Party. The great foreign policy debates thereafter turned on an axis of conservative interventionism versus liberal isolationism. That confrontation reached its final sharp pitch during the battles over President Reagan's anti-communist policies in Central America.

The interventionists of the day emphasized balance-of-power considerations and the consequences of a destabilized Latin America on American order, while the isolationists decried America's covert war making and alliances with corrupt and brutal dictatorial forces.

Throughout those debates, conservative interventionism generally prevailed. But it was a product of World War II and the Cold War, and as the national consciousness slowly absorbed the reality of the Cold War's end, conservative interventionism gradually lost its force. With the Soviet Union's threat to Europe and the rest of the world extinguished, and with no serious external challenge to America's vital national interests, the doctrine's rationale simply unraveled.

And that led to the inevitable intellectual efforts to define the new post–Cold War era—to Francis Fukuyama's End of History doctrine, to the Globalization framework popularized by Thomas Friedman, and to Samuel Huntington's Clash of Civilizations thesis. And through it all the ascendant doctrine became Woodrow Wilson's liberal interventionism. It led the first President George Bush to send troops on a humanitarian mission into Somalia in late 1992 and led President Bill Clinton to expand that mission some months later. It fostered America's particular approach to the Balkans crisis in the mid- to late 1990s, including Clinton's bombing campaign against Yugoslavia in 1999. And it helped fashion major elements of the post-9/11 initiative of the second President Bush as he turned a very real war against Islamist fundamentalism into an expeditionary foreign policy bent on remaking countries and regions across the sea.

What's more, elements of Theodore Roosevelt's brand of imperialism—that Will to Power outlook glorifying American expansionism even to the extent of colonial adventurism—are becoming visible in the foreign policy of George W. Bush. He denies it, of course, as do all of his top officials. But this strain of thinking is unmistakable in both words and deeds emanating from the administration.

America's post–Cold War foreign policy initiatives and the implications behind them will be explored in considerable detail further in this volume. For our purposes here it remains merely to review the legacies of the foreign policy outlooks that emerged, held sway, and then receded through America's great global adventures beginning with the advent of empire in 1898. A number of questions help in the assessment: Which doctrines can actually work? Are there global circumstances that render some more likely or less likely than others to succeed? Which doctrines are consistent with what we know about the unsentimental forces of history and about human nature? And, perhaps most important, which doctrines can sustain America's willingness to accept expenditures of blood, and, if so, how much blood?

The colonial brand of imperialism that captured America's fancy in the early years of the twentieth century had some powerful advocates—President Theodore Roosevelt, Secretary of State John Hay, Senate Foreign Relations Committee Chairman Henry Cabot Lodge. And the American people seemed enthusiastic about this dramatic new development, at least until the emergence of what looked like a Philippine quagmire. Then Roosevelt had to accept the doctrine's limitations. Americans weren't willing to accept significant expenditures of blood in its behalf. Besides, history tells us that this approach to global politics was on the wane anyway. Roosevelt's great model was the British Empire, which didn't survive another two generations beyond his presidency.

Woodrow Wilson's self-righteous liberal interventionism proved disastrous, certainly one of the central contributors to the emergence of German Fascism and the carnage of World War II. His entire purpose for going to war contained little realism or logic. And his effort to bring his naive attitudinizings to Versailles proved nothing short of calamitous. "The single name most inextricably bound up with the Treaty of Versailles, and consequently with its failure," writes Richard Watt, "was that of Thomas Woodrow Wilson." He adds: "The [Wilson] dreams of a world of happy peoples, each assembled into an entity of its own nationality and living in its own historical geographic location, were now seen [at the end of the Versailles negotiations] to have been imbecilic wishes which could not and would not come true." Wilson, sad to say, had been captured by the most radical and most dangerous elements of the Idea of Progress.

The conservative isolationism that emerged after Wilson's failure was probably inevitable, and it was equally inevitable that it would be short-lived. Ultimately it could not survive the crush of events as the world descended into chaos. And yet it would be unwise to dismiss it for all time, because it is a doctrine that could be brought back to life through events. Should America's ventures into the world come to tragedy, with American lives thrown into turmoil and despair, the country's electorate might very well turn to conservative isolationism as an avenue for returning America to a time of stability and safety.

Liberal isolationism never captured the American polity, though it did capture one of its two major political parties. More's the pity for that political party, many believe, because the Democrats' embrace of this doctrine has called into question the party's level of geopolitical realism, if not its patriotism. This no doubt is unfair to a significant extent, and yet the rhetoric that often has emerged through liberal isolationism has given rise to this criticism. What's more, recent history indicates that many adherents of liberal isolationism are more liberal than isolationist—and hence turn interventionist when humanitarian impulses are driving the debate. Thus, liberal isolationism likely will continue to be a significant part of America's ongoing foreign policy debate, but it isn't likely ever to capture the country.

This brings us to conservative interventionism, which is probably the most flexible and least ideological of the foreign policy doctrines. At its best, it focuses on limited goals of stability fostered through strength and balance-of-power global politics. It accepts the world as it is and not as any collection of idealists might want it to be. It embraces the idea of Western civilization and assumes America is not only part of it but remains its primary protector. It extols American-style democracy and fosters it wherever it can take root but doesn't consider its importation to be any kind of policy imperative.

Can an effective brand of conservative interventionism be fashioned for the post-9/11 era, when the West is locked in a clash of
civilizations with major elements of the world of Islam and cultural instability seems on the rise elsewhere around the globe?
That is probably the most pressing question facing the country—
and the world—today.

PART II

THE ELUSIVE NEW ORDER

CHAPTER 6

The Triumph of Wilsonism

O N THANKSGIVING DAY in 1992, a lame-duck American president ordered 28,000 troops into a war-crushed basket-case country in East Africa—and set his nation upon a new azimuth of foreign policy. When George H. W. Bush closed out his four-year presidency by sending his military into Somalia to aid two million starving inhabitants, he set in place a foreign policy doctrine that had been largely eclipsed for sixty years: liberal interventionism. Wilsonism was back.

It wasn't that Wilsonism had played no part in American policy making in those intervening decades. Expressions of the humanitarian impulse had emerged at various times in support of numerous foreign policy actions. Both Franklin Roosevelt and Ronald Reagan were masters at infusing their rhetoric with such expressions to bolster their intentions in the realm of realpolitik. And throughout the Cold War, foreign policy debates often focused on the extent to which global actions should be guided by considerations of morality. But without exception American presidents felt constrained to justify their interventionist actions ultimately on the basis of vital national interests. There could be debates, and often were, about whether particular initiatives did in fact conform to American interests, but the very fact of the debates reflected the political reality that humanitarian arguments alone could not justify sending American troops into harm's path.

Somalia changed all that. Shortly after the troops went in, *Time* magazine correctly labeled Bush's initiative a "precedent." The magazine added: "It is a major military action in the name of morality: addressing a situation that does not threaten American national security and in which the U.S. has no vital interests." Bush himself, *Time* noted, had called the move "a purely humanitarian action." Addressing the Somalis, the president had said, "We come to your country with one reason only: to enable the starving to be fed." Once that task was completed, he said, the Americans would leave.

Within a year, however, enough American blood would flow onto the dusty pavements of the Somali capital that the Bush mission—as expanded by his successor, Bill Clinton—would turn into a military and political embarrassment. And the United States would pull out with hardly a look back at the ongoing predicament of the hapless Somalis. Could such a failure have proved to be anything but a death knell for liberal interventionism?

In point of fact, notwithstanding the Somali debacle, the mission there solidified liberal interventionism as the country's central foreign policy doctrine for years to come. And it led directly to further American adventures in the intractable lands of the Balkans. The story of America's path from the conservative interventionism of the Cold War to the liberal interventionism of Somalia and the old Yugoslavia begins with the presidency of George H. W. Bush, who fancied himself a geopolitical chess master. In foreign policy terms, his presidency was marked by three interventionist initiatives and one abstention.

The first intervention came within weeks of the fall of the Berlin Wall when Bush ordered an invasion of Panama to depose its de facto dictator Manuel Noriega and destroy the corrupt Panamanian Defense Forces that Noriega used to dominate his country. The Panama strongman, once a paid tool of the American CIA, had turned his country into an axis of drug trafficking and money laundering. His drug deals had generated enough evidence in the United States to get him indicted by two Florida grand juries. Bush had wanted him deposed, but he needed enough provocation to justify the action.

Then in December 1989 Noriega's goons summarily killed U.S.

Marine Lieutenant Robert Paz when he encountered a PDF road-
block in Panama City. PDF officials detained another U.S. officer
who had witnessed the shooting, roughed him up and threatened
his life. They pushed his wife against a wall and groped her until
she collapsed. Bush promptly declared the incident to be sufficient
provocation to get rid of this nettlesome dictator. On the morning
of December 20, a contingent of more than 20,000 troops—some
already stationed in the Panama Canal Zone and others flown in as
reinforcements—attacked the PDF and other Noriega paramilitary
units. Within a day they had destroyed or disarmed the government forces and deposed Noriega. A new president was installed,
and Noriega was brought to the United States for trial. The operation cost twenty-four American lives; several hundred Panamani-
ans died.

What was the justification for the invasion? In his memoir, former Joint Chiefs of Staff Chairman (later Secretary of State) Colin
Powell listed several: "Noriega's contempt for democracy, his drug
trafficking and indictment, the death of the American Marine, the
threat to our treaty rights to the canal with this unreliable figure
ruling Panama. And, unspoken, there was George Bush's personal
antipathy to Noriega, a third-rate dictator thumbing his nose at
the United States."

Of these we can dismiss the last as frivolous. If America sought
to depose every tinhorn dictator who stirs the animosity of a U.S.
president, the result would be global chaos. Only slightly more
weight should be ascribed to Noriega's contempt for democracy,
hardly a rationale for spilling American blood. The drug trafficking
indictment gets closer to the mark. America does have an interest
in curtailing the inflow of drugs across its borders. The killing of
Lieutenant Paz constitutes an even stronger justification. The
country can't allow sanctioned elements within foreign countries
to kill Americans with impunity. And this rationale takes on added
weight when combined with the fact that Noriega constituted a
threat to U.S. treaty rights to the Panama Canal. That strategic wa-
terway, built and maintained for a century by America, was sched-
uled to be turned over to Panama at a future date, but the

handover treaty recognized America's right to ensure access to the canal. The Paz killing and the lawlessness it reflected raised serious questions about Panama's willingness to recognize that treaty.

And so the Panama invasion falls neatly under the rubric of conservative interventionism—military action justified largely on the basis of America's own national interests and the need to prevent regional or global instability that could threaten U.S. or Western well-being. Andrew Bacevich, in his book *American Empire*, expounded a broader concept when he called the invasion "a classic assertion of a great power's prerogative to police its sphere of influence." In that sense, the invasion comported with similar actions throughout the Caribbean by just about every president from McKinley to Reagan.

It is also noteworthy that the rhetoric surrounding the invasion was largely devoid of idealistic notions about fostering democracy in Panama. True, the man America installed as Panama's president, Guillermo Endara, had won an election the previous May that Noriega had overturned. Thus, the new ruler enjoyed a welcome legitimacy that went beyond the force of American arms. But there was no full-throated suggestion that this invasion represented a new dawn for democracy in Panama, let alone the world. Panama was still Panama, and the world remained essentially the same place it was before.

A little more than a year later, however, Bush declared a "New World Order"—a product, he suggested, of his own decision to send half a million troops halfway around the world to expel the invading Iraqi forces of Saddam Hussein from the tiny oil sheikdom of Kuwait. Much has been written about Bush's turnaround in the first days following Saddam's invasion—from an initial suggestion that he was "not contemplating any such action" as sending troops into the region to his subsequent statement that "this will not stand." The turnaround is generally credited to British Prime Minister Margaret Thatcher, who admonished the president at Aspen, Colorado, not to "go wobbly."

Less explored is the rationale that ultimately emerged among policy makers for going to war. And the question is muddied by the fact that, once the U.S. force was poised for action in the sands of Saudi Arabia, Congress only reluctantly authorized the president to initiate hostilities to expel Saddam from Kuwait. The question generated abundant underlying partisanship as the resolution authorizing war made its way through the national legislature. Only ten Democratic senators supported the president, while two Republicans abandoned him. In the House, three Republicans voted no, while Democrats split 179–86 against Bush. The primary Democratic argument was that the proposed action was ill-timed, that the administration should give economic sanctions a chance to force Saddam out of Kuwait before resorting to military action.

But inside the administration the focus centered on oil and geopolitical reality, as distilled by Director of Central Intelligence William Webster in a meeting with the president on the Friday following his return from Aspen. With his invasion of Kuwait, said Webster, Saddam had taken control of 20 percent of the world's oil reserves. If he moved just a few miles more into Saudi territory, he could grab another 20 percent. "He'll have easy access to the sea from Kuwaiti ports," Webster told the president. "Jordan and Yemen will probably tilt toward him, and he'll be in a position to extort the others. We can expect the Arab states to start cutting deals. Iran will be at Iraq's feet. Israel will be threatened." In short, concluded the country's top spy, Saddam Hussein would become the preeminent figure in the Persian Gulf.

To which Brent Scowcroft, the president's national security adviser, stated: "We've got to make a response, and accommodating Saddam is not an option."

Thus, although the country was divided on whether to deter Saddam from further expansion and even more so on the question of whether to expel him from Kuwait, in the end the matter boiled down to the balance of power in a strategic corner of the world. And its strategic significance stemmed from one thing only: oil. It was oil that fueled the Western economy, made possible the commerce that fed, clothed, and housed the peoples of the West, and propelled the U.S. military that in turn served as a force for international stability.

Americans weren't entirely comfortable with that rationale, which may be why the administration didn't emphasize it. A typical citizen outlook was expressed to the *Wall Street Journal* by forty-five-year-old Richard Will, a telephone lineman from Towson, Maryland. "Americans," he said, "don't want their sons killed for oil." And, as the war loomed, American acceptance of the oil rationale plummeted. A September poll for the *Wall Street Journal* and NBC News showed 50 percent of respondents listing oil as the chief rationale for Bush's military action, compared with 39 percent who said the primary reason was to repel Iraqi aggression. A follow-up poll a month later showed 46 percent citing the need to repel Iraq while only 35 percent cited oil.

That reflected Americans' characteristic desire to reach a high plane of idealism whenever the shooting starts. And yet in councils of policy making, where officials must deal with real-world forces and imperatives, the rationale was firmly fixed as a need to protect the West from any force that could destabilize the Middle East or interrupt its flow of oil. Thus, the Gulf War, like the Panamanian invasion, fit neatly into the category of conservative interventionism.

But there was an opposition voice less muddled than those of congressional Democrats in the partisan war debate of January 1991. It was the voice of Patrick Buchanan, the conservative commentator and future presidential aspirant, who argued that the Cold War's end called for powerful new thinking about the world and America's role in it. He opposed the Gulf War, said Buchanan, because he didn't think Kuwait was vital to American interests or that the petite regime of a corrupt emir was worth the life of a single U.S. marine. After all, he argued, Saddam stole Kuwait's oil in order to sell it, so there was no reason to anticipate an interruption in supply. And, regarding Persian Gulf stability, he noted that Iraq served as a counterweight to Iran, three times the size of Iraq in territory and population. If America destroyed that counterweight, he suggested, Iran would be the beneficiary, and the United States would have to shoulder the job of containing both countries. Better to maintain that balance of power and let the two countries contain each other.

Though subsequent events after the 9/11 attacks would prove Buchanan's analysis prescient, his was a lonely voice in 1991 as America thrilled to its overwhelming victory over Saddam and George Bush declared his New World Order. But the president couldn't seem to articulate just what this new order was or how his Gulf triumph fit into it. The result was a kind of blank slate upon which others could write their own versions, and soon it became clear that many within foreign policy circles envisioned a world in which America reigned as the lone superpower, directing its wealth and military energy to the service of aims and causes removed from American interests. Liberal interventionism was gaining a foothold, courtesy of George H. W. Bush. Indeed, as Bush himself said shortly after his retirement, "The present international scene is about as much a blank slate as history ever provides."

Liberal interventionism wasn't the only doctrine to be emblazoned upon that slate. Some administration officials sought to inscribe on it a credo that took on an intriguing resemblance to the Will to Power imperialism of Theodore Roosevelt. This impulse was reflected in what Bacevich has called the "Wolfowitz indiscretion," named after Paul D. Wolfowitz, undersecretary of defense for policy in the first Bush administration. The episode concerned a Pentagon position paper, written in Wolfowitz's office by an aide named Zalmay Khalilzad. Circulated in draft form in 1991 and 1992, it identified American preeminence as the premier geopolitical reality in the post–Cold War era. The aim of American foreign policy, declared the document, should be to maintain American global hegemony as far into the future as possible. Thus, America should focus its geopolitical efforts on "convincing potential competitors that they need not aspire to a greater role or pursue a more aggressive posture to protect their legitimate interests." America, said the paper, should "sufficiently account for the interests of the advanced industrial nations to discourage them from challenging our leadership or seeking to overturn the established political and economic order." Further, the country should "maintain the mechanisms [euphemism for military power] for deterring potential competitors from even aspiring to a larger regional or global role."

When this manifesto of American hegemony inevitably was leaked to the press, critics rose up to attack such thinking as arrogant, foolhardy, and un-American. The language was promptly watered down, substituted by more euphemistic pronouncements that masked a lingering reality: within the administration and throughout certain intellectual circles, the idea was gaining force that America should exercise its power to dominate the world to the fullest feasible extent into the future indefinitely.

Bush himself, however, opted for a more cautious approach. Whatever his New World Order signified, it did not seem to include American action to counter the bloody disintegration of the old Yugoslavia, where Serbs, Croats, and Muslims were locked in ethnic-territorial wars that generated the greatest human carnage on the European continent since the end of World War II. "We don't have a dog in this fight," said Secretary of State James A. Baker III when pressed as to why America stood by amid such bloodshed. Crudely put, to be sure, but a succinct expression of conservative interventionism. American interests were not affected by events in the Balkans, and therefore America would not intervene.

But the forces of liberal interventionism were gathering, and they had found their cause and their enemy. The cause was Bosnia, where the Muslim plurality found itself pummeled by heavily armed Serbs bent on carving out large patches of territory for inclusion into a Greater Serbia. The enemy was the Bosnian Serbs and their Serbian patron in what was left of Yugoslavia, Slobodan Milosevic. Bosnia was where liberal interventionism, a kind of neo-Wilsonism, would capture American foreign policy.

As Andrew Bacevich points out, Bosnia became for 1990s progressives what Spain had been for their 1930s predecessors—"a horrific war in its own right but one freighted with moral and political significance transcending the issue immediately at hand." Like Spain, Bosnia symbolized a much larger struggle, described by Bacevich as "the hopes for human, secular multiculturalism against the dark forces of ethnic intolerance infused with religious fervor." Liberal interventionists turned this sad story of ancient cultural animosities into a morality play, adds Bacevich, "through the artful selection and arrangement of facts."

Their opening came with Bush's Somalian incursion, which established the precedent for purely humanitarian military adventures. Liberal critics immediately identified a flaw in the president's approach. He had sent in the troops, he said, merely to ensure the distribution of food by relief organizations and halt the famine that had gripped the country. His aides said publicly they expected the troops home by inauguration day. But the famine, as the critics pointed out, stemmed from brutal infighting among nasty warlords who fostered starvation as a weapon against their enemies' followers. Can America really help in Somalia, asked the critics, without dealing with those warlords? And wouldn't that take a lot longer than a few weeks? "There is no agreement," wrote *Time* magazine, which emerged quickly as a leading exponent of expansive humanitarian interventionism, "on whether the U.S.-led troops are only to guard supply routes or are to go out and disarm the thousands of ragtag fighters who are terrorizing the country." *Time* left no doubt about its own position. The magazine pointed out that Somalia had no working economy, no police force and no government. "Unless a contingent of peacemakers stays long enough—which could be years—to fashion some kind of effective national authority, the causes of Somalia's chaos will only re-emerge," said *Time*, adding that "many experts" doubted that military steps to guard food convoys could or should be separated from rebuilding the nation.

According to this brand of thinking, the hour had arrived for America to declare her Wilsonian intention to place her military power at the disposal of humankind and not just Americans. "With wrenching pictures of starving Somalis on view," said *Time*, "anyone who raises questions about succoring them risks being labeled heartless. Nor is there a strong case to be made against applying a moral standard to diplomacy: using military might in the name of humanitarianism is an estimable principle."

A week later the magazine employed its cover to apply some editorial pressure on the incoming president: "Clinton's first foreign challenge: If SOMALIA, why not BOSNIA?" The inside pages put it more starkly: "The startling new way American forces are being used in Somalia—for humanitarian purposes, with no national interest at stake—has instantly opened the debate about where the new President . . . will be inclined to take the country." Rather than inoculating America against Bosnian involvement, declared *Time*, "the Somalia venture has only intensified the pressure to apply the same moral approach there." That same issue revealed that U.N. Secretary-General Boutros Boutros-Ghali had issued demands that America keep troops in Somalia until the warlords could be disarmed and the country restored to some kind of civic health. Liberal interventionism was on the march.

The new president proved receptive but wary. In Somalia, Bill Clinton quickly expanded the Bush mission to include, first, the restoration of the country to some kind of internal stability and, second, the apprehension of the top warlords, most notably an elusive and brutal clan leader named Mohammed Farah Aidid. Ostensibly, this mission was turned over to the United Nations, which assembled a motley peacekeeping force from some two dozen armies from around the world. But in reality the United States retained control over its own substantial Somalia-based force, which included battle-trained contingents of elite Ranger and Delta Force warriors. The Americans were commanded by a retired four-star admiral named Jonathan Howe, who was handpicked by Washington and took his orders from there. Howe's troops and their counterparts in the U.N. force quickly found themselves in the middle of a dangerous environment of civic chaos. At one point some two dozen Pakistani soldiers were killed in a firefight with Aidid's followers. U.N. "peacekeepers" responded with a significant degree of brutality.

That led columnist Charles Krauthammer, a penetrating if occasionally inconsistent analyst of world affairs, to issue a stinging critique of humanitarian interventionism. "We waded ashore in Somalia to feed the hungry," he wrote in a *Time* essay (a neat counter to the magazine's news pages). "Now our gunships hover over Mogadishu shooting rockets into crowded villas." He called it the "humanitarian's ultimate nightmare. Famine relief turns into counterinsurgency. From Red Cross to Green Beret in six months."

Somalia, wrote Krauthammer, revealed a fundamental reality about the world—namely, that humanitarian intervention rarely remains humanitarian: "In a country racked by civil war, what starts with feeding ends with killing. There is no immaculate intervention." He concluded: "There is no new world. There never is."

But the humanitarian impulse was driving American policy in Somalia, and there was no evidence that policy makers were noticing that liberal interventionism often contains an underlying brutality. To accomplish the stated humanitarian mission of subduing the warlords, Howe's troops initiated a series of daylight raids into the Somali capital of Mogadishu to ensnare Aidid and bring him to justice. Not only were these efforts unsuccessful, but over time they provided the enemy with a working knowledge of U.S. tactics, which didn't change from raid to raid. The result was the debacle of October 3, 1993, when Aidid's warriors shot down three Blackhawk helicopters, damaged three others, and ambushed a unit of rangers in downtown Mogadishu. The ensuing firefight lasted several hours, with the Americans surrounded by angry and well-armed Somalis out for blood. The natives managed to kill eighteen Americans, wound another seventy-eight, and cause a worldwide stir by dragging a dead U.S. soldier through the streets of the dusty capital. The televised image of a seriously injured American pilot in captivity also was broadcast worldwide. Some five hundred Somalis died, many of them civilians, and another five hundred were wounded.

For the president it was a military failure and a political disaster. Clinton quickly quashed the Somali mission, then retrieved his troops and offered up the head of Defense Secretary Les Aspin as a gesture of submission to an agitated Congress. But the lesson embraced by the administration in the wake of the Somalia debacle was not the Krauthammer lesson. It was not that humanitarianism had its limits or was fraught with potential for unforeseen and unwelcome bloodshed. It was simply that the American people would not accept casualties in behalf of humanitarian missions, and hence such interventions had to be crafted in ways designed to eliminate or minimize the prospects for American soldiers returning home in body bags.

That posed a dilemma for Clinton as events in Bosnia became more and more bloody and American interventionists issued increasingly shrill cries for action. The president shared the humanitarians' underlying sentiments, but the lesson of Mogadishu was vivid in his mind. He shied away from any intervention that could pull America into a brutal ground campaign and shed American blood. But the pressure on the president was growing, and it was immense. The media unleashed a steady drumbeat of agitation in behalf of intervention. Some members of Congress joined the chorus. Always there were echoes of the *Time* formula for assessing humanitarian ventures overseas—if you oppose them, you must be heartless.

What's more, the issue was complicated by the fact that it seemed to scramble up political fault lines in entirely new ways. Among Democrats, former doves became hawks on Bosnia—notably Senator Joseph Biden of Delaware, who had opposed Ronald Reagan's invasion of Grenada in 1983 and George Bush's Persian Gulf operation eight years later; and Senator Paul Wellstone of Minnesota, a fiery liberal and product of the antiwar furies of the Vietnam era. But John Glenn of Ohio, a Democratic conservative on foreign policy issues throughout the Cold War, opposed intervention. And Representative Robert Torricelli of New Jersey (later a senator) predicted that Democratic support would crumble "when the bombing starts, and those now chanting for military involvement see the enormous collateral damage against civilians."

Republicans were similarly split, with many steadfast hawks from the Cold War era now expressing strong misgivings about any major U.S. involvement in Bosnia. These included Senators Trent Lott and Thad Cochran of Mississippi and John McCain of Arizona. "What is viable?" asked McCain at one point. "We cannot confuse a desire to do good with viable military options." The Republican floor leader, Robert Dole of Kansas, however, issued intermittent emotional pleas in behalf of intervention.

It was easy to see how these new and scrambled-up fault lines would give the new president pause as he weighed the political dangers inherent in taking action in Bosnia. Meanwhile, the media drumbeat gained intensity. *Newsweek,* over an article published just before Clinton's inauguration, headlined: "Bosnia Waits for Clinton." A subhead suggested that the recent killing of a Bosnian government official by Serb irregulars "dares the West to intervene." The magazine suggested that "the end of the cold-war rivalry appears to be broadening the constituency for a muscular defense of human rights."

Publications such as *Time, Newsweek, The New Yorker,* and even the conservative *National Review* freely employed the term "genocide" to describe the "ethnic cleansing" that was going on in Bosnia. Headlines shouted out the moral fervor that engulfed most of the media elite. "A LESSON IN SHAME," declared *Time* when Clinton pulled back from the idea of a major air attack. A subhead suggested the failure to act was "the West's most disgraceful mistake since World War II," presumably referring to the "appeasement" of Hitler before his invasion of Poland. Another large-type statement declared that "the West will be tormented for years to come by the question of genocide."

Even before Clinton took office, the *New York Times* had pushed hard for American intervention in the Balkans. In an autumn 1992 editorial entitled "At Least: Slow the Slaughter," the newspaper attacked General Colin Powell, then chairman of the joint chiefs, for his stated aversion to "limited" military actions. The newspaper particularly ridiculed a Powell statement to a *Times* reporter some days earlier: "As soon as they tell me it's limited, it means they do not care whether you achieve a result or not." This reflected, said the newspaper, a tendency to "dither" while the bloodshed proceeded. And it compared Powell to George McClellan, the Civil War general who frustrated Abraham Lincoln with his aversion to taking his troops into battle. Powell argued in an op-ed reply that his point had been simply that the military needs a clear set of objectives before sending troops into harm's way. Otherwise, there is no definition for success but high prospects for perceived failure and half-baked escalation, as in Vietnam. As for McClellan, Powell pointed out that Lincoln's general had refused to fight *after* a clear set of objectives had been laid out, and thus the situations were not analogous.

Powell had no way of knowing it, but the *Times* drumbeat that rankled him and stirred his reply was just the beginning. Through the fall and into the new year, straddling the presidencies of Bush and Clinton, the media bombardment continued. When in May 1993 Clinton revealed plans to move toward a bombing campaign and an end to the international arms embargo then in place, the media applauded. Wrote Mark Whitaker in *Newsweek:* "Our status as the last true superpower . . . demands that we be prepared to use force not only in our own defense but in defense of international law and democratic values." If ground troops prove necessary to push back the Serbs from their captured territory, he added, "public squeamishness about casualties shouldn't keep Clinton from considering that option."

Time agreed, noting the "moral imperative" involved and saying Clinton now faced the task of persuading Americans "that their children and their billions should be spent on Bosnia." *The New Republic* described the policy shift under a headline that read, "A Star Is Born." And *National Review* praised Clinton for getting beyond his previous tendency to "let the weenies get to him."

But when Clinton's statements of resolve melted in the face of European timidity, the drumbeat returned at a heightened pitch. In an article entitled "Slouching Towards Bosnia," *The New Yorker* called Clinton "childish" for suggesting the Balkans tragedy was largely a European problem. The president's "toothless" efforts to foster U.N. suasion on the matter, said the magazine, was "obscene," and Clinton's approach was being undertaken from a "cowardly slouch."

Meanwhile, Clinton had to consider a political factor significantly larger than the humanitarian impulses of the media elite—namely, the collective sentiment of the electorate. And it was clear that the American people remained decidedly wary of any Balkans involvement. In a *Time*/CNN poll published in May 1993, fully 52 percent opposed any military action beyond the country's largely empty gestures up to that point. Some 36 percent favored greater involvement. A *Newsweek* poll around the same time revealed that 60 percent of respondents opposed sending U.S. ground troops into the region, while only 27 percent favored such action. Some 45 percent opposed U.S. air strikes, compared to 40 percent who favored them. Half of the respondents agreed with the statement that Bosnia was not America's problem, while 44 percent disagreed.

Clinton, by all accounts, agreed with the media elite, but he took his cues from the polls. And for nearly two years his actions on the issue were best characterized by indecision. It wasn't until the summer of 1995 that he took action, approving a large-scale bombing campaign against Serb positions designed to force them to the bargaining table. America had moved into the Balkans.

THE STORY OF WHAT actually happened on the ground in old Yugoslavia and in Washington's warrens of decision making, as well as the historical context in which those developments unfolded, will be told in the following chapters. The point here is that from late 1992 to mid-1995—from George H. W. Bush's Somalia decision to Clinton's Bosnia bombing decision—a profound shift had occurred in the country's foreign policy thinking. Though it was little noted and seldom analyzed seriously, the country had been captured by liberal interventionism. Some sixty years after Woodrow Wilson's dreamy notions had been tossed aside by the electorate, Wilsonism had become America's prevailing foreign policy doctrine.

A corollary development that helped drive all this was the transformation of many of the country's old liberal isolationists into hardened interventionists. As noted, this was particularly visible among certain politicians, such as Senators Joseph Biden and Paul Wellstone. But the same was true of the media elite that pounded the drums so earnestly for America's march into foreign wars. *Newsweek,* during the Vietnam era, was a hotbed of antiwar sentiment. *Time* actually experienced a kind of corporate civil war brought on by the Vietnam emotions of the late 1960s; a managing editor who favored America's war policy ultimately was ousted amid widespread internal hand-wringing. One could trace similar ideological journeys at the *New York Times* and *The New Yorker,* among other publications.

Such a transformation would not have seemed particularly surprising to students of Samuel Huntington's critique of liberal foreign policy thinking, as described in his *The Soldier and the State.* Huntington noted in this early work that Americans have tended to be extremist on matters of war, either embracing it wholeheartedly or rejecting it completely. This, he writes, is required "by the nature of the liberal ideology," which deprecates the moral validity of the state's security interests and focuses instead on humanistic ideals. Thus, war must be either condemned as incompatible with liberal goals—freedom for the individual, for example, or self-determination—or justified as an ideological movement in support of those goals.

"It is a common observation," writes Huntington, "that American nationalism has been an idealistic nationalism, justified, not by the assertion of the superiority of the American people over other peoples, but by the assertion of the superiority of American ideals over other ideals." He quotes the prominent Harvard professor of government Carl J. Friedrich as noting that to be an American is an ideal, while to be a Frenchman is merely a fact. While this identification with abstract ideals is an American trait, it is particularly pronounced among American political liberals, who tend to see the world in humanistic terms. Some traditionalists have been more inclined to view war in the conservative-military sense as an instrument of national policy, in the vein of Clausewitz or George Washington's detached and analytical admonition that the nation should "choose peace or war as its interests guided by justice shall counsel."

In analyzing the Huntington critique, the writer Robert Kaplan explains that the liberal embrace of universal principles as foreign policy guidance "leads to a pacifist strain . . . when it comes to defending our hard-core national interests, and an aggressive strain when it comes to defending human rights." He adds: "It came as no surprise to readers of *The Soldier and the State* that the same intellectuals and opinion-makers who consistently underappreciated NATO in the 1970s and 1980s, when the outcome of the Cold War remained in doubt, demanded aggressive NATO involvement in the 1990s, in Bosnia and Kosovo, when the stakes for our national security were much lower, but the assault on liberal principles was vivid and clear-cut."

Behind this passion for liberal assertiveness in behalf of universal principles lay the Idea of Progress as embraced by American liberalism in the post–Cold War era—that mankind had been developing for centuries and millennia to reach Fukuyama's "universalization of Western liberal democracy as the final form of human government." For the new liberal interventionists, this represented a cluster of humanitarian ideals worthy of America's sacrifice in treasure and blood, not like that Cold War bellicosity in behalf of American interests or mere global stability. This was the outlook that got America into the Balkans. And it was the outlook that would shape America's approach to that dark sump of ethnic and religious animosities that stretch back over six centuries.

CHAPTER 7

Balkan Ghosts

I T WAS A DRIZZLY SPRING DAY in the Balkans, and Sarajevo was astir with anticipation and cultural fervor. The year was 1937, and the Bosnian capital soon would welcome the Turkish prime minister and his top military official, guests of the mayor, who would lead them in a procession from the museum to the railway station. Some thirty thousand inhabitants—nearly the city's entire Muslim population—filled the boulevard, clutching little Yugoslavian flags and holding up banners inscribed with Turkish script. For those crowded upon the dampened pavement, this was a special day.

But for the Serbs of Sarajevo, it was a day of humiliation. They viewed the foreign visitors as emissaries from the Ottoman tyranny that had held their people in subjugation for nearly five centuries. There was hardly a Christian to be seen on the streets of Sarajevo that day.

One non-Muslim who ventured forth was Dame Rebecca West, the British writer, critic, sexual dissident, and intellectual gadabout, whose presence was part of a months-long tour of Yugoslavia during this shivery spring. Her thoughts, observations, and reactions from that trip, along with the fruits of a prodigious inquiry into the dark recesses of the region's history, were thrown together into her famous travel volume, *Black Lamb and Grey Falcon*, probably the greatest of her twenty-one books. First published in 1940, it remains to this day an indispensable window on the Balkans for anyone who wants truly to understand these tragic lands.

Looking out a café window that morning, Dame Rebecca saw streams of passing people—"none of the men without fezes, all of the women veiled." Though an ardent liberal who loathed bigotry, she found herself a little disconcerted by the sight. "I do not mind there being such men and women," she wrote, "but one sees them with a different eye when they are in a majority and could put at a disadvantage all those not of their kind." Later, outside in the damp inner city, Dame Rebecca got a closer look at these earnest Muslims demonstrating their affinity for the now gone Ottoman ascendancy. "They were rapt, hallucinated, intoxicated with an old loyalty," she wrote, "and doubtless ready to know the intoxication of an old hatred."

The Turkish ministers comported themselves with impeccable diplomacy that day. They praised the concept of Yugoslavia—the unity of the South Slavs into a nation able to withstand the will of the great powers—and uttered not a word about the ancient link between the region's former Turkish overlords and their indigenous Muslim allies. Dame Rebecca noted that the prime minister, seeing the old green banner of the Ottoman heritage waving in the distance, visibly winced. But this good behavior could not dispel the fundamental reality that the Balkan lands were blighted with crosscurrents of cultural venom injected into the hearts of the peoples there through half a millennium of Turkish rule. And it would not go away even though the Turks themselves had departed. "The Turks ruined the Balkans," wrote Dame Rebecca, "with a ruin so great that it has not yet been repaired."

Half a century later, the itinerant journalist Robert Kaplan retraced much of Dame Rebecca's journey as part of his own effort to probe the complexities of the old Yugoslav societies. The result was a best-selling volume called *Balkan Ghosts: A Journey Through History,* published in 1993, just as the latest wave of Balkan bloodshed began to stir the Western consciousness. Kaplan had been dazzled and inspired by *Black Lamb and Grey Falcon,* and he came to see these lands through eyes similar to those of his distant mentor. In the meantime, of course, the region had seen the emergence of the communist fist of Josip Broz, known as Tito, whose rule Kaplan viewed as parallel to the Ottoman overlordship. He traveled to Pristina, capital of the Serbs' ancestral homeland of Kosovo but now firmly in the hands of Albanian Muslims. He called it "the Tito-built, Albanian-dominated, slum capital of 'autonomous' Kosovo" and noted it was situated between two Serb pilgrimage destinations as a kind of insult to Serb sensibilities. "Not until I traveled to Pristina," he wrote, "did I fully grasp the extent of the crime committed by Tito and the other sultans going all the way back to Murad," the first Ottoman victor over the Serbs in the fourteenth century.

The writings of Rebecca West and Robert Kaplan are notable for their sympathetic effort to understand the history and plight of the Serbs and the political sensibilities that have emerged among them through centuries of struggle and frustration. Throughout much of the 1980s, Kaplan sought to get Americans to take note of the cultural typhoons gathering in the Balkans, to no avail. It wasn't until the Serbs began moving against their perceived enemies, displaying the brutality and heartlessness so prevalent in the region's history, that the American media elite began its drumbeat call for action. By then the story line had cast the Serbs into the role of villain; demonized by the media, the Serbs became demonized also in the eyes of the American government and people.

This Serb demonization flowed inevitably from the triumph of liberal interventionism. The liberal impulse, applied to foreign affairs, almost always leads to a view of the world in terms of good and evil. That in turn creates an analytical framework best characterized as the search for villains—a simplistic but highly satisfying way of looking at world events. This outlook takes on added power when coupled with the End of History notion that Western democratic capitalism represents the culmination of human development. If only these benighted people would join us at the culmination stage, the reasoning goes, they wouldn't be so brutal and evil, and then we could chalk up one more world region into the column of civilization and peace. In the meantime, we'll just have to bomb them.

TO UNDERSTAND HOW American policy went awry in the Balkans, it is necessary to understand the Balkans, including the region's history going back some eight hundred years. The story naturally gives prominence to the Serbs, whose historical significance began with the twelfth-century emergence of the Nemanjic kingdom. It lasted two hundred years and gave the Serbs an identity that would sustain them through centuries of Turkish dominion. The dynastic founder, Stefan Nemanja, established Serbia's connection to the Byzantine ascendancy at Constantinople and to its Orthodox Christian Church. He built numerous chapels and monasteries, including the Studenica Monastery that was to become a focal point of the Serbian civilization through the coming centuries. He also gained sway over wide-ranging lands, including what is now Herzegovina, much of modern Kosovo, and today's central Serbia.

His son, also called Stefan, had the good fortune to rule at a time when the Fourth Crusade was putting an end to the Greek empire and seriously eroding the power of Byzantium. Thus Stefan got himself recognized as king of his domain by both the pope in Rome and the patriarch of Constantinople. While accepting the central Orthodox authority, he nevertheless gave his Serbian church a national character and unity by naming his brother Sava as archbishop. Sava, a civic genius, put forth a code of canon and civil laws aimed at harmonizing relations between church and state; he also canonized his father, beginning a dynastic practice that would bind the church forever to the Nemanjic heritage.

Within a few decades Serbia had become an expansive and civilized Christian Orthodox empire. As Robert Kaplan notes, Stefan could sign his name at a time when the Holy Roman Emperor in Germany could only manage a thumbprint. Serbia surpassed the Byzantine Empire in wealth and the early Western Renaissance in artistic expression. Viewing the fourteenth-century paintings on the walls of the famous Grachanitsa Monastery in Kosovo, Kaplan perceived a "sense of anatomy and bodily sexuality" that would not emerge in the West until Michelangelo and Leonardo. "But never," he added, "could any Renaissance artist duplicate the supernatural and spiritual element achieved here by the medieval Serbs."

By the fourteenth century, the Serbian empire stretched from the Danube to the Peloponnese. It was the most powerful and most civilized state in the Balkans, with a modern civil code, rule of law, trial by juries, religious freedom, an effective tax system. But when the last Nemanjic king, an ineffectual monarch named Uros, died in 1371, the Serbian lords elected one Knez ("Prince") Lazar as imperial leader. It fell to him to repel the Ottoman armies that had ventured into the Balkans in search of conquest. Lazar failed.

He failed on a hot June day in 1389 on a drab plain called Kosovo Polje, the Field of Blackbirds—a locus burned into the Serbian consciousness ever since. Scholars have noted that Kosovo Polje didn't immediately usher in the Turkish overlordship. But the battle marked the beginning of the end of Serbian control over Serbian destiny. And the defeat took on all the more power in the Serbian mind because of the large number of battlefield deaths, including that of Lazar himself, and because of the long night of subjugation that shortly would ensue.

From their previous status as an independent and conquering people, the Serbs now became the vassals of a vassal state. "As against their Moslem lords, who took possession of the land and for whom they laboured," wrote British historian R. G. D. Laffan, "they had few rights and little chance of a successful appeal to the distant government of the Sultan." Their sons were whisked away for service in the peculiar institution of the "Janizaries," an elite guard of the Turkish military manned by soldiers indoctrinated into service after being taken at a young age from Christian homes. Thus did the Turks employ Serbian manhood against the Serbian people. Further, as Laffan notes, the Serbs could not protect their daughters from being forced into the harems of the "dominant race."

Only one ancestral institution was left to them—their church. True to the Muslim tradition, the Turks did not attempt to force their religion on the conquered peoples. But they did impose a three-way choice—Islam, tribute, or the sword. The Serbs could convert to the conquerors' religion; or they could submit to substantial taxation not imposed upon the region's Muslims; or they could die. Not surprisingly, most chose taxation, and thus did the sultan of Turkey draw his revenues from subjects who were allowed to disdain his faith.

But in Bosnia-Herzegovina there was a population group that had already abandoned many elements of the established religion. These were the "Bogomils," a kind of breakaway sect that practiced ecstatic prayer, rejected the more puritan aspects of the Orthodox religion, and embraced certain pre-Christian beliefs and customs. According to Dame Rebecca, this sect had attracted a significant proportion of the Bosnian people, including both feudal lords and peasants. Having been persecuted to varying degrees in the past by Christian authorities, these people had little difficulty in accepting the Turkish entreaty of conversion. "The Bosnian Moslems," wrote Dame Rebecca, "felt that they had won their independence by a concession no greater than they would have made had they submitted to the Roman Catholic Church. So they sat down in their new town [of Sarajevo], firm in self-respect, and profited by the expanding wealth of their conquerors."

These were the people whose descendants in 1937 filled the pavements of Sarajevo to catch a glimpse of the Turkish prime minister. And through the centuries they were seen by the Serbs as collaborators in the Serbian abasement. But during that dark time the Serbs could do little about the collaborators, and they concentrated their intellectual energies on preserving their identity through their winter of adversity. They did this through two institutions: first, the church and its network of medieval monasteries constructed so zealously during the Nemanjic period—"safe-boxes of art and magic," as Kaplan described them; and, second, the sinews of poetic myth and legend that developed around the tragic story of Kosovo Polje, employing that defeat to fashion the nation's historical and national consciousness.

Students of these epic poems wax eloquent about their power and beauty. Their "Homeric grandeur," Aleksa Djilas informs us in *Foreign Affairs* magazine, so captivated Goethe's imagination that he learned Serbian in order to read them. The legend focused on the character of Lazar, who was said to have faced a choice that fateful day in 1389—an earthly kingdom or a heavenly kingdom; victory or defeat. According to the legend, by erecting a church on the plain before arraying his army in preparation for battle, Lazar chose the kingdom of heaven, a supreme sacrifice that would be redeemed someday when Lazar would return in some guise to restore the earthly kingdom.

As one epic poem concluded:

> *All was holy, all was honorable*
> *And the goodness of God was fulfilled.*

Kaplan observes after quoting this poem: "As the living death of Ottoman Turkish rule began to seep in, with its physical cruelty, economic exploitation, and barren intellectual life, the Serbs perverted this myth of noble sacrifice. They filled their hearts with vengeful sadness and defeat." And with a lingering hatred. Kaplan quotes journalist John Reed, writing during World War I: "Every [Serbian] peasant soldier knows what he is fighting for. When he was a baby, his mother greeted him, 'Hail, little avenger of Kosovo!'"

These vengeful passions sustained the Serbs through the dark centuries as the invaders pushed north and west. Twice, in 1529 and 1683, the Ottomans moved all the way to Vienna and laid siege to the Habsburg capital. But they could not prevail against Austria or Hungary because the Habsburgs had established what became known as the Military Frontier (or *Krajina* in the Serbo-Croatian language), populated in part by Serbs who had fled the advancing Turks and settled in this fortified area at the behest of the Habsburgs. In exchange for their willingness to fight, these migrants were offered land, freedom of worship, and a free hand in establishing many of their own societal institutions.

Ottoman brutality in the occupied lands served as further inducement. Whenever the Habsburgs mounted a military campaign against the Ottomans, many Serbs avidly joined in; then in the wake of Habsburg defeat the participating Serbs had to flee Turkish-dominated lands to escape the inevitable reprisals. In

1690, for example, a Habsburg army was forced to withdraw from Kosovo, and some hundreds of thousands of Serbs followed the retreat path to safety in the *Krajina*. Their homes and lands were quickly expropriated by Albanian Muslims who moved down from their mountain enclaves to claim Serbian property under Ottoman protection.

Also taking their place in the *Krajina* were the Croats, whose Balkan lands curved like a boomerang along the Adriatic Sea and then down to the border of Hungary. Nestled into this curvature was Bosnia. Like their brethren the Serbs, the Croats were Slavic peoples whose tribal ancestors arrived in the region in the sixth and seventh centuries A.D. The two groups shared the same ancient heritage, spoke the same language, manifested the same fierceness in war. But, while the Serbs cast their lot with Byzantium and the Orthodox Church, the Croats were the first Slavic tribe to pull free of the Byzantine influence and establish their own kingdom. Soon they were aligning their identity with the West, embracing Roman Catholicism and accepting Hungarian and Habsburg influence.

As Kaplan points out, the differences in religion, after centuries of custom, turned out to be "no mean thing." He notes that Western religions emphasize ideas and deeds while Eastern religions emphasize beauty and magic. This distinction is seen in nearly every aspect of the two religions, including their uses of ceremony, the tone of their respective services, the duties of their priests, the length of their weddings, and eventually their way of looking at the world. These distinctions seeped over into secular habits as well.

Moreover, the Turks arrived upon the Croatian lands later than upon Serbian territory, and they were forced out some two hundred years earlier. Thus the Croats never suffered the same long winter of overlordship. During the worst of it, they took their place within the Military Frontier and afterward cemented themselves to the Habsburg ascendancy with an enthusiasm born of destiny. Over the centuries of Western expansion and material progress, the Croats came to regard themselves as part of the West and hence somewhat superior to their fellow Slavs to the south.

This drove Dame Rebecca to fits of bemusement. She didn't much care for Germans in general, still less Austrians in particular, and even less the Habsburg dynasty, which she considered feckless and unscrupulous. And she viewed the Croats' "burning, indestructible devotion" to the Habsburgs as "one of the most peculiar passions known in history." The Habsburgs repaid this devotion, writes Dame Rebecca, with a series of indignities—forcing Croatia into Hungarian annexation, denying Croatian requests for autonomy, sanctioning a Magyar assault on the Serbo-Croatian language, and finally by placing Croatia directly under the dominance of the central government in Vienna. And yet the Croats' passion for Austria remained "idiotically stable." As Robert Kaplan puts it, "Fear of the East, as manifested by Constantinople—whether Byzantine or Turkish—swept the Croats willingly into the arms of Catholic popes, Hungarian kings, and Austrian-Hapsburg emperors."

This sentiment was to play a major role in the Balkans after the nineteenth century dawned amid signs of Ottoman decline. This stirred Serbian optimism and resistance. A Serb army defeated an Ottoman force at Ivankovac in August 1805, prompting the sultan to declare a *jihad* or holy war against the insurgents. Following a Serb defeat in 1813, the Turkish vengeance was terrible and swift. Serb villages were burned and thousands of inhabitants sold into slavery. On a single October day, 1,800 women and children were sold as slaves in Belgrade. But the Serbs rallied and succeeded in freeing a large portion of Ottoman dominance by mid-1815. From that moment forward, the Ottoman retreat proved inexorable. The last Turkish soldiers left the region in 1867, and Serbia gained international recognition in 1878.

But, while little Serbia managed to free itself of the Turkish yoke, it could not avoid the pressures and forces of great power maneuverings. Particularly troublesome were the ambitions of the new Austro-Hungarian Dual Monarchy, which in 1878 gained international authority to occupy and administer Bosnia-Herzegovina. Naturally this caused grave concern among the region's Serbs, not only in Serbia proper but also in Bosnia, Croatia, Slavonia, and Dalmatia. After the Habsburgs had abandoned the old Military Frontier in the wake of the Ottoman retreat, many Serbs had entered the political mainstream of these regions. By the late nineteenth century, Serbs made up a quarter of the population in Croatia and 16 percent in Dalmatia. In Bosnia, they constituted 43 percent of the populace, to the Muslims' one-third and the Croats' 20 percent. These Bosnian Serbs wanted to be part of independent Serbia, not absorbed into the vast polyglot Austro-Hungarian Empire. They dreamed of a unified pan-Serbian nation encompassing all the Serbian peoples of the region and harking back to the hallowed Nemanjic kingdom of old. That dream was shared by most Serbs throughout the region.

The dream was dealt a powerful blow in 1908 when the Habsburg Empire annexed Bosnia-Herzegovina through force of arms. Serbia, with its three million inhabitants, couldn't bring much sway against an empire of fifty million. So the region settled down to a period of seething anger, which in turn fostered a network of underground terrorists bent on expelling the Austro-Hungarians by any means possible.

One of their number, a student radical named Gavrilo Princip, concluded the best means available was assassination, and his opportunity came on June 28, 1914, when the heir to the throne, Archduke Franz Ferdinand, made a state visit to Sarajevo. It was a provocative day for such a visit by the Austrian royal family—the very day, venerated by Serbs everywhere, commemorating their 1389 defeat on the plain of Kosovo Polje. Thus was the royal visit viewed by many Bosnian Serbs as an insult. As the duke's motorcade made its way through inner-city Sarajevo, Princip rushed from the crowd and killed Franz Ferdinand and his wife, Sophie.

Every schoolchild knows what happened next: although no evidence established an official Serbian connection to the assassination, Vienna used the event as a pretext to gain control of Serbia. Russia promptly mobilized to protect its little client state, which in turn prompted Germany to mobilize in support of its Austrian ally. That brought declarations of war from Russia's military partners, Britain and France. And soon the entire European continent was consumed in a conflagration every bit as ominous, bloody, and seminal as that obscure German pessimist, Oswald Spengler, had foreseen. The passions unleashed by the Ottoman invasion half a millennium before had detonated what history likely will perceive as the culminating crisis of Western civilization.

EVEN BEFORE THE FAMOUS guns of August could be heard in 1914, Austria-Hungary invaded Serbia and set out to cleanse Bosnia of as many Serbs as possible. The old empire, sparing no brutality, received willing help from Croatian and Muslim mobs that rampaged through Bosnian towns, destroying Serbian houses and businesses. The authorities in Bosnia fostered special military units called *Schutzkorps,* with "full powers to deal with the Serbian population." Within weeks, five thousand Serbs had been imprisoned, Cyrillic spelling banned, and Serbian schools closed. If a Bosnian Serb vacated his home to join the fight to save Serbia, his property was promptly seized and his family expelled. A network of concentration camps was established in Hungary to which some 150,000 Serbs, from Bosnia and later from occupied Serbia, were sent during the ensuing war. Another thirty thousand were sent to camps in Austria. Many died from disease and starvation.

Serbia initially repelled the invaders, but by October 1915 a combined force of Austria-Hungary, Germany, and Bulgaria had conquered the country and placed it under occupation. There followed a remarkable mass migration of Serbian troops, civilians, government officials, and the ruling family—across Montenegro and over the Albanian mountains. They took heavy losses from disease, the elements, and intermittent fighting, but eventually 150,000 reached the Greek island of Corfu, where the army regrouped and threw itself back into the fray at Salonika.

The war's end marked the end also of the Habsburg Empire and the Austro-Hungarian presence in the Balkans. And so in October 1918 a National Council of Slovenes, Croats, and Serbs took power and two months later declared the new Kingdom of Serbs, Croats, and Slovenes, later renamed Yugoslavia (kingdom of South Slavs). This was a powerful idea—a unified Balkan kingdom encompass-

ing twelve million people including Serbs, Croats, Slovenes, Slavo-
nians, Montenegrins, Bosnian Muslims, and Albanian Muslims
from the old ancestral region of Kosovo. Of the twelve million,
some 39 percent were Serbs, another 24 percent Croats.

Embedded within these percentages was cause for endless wran-
gling between Serbs and Croats about the nature of the kingdom.
Croats feared that a strong centralist state would lead to domination by the single largest group, the Serbs, and that other groups
would soon lose standing in the new polity. The Serbs argued that
the Croats' concept of a loose confederation of autonomous states
would leave the entity too weak to survive. Besides, recalling the
Serbs' fate during World War I, they worried about the safety of
large numbers of Serbs living outside Serbia as minorities in Croatia, Slovenia, and elsewhere.

The Serbian argument prevailed, and soon the new Yugoslav
government did in fact come under the domination of Serbian influences. Some Croats accepted this, but many others seethed under this new Serbian ascendancy. As Tim Judah puts it in his *The
Serbs: History, Myth and the Destruction of Yugoslavia,* "The Yugoslavia that tottered through the 1920s and 1930s was a poor, unstable and mostly sullen country."

Just how sullen was made clear in 1928 when a Montenegrin
deputy rose in the Yugoslav parliament and shot two Croat legisla-
tors dead. Croatia's leading patriot, Stjepan Radic, was wounded in
the spree and later died. Then in 1934 an agent of a Croatian nationalist underground group, the Ustasha, assassinated Yugoslavia's King Alexander during a royal visit to Marseilles, France.
The Serb-dominated government responded with remarkable for-
bearance—"one of the most extraordinary feats of statesmanship
performed in post-war Europe," as Dame Rebecca characterized it.
Thus the rickety Yugoslav state held together—barely.

This was the Yugoslavia that beckoned Dame Rebecca in the
mid-1930s. She had not heard the name of the country until one
October day in 1934. Languishing in the hospital and listening to
the radio following a major surgery, she heard the news of King
Alexander's assassination in Marseilles. Instantly she conjured up

visions of the war that was likely to ensue, brought about by a chain of events reminiscent of the 1914 summer. That anticipated war never materialized, but those instinctive fears stirred in her a passionate fascination with the region. She vowed to visit, which she did in 1936. A year later she returned with her husband for the tour that was to become the foundation for her great book. Waiting to greet them at Croatia's Zagreb train station on a rainy spring evening in 1937 were three friends from her previous visit.

These were men who never would have lingered with each other in any setting had they not been brought together by their friendship with Dame Rebecca. One was a Serb poet named Constantine, a passionately voluble Orthodox Christian whose fealty to the concept of Yugoslavia stirred him to sudden flights of eloquence in behalf of this new civic structure. Another was an instantly likable mathematician named Valetta, a Roman Catholic from Dalmatia who hated the very thought of Yugoslavia; as a Croatian patriot, he reserved his passion for the idea of an autonomous Croatia. Then there was Gregorievitch, a Croatian writer and critic whose primary civic passion was a hatred for the Austro-Hungarians; he revered the new Yugoslav kingdom as a bastion against external encroachments and dismissed Valetta as "quite simply a traitor," as Dame Rebecca put it.

"They greet us warmly," she writes, "as in their hearts they cannot greet each other, and they dislike us a little because it is to meet us that they are standing beside their enemies in the rain." As her narrative unfolds, the political tensions among these Balkan men come into focus to form a kind of microcosmic view of the underlying tensions within the Yugoslav experiment. They can come together if they must to serve the interest of their friendship with this British outsider and her husband, but their inevitable bickering, often friendly but sometimes displaying strains of bitterness, reflects the broader crosscurrents of political sentiments in their country. As long as stability reigned, however precariously, they could deal with one another and remain civil. But one had to wonder what would happen if the precarious kingdom were to collapse.

As the storm clouds of World War II gathered nearby, the precarious kingdom did collapse. In August 1939, bowing to Croatian pressure and fearing the growing power of the Third Reich following the previous year's German-Austrian *Anschluss,* the Yugoslav prime minister negotiated a new status for Croatia. It became autonomous within a Yugoslav federation, encompassing not only the lands of Croatia, Slavonia, and Dalmatia but also a large portion of Bosnia. Its population of 4.4 million included 866,000 Serbs. Serbian nationalists naturally were outraged. But, as historian Tim Judah notes, this was to be the beginning of a thoroughly new Yugoslav federation, with further carvings anticipated to accommodate Serbian interests. He adds: "Bosnian Muslim anger at the utter disregard for their interests in the . . . division of Bosnia was of no interest to the Serbian or Croatian parties concerned." Six days after this agreement was signed, Europe was at war.

World War II visited upon the Serbs even greater catastrophe than World War I. The German-Italian Axis moved in and crushed Yugoslavia in April 1941, then installed a puppet regime in Croatia under the brutal Ustashi terrorist organization, headed by an anti-Serb strongman and Nazi sympathizer named Ante Pavelic. He promulgated a killing spree against Serbs, vowing to eliminate a third of them, drive out another third, and convert the rest to Catholicism. Robert Kaplan writes: "In primitive ferocity—if not in sheer numbers—the massacre in Catholic Croatia and neighboring Bosnia-Herzegovina of Orthodox Serbs was as bad as anything in German-occupied Europe."

To this day it isn't known just how many Serbs perished. Kaplan writes that if you talk to a man in the Balkans who pegs the number at sixty thousand, you know you're talking to a Croat nationalist; if he puts the number at 700,000, you can assume he is a Serb. In his book, *Serbs and Croats: The Struggle in Yugoslavia,* Alex N. Dragnich credits the 700,000 figure, while two credible post–Cold War studies suggest the total number of Serbian deaths during the war was 530,000, compared to 192,000 Croat deaths and 103,000 Muslims. What isn't in dispute is the brutality of the pogrom. As one ethnic Serb said to Kaplan during a Balkan train ride, "The Croatian fascists did not have gas chambers. . . . They had only

knives and mallets with which to commit mass murder." It is esti-
mated that Pavelic's regime also killed fifty thousand Jews and
twenty thousand Gypsies.

In Serbia, meanwhile, large numbers of troops fled to the
mountains to form cadres of resistance fighters under the command of a World War I veteran named Draza Mihailovic. This
Homeland Army, or Chetniks, as they were popularly called,
waged a guerrilla war against the occupiers and received recognition from the Yugoslav government in exile, which promoted Mihailovic to general and named him minister of war. But the
general soon found himself locked in a civil war against another
guerrilla outfit, Tito's communist Partisans. Mihailovic's aim was
liberation from the occupiers and a postwar restoration of the Yugoslav federation, to be molded and shaped through freedom of
choice. Tito wanted a postwar dictatorship of the proletariat
aligned with the Soviet Union. Mihailovic managed to expel the
Partisans from Serbia and Montenegro, though it should be noted
that in the process his troops, in fits of vengeance, also visited brutal treatment upon Croats and Muslims in the region, killing some
and forcing others to flee their homes.

But with the arrival of the Soviet army the balance of power
shifted, and soon the Soviets were handing Belgrade over to Tito,
who proved to be as cunning and ruthless as his ally Stalin. He
quickly consolidated power throughout the region, established a
communist police state, and moved harshly against his enemies,
including the middle class, the intellectuals, and anyone who opposed his aims. Croat collaborators and Ustashi warriors, returned
to Tito after fleeing to British-occupied territory, were executed in
the tens of thousands.

Tito, half Croat and half Slovene, melded together his new
communist Yugoslavia by diminishing the power of the largest
population group, the Serbs, and enhancing the power of the
Croats and Slovenes. He awarded republic status to Slovenia and
Croatia without regard to the fate or wishes of the minority Serbs
in those areas, but in Serbia he carved out autonomous regions to
accommodate the wishes of minority Albanian Muslims in Kosovo

and Hungarians and others in Vojvodina. By restoring Bosnia to its historic 1878 boundaries, he thwarted Serbian interests there. In Kosovo, the Serbian ancestral lands, Albanian Muslims soon outnumbered Serbs, largely because Tito prevented the return of dislocated Serbs to the region while allowing an influx of some 100,000 Albanian Muslims. Economically, he fostered development in Croatia and Slovenia at the expense of Bosnia and Serbia.

Tito simply declared an end to the region's cultural strife and employed his military police to enforce it. He issued a decree that stated: "There can be no change because the new federal Yugoslavia has been accepted by the overwhelming majority of all Yugoslav nations. Nothing can be changed because we are all aware that this is an historic necessity. There can be no change because we know that the Yugoslav nations cannot exist without genuine unity, that they would be unable to develop on the economic and social plane." In exchange, he offered words of protection to calm the fears of Serbs living in minority status outside Serbia.

Even after he boldly broke away from Soviet hegemony in 1948, Tito enforced his hold on the Yugoslav state with the iron fist of totalitarianism. For thirty-five years he ruled, until his death in 1980 at age eighty-seven. During that time he thwarted any serious historical inquiry into the bloody events of World War II, thus ensuring that the wounds of the consciousness stemming from those dark days would remain unhealed. He held at bay the aims and dreams of the various peoples within his domain. He dictated the continuance of an artificial regime that inevitably would collapse one day under its own weight. And when that day came and that collapse materialized, the driving force of Balkan nationalism would rise again, stirring those old passions and hatreds and aspirations that had swirled with such force around the region since that fateful June day at Kosovo Polje in 1389.

CHAPTER 8

Balkan Tragedy

I N EARLY 1989 A VETERAN Foreign Service officer named
Warren Zimmermann paid a visit to the freshly nominated
deputy secretary of state, Lawrence Eagleburger, to discuss
Zimmermann's new assignment as ambassador to Yugoslavia. The
two men shared extensive experiences in the Balkans, where they
had developed a deep affection for those tormented, spellbinding
lands. "By the way," said Eagleburger with a grin as they con-
versed, "I'm going to get you in trouble during your first few weeks
in Yugoslavia." At his forthcoming appearance before the Senate
Foreign Relations Committee, he explained, he planned to issue a
sharp rebuke to Serbian President Slobodan Milosevic over the
Serbs' treatment of Albanian Muslims in the Serbian region of
Kosovo. Zimmermann quickly welcomed the planned remarks as
being consistent with what he intended to say privately to Yugoslav officials.

That casual exchange, recounted in Zimmermann's memoir of
his tumultuous Belgrade tenure, reflects America's foreign policy
transition from the realpolitik of the Cold War to a more moralistic and at times hubristic approach as the East-West confrontation
subsided. Zimmermann's memoir, *Origins of a Catastrophe: Yugoslavia and Its Destroyers—America's Last Ambassador Tells What Happened and Why*, reveals a diplomacy based on the view that
America served as a kind of world model posing solutions for other
nations' problems, however disparate those problems might be.

"This is a story with villains," writes Zimmermann. They were

130

villains, he says, because they destroyed the multiethnic state of Yugoslavia and wrenched it away from any prospect of pursuing the American model, "the most successful multiethnic experiment in existence." To Zimmermann and his government, the primary imperative was that a united Yugoslavia should evolve into a multiethnic democracy. Barring that, the individual republics formed from any breakup should all take on the multiethnic mantle.

From this outlook, certain perceptions and convictions followed. Zimmermann fingered the Serbs as most responsible for the unfolding Balkan tragedy. The Bosnian Muslims, on the other hand, were viewed largely with equanimity. Nationalist impulses in the region were "a cancer," "the arrow that killed Yugoslavia." Zimmermann believed this malignant outlook had been artificially inserted into the Balkan consciousness by manipulative Balkan leaders. "What we witnessed," he writes, "was violence-provoking nationalism from the top down."

These thoughts and perceptions led Zimmermann and his government to oppose any solution involving partition—separating these warring contingents into national ethnic enclaves. That would violate American principles. "Most of all," he writes, "we stand for the simple proposition that people of all ethnic strains can live together, not without tensions, but with tolerance, civility, and even mutual enrichment."

Warren Zimmermann, who died in February 2004 after a brave fight against cancer, represented in many ways the very best traits of the American Foreign Service officer—intelligence, patriotism, personal rectitude, charm. And his book offers abundant insight into the unfolding Balkan tragedy as the Cold War era faded into a new and at times bewildering season. But the geopolitical sensibility he brought to his Belgrade posting, reflecting the outlook also of his bosses back in Washington, obscured the region's fundamental realities. The result was diplomatic failure.

Zimmermann repeatedly dismissed the notion that the Yugoslav turmoil was the product of what had become known as "ancient ethnic hatreds"—reflecting, in the view of some, characteristic traits of the region's peoples. He argued instead that these passions had been synthetically infused into the Balkan consciousness by cynical demagogues seeking legitimacy for their post-communist leadership. But, says Professor William W. Hagen of the University of California at Davis, neither school had it right. In a penetrating 1999 essay in *Foreign Affairs*, he argues that the region's ethnic strains were neither as ancient as time nor as recent as Slobodan Milosevic. Echoing Rebecca West and Robert Kaplan, he suggests these passions were the lingering result of that five-hundred-year winter of Ottoman tyranny that descended upon the Balkans in the fourteenth century. With its dissolution, says Hagen, came a "crippling dependence of all Balkan peoples on the ideology and psychology of expansionist nationalism."

As we have seen in the previous chapter, the Ottoman centuries led to the dispersion and intermixture of the region's various ethnic groups. And the kind of pre-modern state formation seen in other regions of Europe could never take root in the Balkans. Thus, the subject populations were organized largely by religion. As noted previously, the Serbs managed to maintain their identity through this dark winter largely through their fealty to the Orthodox Church and the church's reciprocal devotion to the identity of its flock. The same was true of the Catholic Croats and, in a different way, the Bosnian Muslims who rode the wave of Ottoman hegemony. Thus did religious identity drive a powerful wedge between peoples who spoke the same language and in fact shared the same ethnic provenance.

With the first signs of the Ottoman retreat, the ideology of European nationalism became the rallying cry for those seeking liberation from Turkish rule. From 1815 to 1913, independent national states were established in Serbia, Greece, Romania, Bulgaria, and Albania. But these states emerged amid two fundamental and potentially troublesome realities, both products of the Ottoman ascendancy. First, each contained various minorities besides the ruling nationalities. And, second, none of them encompassed all of the territory that the various ruling elites considered necessary for national cohesion.

Thus the Balkan states all emerged as "irredentist nations," as

Hagen puts it—"nations committed to the recovery of their 'unredeemed' national territories." Their legitimacy was tied inextricably to their commitment to the imagined national community.

The Ottoman overlordship yielded another societal reality that helped give shape to most of the Balkan territories in the twentieth century—strains of extreme populism. The Turks consciously set out to destroy the medieval dynasties and nobilities of the conquered societies in order to reduce them to peasant lands. Thus, most of the nations that emerged with the Ottoman dissolution did not have significant commercial or manufacturing classes. The elites of the Ottoman years had been the Turks themselves and their indigenous Muslim collaborators, but the Turks were now gone and the Muslims had been stripped of their previous status.

The result was that the emergent post-Ottoman nations lacked not only prospects for commercial prosperity but also the bourgeois sensibility that can lend stability and moderation to society. Meanwhile, the intellectual classes gravitated to the goal of building the national state and its armies as a means of regaining unredeemed territories. Thus we see the emergence of societies that possessed almost nothing of the West's liberal tradition and where there was little regard for the Western devotion to capitalism, individualism, or minority rights. In these societies national minorities faced intrinsically dangerous circumstances. Muslim minorities particularly lacked standing to claim effective citizenship in a Balkan Christian nation forged only through the ejection of the hated Turkish Muslims. But even Christian minorities were forced to bend to the majority culture, confining their demands to linguistic and religious rights. To demand more, as Hagen notes, "risked the charge of hostility to their new fatherland."

The political climate engendered by these circumstances favored rightist oligarchies. During the interwar period, rightist dictatorships soon overwhelmed the peasant parties, themselves highly nationalist in outlook, that had emerged to assert class rights over the oligarchies. And after World War II, Tito's Yugoslav communism was deeply nationalist in nature, legitimized in large measure through Tito's delicate effort to satisfy the nationalist aims of his various peoples while balancing them off against each other. Some intellectuals have argued that democratic sentiments during the Tito decades emerged in nationalist garb because that was the only dissident language that was allowed. Hagen dismisses this as "liberal wishful thinking" and adds, "Exclusivist nationalism triumphed in Yugoslavia because it expressed the deepest yearnings and values of most of those who were disaffected from the communist regime."

And so we come back to the demarcation year of 1989, when it became clear that the political essence of Yugoslavia—and perhaps its map—was about to change. There were many possibilities, but they all fit into two fundamental philosophical frameworks—one based on the concept of progress, the other based on the force of culture.

The former, embraced by the U.S. government and eloquently articulated by Ambassador Zimmermann, held that the problems of Yugoslavia boiled down to one nefarious influence, the mania of nationalism. Only by eradicating the nationalist impulse, according to this view, could Yugoslavia find its destiny as a liberal democratic nation and join the Western community. The other framework, based on cultural realities, was widely embraced in Yugoslavia itself but also by some Western intellectuals. It held that nationalism was part of the essence of Yugoslavia and its peoples. Just as the Balkan problem could not be understood without that acknowledgment, neither could any solution be crafted without it.

The story of how the Idea of Progress guided American policy in the region begins and ends with Kosovo, the Serbs' ancestral homeland where Serbs accounted for only 10 percent of the population by 1989. Through centuries of migration and birthrate patterns, the province had become nearly 90 percent Albanian Muslim. During World War II, when the region was under Italian control, Muslims killed some ten thousand Serbs and forced another 100,000 to flee. After the war, as a concession to the Kosovo Muslims, Tito barred the expelled Serbs from returning while allowing Albanians who had arrived during the war to remain. As a further concession, he declared Kosovo an "autonomous region" within Serbia, to be run by majority Muslims as an essentially independent republic.

Soon Kosovo's Albanian nationalists initiated what Robert Kaplan calls "the Albanian *intifada*"—a secession campaign to meld the region to Albania and an intimidation campaign against the region's minority Serbs. One relatively neutral observer, a Croatian Protestant, described the anti-Serb campaign as "numerous violent incidents . . . which included property damage, loss of jobs, harassment, rapes, fights, and killings." More than 200,000 Serbs fled the area in the face of this intimidation during the Tito years and immediately after, and those who remained felt increasingly vulnerable. Thus, Serbs throughout Yugoslavia began agitating in behalf of their Kosovo brethren.

That's when Slobodan Milosevic, the sly communist functionary with the baby face and ruthless instinct for political opportunity, essentially ended the Tito era with a speech. On June 28, 1987, the anniversary of the Serbian defeat at Kosovo Polje, he traveled to that hallowed ground, pointed his finger toward the horizon, and declared, "They'll never do this to you again. Never again will anyone defeat you." Kaplan writes, "As the crowd roared, the Serbian revolt against the Yugoslav federation began." Instantly, Milosevic became the voice of Serbian nationalism and the most popular Serbian leader of the twentieth century. He rode that popularity to the Serbian presidency in May 1989.

In the meantime he had revoked Kosovo's autonomy and reversed the flow of intimidation. Now it was the Muslims who were subjected to abuse. Serbian police units conducted search raids on villages and businesses. Armed Serb civilians paraded around menacingly. Muslim families were harassed, parents sometimes beaten in front of their children. Muslims were fired from their jobs. The ostensible reason for all this was the need to control the Albanian separatist movement, which was in fact gaining force. But the intimidation campaign clearly was brutal and soon caught the eye of America.

Members of Congress attacked these Serbian actions and warned darkly that they could affect U.S. relations with Yugoslavia. Lawrence Eagleburger, as he had promised Zimmermann, echoed those sentiments during his Senate confirmation hearings. And upon arriving in Belgrade Zimmermann wasted no time in demonstrating that American policy favored Albanian interests over those of the Serbs in this complex embroilment. When Milosevic again traveled to Kosovo Polje in June 1989 for a commemorative speech that drew more than a million people, Zimmermann and other Western diplomats declined to attend. He didn't want to associate himself with Milosevic's brand of Serbian nationalism, he explained in his memoir. But, when American dignitaries visited Belgrade, he routinely congregated around his dinner table leading opposition figures.

Nowhere in his book does Zimmermann express concern about the fate of Kosovo's minority Serbs under Albanian autonomy, either past or future. As a kind of "truth test," he asked Albanian leader Ibrahim Rugova how his people had treated the Serbs before Milosevic revoked autonomy. "Unfortunately," replied the Muslim leader, "there were many crimes committed against Serbs." But Zimmermann in his book provides no elaboration on these abuses, expresses no outrage about them, and remains silent on how this potential threat to Serbian security might be addressed in any Kosovo solution.

Given the demographics of Kosovo, it probably wasn't possible to fashion a solution to the problem that could accommodate Serbian interests and ambitions. The matter could be handled, if at all, only within the broader context of the entire Yugoslav puzzle. But that was all the more reason for American policy to demonstrate a degree of understanding for the Serbian predicament. The Serbs, after all, held the largest proportion of power in the region, and no peaceful solution could be possible without their ultimate acceptance.

Rather than accept the political standing of Milosevic, who could draw more than a million followers to a speech, America cast its lot with the Yugoslav prime minister, Ante Markovic, described by Zimmermann as "one of the few admirable figures in a landscape of monsters and midgets." He shared America's hopes for

Yugoslavia as a "Western democratic country with a capitalist system." There was only one problem: he had no following. In part this was because he voiced a kind of civic idealism that simply couldn't take root in the nationalist soil of post–Cold War Yugoslavia. But perhaps in larger part it was because he was the advocate of brutal economic reforms—so-called shock therapy policies imported from the West—that included currency devaluations, mass layoffs, and increased tax burdens. These hopeless nostrums, pushed avidly by the International Monetary Fund, were strangling Yugoslavia's commerce and further enflaming civic passions in the region.

Even more curious was America's early attitude toward the Muslims of Bosnia and Aliza Izetbegovic, the Muslim leader whose aim, to judge from his writings, was creation of an Islamic fundamentalist state in Bosnia. The primary evidence was his political platform, called *The Islamic Declaration: A Programme for the Islamization of Muslims and the Muslim Peoples.* Published in 1990 but written twenty years earlier, the book asserts "the incompatibility of Islam with non-Islamic systems. There can be neither peace nor coexistence between the Islamic religion and non-Islamic social and political institutions." Further, Izetbegovic declared that the Islamic movement "should and can start to take over power as soon as it is morally and numerically strong enough to be able to overturn not only the existing non-Islamic movement, but also to build a new Islamic one." Once this Islamic republic was created, said Izetbegovic, it was imperative that both education and the media "should be in the hands of people whose Islamic moral and intellectual authority is indisputable."

America repeatedly rebuffed warnings from Serb and Croatian leaders about the Muslims' true intentions. In his memoir, Zimmermann ignores Izetbegovic's provocative language and dismisses his manifesto as "dreamy" musings "wrongly thought to be a Muslim call to arms." Thus, America missed an essential reality in Yugoslavia that was contributing to its looming civil war.

The civil war came in June 1991 when Slovenia and Croatia issued declarations of secession. Slovenia, whose population was 91 percent Slovenian, was allowed to go, but Croatia was another matter. There some 700,000 Serbs found themselves a 15 percent minority in a new nation dominated by Croats. The Yugoslav military, now "Serbianized," responded by capturing more than a quarter of Croatia for the Serbs.

America, which for months had opposed Slovenian and Croatian secession, wheeled about and recognized the two breakaway republics. This emboldened Izetbegovic to declare Bosnian independence. Then America quickly recognized that breakaway republic as well. Both actions were serious diplomatic mistakes. The Yugoslav civil war, relatively contained until now, suddenly turned vicious and bloody. The Muslims, representing 43 percent of the Bosnian population, wanted a multiethnic state dominated by themselves. This was utterly unacceptable to the Serbs (33 percent) and Croats (17 percent), who set about to carve out their own territories and meld them to Serbia and Croatia. The age-old Balkan tool of "ethnic cleansing," as it was now called, was applied with a vengeance, and of course the dominant power in the region, the Serbs, applied it most effectively. The United Nations imposed an arms embargo on the whole of Yugoslavia in September 1991 and economic sanctions against Serbia, considered the aggressor, in May 1992.

But by the end of 1992 the Serbs had won what historian Tim Judah called "a coward's war" in which Serbian wrath was directed primarily at civilians. But the Serbs now held a quarter of Croatia and had extended their Bosnian landholdings, now called Republika Srpska, to 70 percent of the region. From that time to the summer of 1995, despite ongoing combat, the front lines hardly changed, and ethnic cleansing operations became scattered and desultory. But the Serbs had paid a fearsome price for their brutality in the summer of 1992, when they killed thousands of innocents in their effort to wipe out Muslim enclaves. The 1992 massacres, particularly the famous episode at Srebrenica, writes Tim Judah, proved to be a "catastrophe" for the Serbs. "From the moment of their discovery, all lingering doubts in the international community about whether all sides in the war were guilty . . . were driven into the background. The Serbs were branded as . . . the Balkan successors to the Nazis."

Throughout this time America's President Clinton struggled with indecisiveness. As a liberal interventionist the president wanted to act. But as president of a country with no direct national interest in the Balkans, he knew that any sacrifice of American blood would be politically untenable. Meanwhile, his halfway measures—economic sanctions, verbal attacks, and occasional pinprick air strikes against the Serbs—only prolonged the Balkan agony. Muslims had no incentive to negotiate so long as they believed the Serbs would buckle under American pressure. A better approach would have been to convince the Muslims that the American cavalry wasn't coming, that the outcome needed to reflect the power realities on the ground, and that ultimately 1.2 million Muslims could not stand up against nine million Serbs.

But Clinton had other ideas, and by fall 1994 a government-sponsored private organization called Military Professional Resources Inc. was giving the Croat army a crash course in sophisticated American combined-arms tactics. A year later the Croats launched the U.S.-sanctioned Operation Storm, a potent ground offensive targeted at Serb positions in Croatia's *Krajina* region. Shortly thereafter, Clinton authorized a NATO air campaign called Operation Deliberate Force, aimed at forcing the Bosnian Serbs to negotiate a settlement on Western terms.

The highly effective Croat offensive was accompanied by a brutal wave of ethnic cleansing against the *Krajina* Serbs. The harassment and threats against the civilian population began at 5:00 A.M. on August 4, and within two days some 175,000 Serbs were on the roads. "That was all the time it took," writes Tim Judah, "for the Serbian Orthodox population of these lands, which had lived there for several centuries, to vanish." In America, the forces of liberal interventionism raised hardly a murmur of angst against this particular episode of ethnic cleansing, though it was comparable to the Serbian cruelty that had been generating cries of anguish from the humanitarians for years.

Clinton's approach worked and led to negotiations in Dayton,

Ohio, that culminated in what became known as the Dayton Accords. Under the agreement, the Bosnian Serbs got 49 percent of the Bosnian land, incorporated into the now recognized Republika Srpska, while a federation of Croats and Muslims received 51 percent. Thus, Bosnia was to remain one state divided into two entities. Theoretically, dislocated peoples were to be allowed to return, but that never happened. And theoretically the new country was to have a central government, with a multiethnic presidency, a bicameral parliament, and a court system. But the government rarely met unless pressured by the West to do so. The whole thing ultimately was held together by NATO troops and later by European Union troops, who remain in place as of this writing.

AMERICAN POLICY IN the Balkans through the first half of the 1990s can only be described as feckless. The country ignored the historical and cultural forces that would have to be accommodated in any solution and instead promoted a civic outlook that stirred no passion among the Yugoslav peoples. It fostered economic policies that strangled commerce throughout the region. It embraced a politician, Markovic, who had no following and rebuffed the leaders who actually enjoyed political support. It entirely missed the emergence of Islamic fundamentalism upon the soil of Europe and prolonged the agony by giving Bosnian Muslims hope for Western intervention. And it firmly opposed, until the very end, the only solution that could have seriously addressed the Balkan agonies and thus proved successful. That was partition.

Had the West been less preoccupied with visions of multiethnic harmony and more realistic about the cultural and political realities of the region, it might have seen merit in fostering the creation of three ethnically homogeneous entities in Bosnia, with the Serb and Croatian entities being free to join Greater Croatia and Greater Serbia, respectively, and the independent Muslim state fortified and protected through international guarantees. The plan could have included a large population-exchange program, established and run by the United Nations, that could have guaranteed safe passage for ethnic minorities trapped behind the new boundaries. And it could also have included a new development bank dedicated to financing relocations and fostering economic development in relocation areas.

As it turned out, the Dayton formula was essentially a partition solution. But it came about only grudgingly after the region's latest irredentist wars had scrambled up its demographic map through bloodletting rather than through negotiation and peaceful relocation. Besides, as academics John J. Mearsheimer and Robert A. Pape have pointed out, a peaceful partition approach conceivably could have included a resolution of the Kosovo problem. The idea was that the Serbs may have seen merit in relinquishing Kosovo, where Serbs had become a tiny minority, if that sacrifice were accompanied by substantial irredentist gains in Bosnia, by relocation assistance for Kosovo's remaining Serbs who wished to leave, and by internationally enforced protections for those Serbs who chose to remain and for their ancient churches and monasteries. We'll never know if that could have worked. But we do know the Dayton solution left Kosovo unresolved, which guaranteed that it would erupt in blood a few years later.

THAT'S PRECISELY WHAT happened by early 1998, when Kosovo's peaceful resistance movement led by the remote and ascetic Ibrahim Rugova gave way to a powerful new force called the Kosovo Liberation Army, or KLA. This was a dedicated cadre of Albanian Muslim fighters who were described by *New York Times* correspondent Chris Hedges, writing in *Foreign Affairs*, as "militant, nationalist, uncompromising, and deeply suspicious of all outsiders." Financed largely by the large Albanian diaspora in Europe and North America, armed by next-door Albania, and manned by seething Kosovar youths struggling in a region beset by 70 percent unemployment, the KLA initiated a series of attacks on Serbian officials and positions in the region. Its aim was secession and eventual absorption into a Greater Albania. Not surprisingly, Milosevic soon sent his army in to subdue this paramilitary rebellion.

What followed was a civil war within the undisputed boundaries of Serbia. Relatively contained, it claimed about 2,500 lives
and displaced some 230,000 persons. During one particularly brutal offensive in October 1998, some 400,000 Kosovars were chased
from their homes. But after a subsequent cease-fire most of them
felt safe enough to return. Thus, Serbian ethnic cleansing in
Kosovo seemed to many as largely a tactical offensive directed primarily at KLA-held territory and aimed at driving a wedge between
the insurgents and their civilian supporters.

But back in Washington the humanitarian juices were flowing,
and soon the government was expressing official outrage at Milosevic's latest military initiative. Moreover, a new power player had
emerged to press the case for American action. Secretary of State
Madeleine Albright combined fervent sentiments of liberal interventionism with an even stronger conviction of American exceptionalism (a variant of the Eurocentrism that so often emanates
from the Idea of Progress). She was fond of referring to her country
as "the indispensable nation" and often added: "We stand tall and
hence see further than other nations."

Her presumed far-seeing talents led her to conclude that America must destroy the Milosevic government and break the Serbian
effort to preserve its sovereign borders. She maneuvered tirelessly
throughout official Washington and among her NATO colleagues
in behalf of NATO action. And eventually she engineered a round
of talks in the French resort town of Rambouillet, where she sum-
moned KLA and Serbian officials, outlined a blueprint for Kosovo
autonomy under NATO protection, and enjoined them to embrace
it upon threat of military punishment. Initially, both sides rejected
the plan, but eventually the KLA accepted it. Within days NATO
began a bombing campaign aimed at inducing Serbian acquies-
cence. It would all be over, said Albright on national television, "in
a relatively short period of time." She characterized Milosevic as a
"schoolyard bully" who would cave under pressure. Once again
the American government misread this man and the political imperatives he faced. As it happened, the bombing lasted seventy-
eight days, reduced large sections of Kosovo to rubble, and

destroyed much of Serbia's physical infrastructure. The Serbs responded by taking their ethnic cleansing campaign to a new level of brutality, forcing 1.4 million Albanians from their homes, some 860,000 of them into refugee camps outside Kosovo.

In the end Milosevic did cave, but only after America had helped forge the KLA into ground units capable of forcing the Serbian army into the open to defend territory, subjecting it to the slaughter of American air attacks. NATO troops promptly entered Kosovo to secure it and turn it into an autonomous region of Serbia run by the majority Albanian Muslims under United Nations auspices. NATO, created at the dawn of the Cold War as a defensive alliance, had invaded a sovereign nation under the banner of humanitarian interventionism and Western universalism. The Idea of Progress had prevailed.

AN ASSESSMENT OF America's Kosovo action and its consequences must begin with the moralistic impulses of Madeleine Albright and her boss, Bill Clinton. True, Serbian actions in Kosovo prior to the bombing were barbaric. But in fact they never matched the kinds of abuses the administration had been willing to accept in Turkey, Kashmir, Sudan, and Rwanda—or in Croatia, for that matter. Thus did the United States action reveal a fundamental reality of any moralistic foreign policy: inevitably it exposes a selective morality.

Clinton and his aides argued after the fact that the massive ethnic cleansing unleashed by Milosevic at the start of the bombing revealed his true intentions from the beginning. Others dispute this, saying we really don't know what his intentions were. In any event, it is difficult to justify a bombing campaign against a sovereign nation based on speculation about what might happen.

Furthermore, Albright emphasized repeatedly that her government and its European allies "went the extra mile" in an exhaustive search for a peaceful solution before the bombing. Milosevic, she argued, was just too obdurate. But, as Johns Hopkins Professor Michael Mandelbaum pointed out in a 1999 *Foreign Affairs* article, the unfolding drama revealed this to be untrue. In the end America accepted terms for cessation of the bombing that represented significant concessions from Albright's hard-line Rambouillet stance. For one thing, Kosovo became a United Nations protectorate, something Albright adamantly had opposed prior to the bombing. Secondly, the Rambouillet plan had envisioned a Kosovo referendum after three years to determine its fate. This amounted to a guarantee to the region's Albanians that they could secede from Serbia on that timetable, a provision that no Serbian leader could possibly have accepted. The bombing cessation agreement made no mention of a referendum.

Most significantly, whereas Albright's Rambouillet plan would have given NATO unrestricted troop access to all of Serbia (again, something no Serb leader could accept without undermining his own legitimacy), the later terms restricted NATO troops to Kosovo. These examples suggest American obduracy at Rambouillet exceeded Serbian obduracy and reveal further that America made little effort to understand the intricacies of Milosevic's political circumstances. That led in turn to the Clinton-Albright miscalculation that Milosevic would back down quickly, before America had to demonstrate its own brutality through an extended bombing campaign.

Indeed, the entire episode revealed a fundamental contradiction in the very essence of humanitarian interventionism. Because no national interest was at stake, America couldn't undertake the mission so long as there was any prospect of serious military casualties. That meant the action was restricted to high-altitude bombing. But that in turn meant that America couldn't redeem the rationale for military action in the first place—namely, protection of Kosovar Albanians. Their fate proved far worse after the NATO war began than it had been before.

Further, Mandelbaum argues that in the name of humanitarian interventionism America and its allies violated a fundamental tenet of international law—namely, the prohibition against interference in the internal affairs of other sovereign states. There is a body of thought that exceptions are permitted under two well-defined conditions—first, when there is a gross violation of fundamental human rights; and, second, when there is authorization by what Mandelbaum calls a "legitimate authority," meaning the United Nations. Whether either of these conditions was met would seem at least debatable. Certainly, the plight of Kosovo's Albanians didn't rise to the level of serious atrocities being committed elsewhere in the world around the same time. And NATO acted without U.N. authorization—"implying," writes Mandelbaum, "either that the Atlantic alliance can disregard international law when it chooses—a precept unacceptable to nonmembers of the alliance—or that any regional grouping may do so . . . —which is unacceptable to NATO."

It's arguable also that America's air assault on the Serbian infrastructure violated international law, specifically Article 14 of the 1977 Protocol to the 1949 Geneva Convention, which proscribes destruction of "objects indispensable to the survival of the civilian population." Although the actual civilian deaths in the precision strike bombing campaign were held under a thousand, by striking Serbia's electrical grids, water facilities, and bridges, the alliance seriously damaged the civilian population.

Finally, the bombing war had diplomatic repercussions far beyond the Balkans, most notably in relations between the West and Russia. With the breakup of the Soviet empire, Russia found itself a much diminished power, bereft of its ability to pose a serious challenge to America and the West. But it remained a significant regional power and the core state of the Orthodox civilization. Besides, it harbored historical and cultural ties to the Serbs that far outweighed any American interests in the region. The NATO bombing campaign continued a post–Cold War pattern of Western inclinations to trample upon Russian sensibilities.

It began with the inclusion of a reunited Germany into NATO. To allay Russian concerns, the West disavowed any interest in NATO's eastward expansion. Upon assuming office, President Clinton promptly reneged on that promise. But in return Russia was given three assurances: that NATO's military intentions would remain entirely defensive; that it would become essentially a political alliance dedicated to the spread of democracy and capitalism;

and that it would invite Russian participation in matters involving European security. "The war in Yugoslavia," writes Mandelbaum, "gave the lie to all three."

FROM THE VERY BEGINNING and continuing to this day, America misread, misjudged, and misinterpreted the Balkan crisis. It brought to the challenge an outlook—Western universalism wrapped in geopolitical humanitarianism—that obscured the fundamental reality of that tragic story. The fundamental reality was that the Balkan crisis constituted the first great civilizational war in a new era that would be characterized by clashes of civilizations. As the tragedy unfolded the world divided along civilizational lines corresponding precisely with the cultural fault lines of the former Yugoslavia itself.

In Bosnia, policies of Muslim nationalism rapidly supplanted the multicultural sentiments expressed by Izetbegovic to soothe American diplomats. The elements of this development were catalogued by Samuel Huntington in his book *The Clash of Civilizations and the Remaking of World Order*. The schools turned more and more to religious teachings and extolled the region's Turkish heritage. The Serbo-Croatian language was pushed aside in favor of a Bosnian dialect that employed more Turkish and Arabic words. Mixed marriages were attacked along with "aggressor" Serbian music. Muslims received preference in hiring and promotions. By 1995, 90 percent of the Bosnian army's personnel were Muslims, and many elite units identified themselves with Islamic symbols and titles. Izetbegovic's Muslim party, the SDA, took on the trappings of Islamic authoritarianism and gained sway over the army, the civil service, and all public entities.

In short, Izetbegovic and his governing philosophy turned out to be closer to what Serb and Croat leaders had predicted than to the benign multicultural protector envisioned by Warren Zimmermann and his government. The Bosnian Muslims had not escaped Balkan history any more than the Serbs or Croats. Neither did the Muslims' fate escape the notice of other Muslim governments and organizations, which rallied to the cause of their Bosnian coreligionists in a wave of cultural solidarity. The Organization of the Islamic Conference, spurred on by Iran, created an organization to lobby at the United Nations in behalf of the Bosnian Muslims. The prime ministers of Turkey and Pakistan visited Sarajevo to express their cultural interest. In August 1995 nine OIC foreign ministries repudiated the U.N. arms embargo, and in September the OIC itself approved arms and economic assistance for the Bosnians. The fate of the Bosnian Muslims became a major political issue in Turkey, where Bosnian immigrants and refugees made up nearly 5 percent of the population.

Despite the U.N. arms embargo, Muslim military assistance flowed into the area in the form of weapons, money to buy weapons, military training, and volunteers. Some four thousand *mujahedeen* volunteers from the Afghan war against the Soviet Union arrived early in the conflict. Guerrillas from the Shi'ite Lebanese Hezbollah and the Iranian Republican Guards provided military training. One Republican Guard unit of four hundred men helped organize extremist guerrilla and terrorist units. A United Nations paper reported that *mujahedeen* troops trained up to five thousand Bosnians for special Islamist brigades. Meanwhile, Muslim countries poured in weapons and military aid worth up to $1.8 billion, most of it from Iran but large amounts also from Saudi Arabia, Turkey, and Malaysia.

Meanwhile, nations associated with the Orthodox civilization rallied to the Serbian cause. Greece, a NATO member, consistently supported the Serbs in United Nations debates, opposed NATO military action in Bosnia, and pressed the United States to lift economic sanctions against Serbia. Russia, despite the desire of its leader, Boris Yeltsin, to forge close relations with the West, frequently extended strong rhetorical and diplomatic support for the Orthodox Serbs, employing its United Nations Security Council veto on a number of occasions to block anti-Serb resolutions. Serbia also received arms support from Russia as well as other Orthodox nations, notably Romania, Bulgaria, and Ukraine. And Western governments and elites generally supported the Croats while denouncing the Serbs and manifesting indifference toward the Muslims.

There was one "partial exception" to this pattern, in the view of Samuel Huntington, and it was the United States, whose leaders rhetorically favored the Muslims and kept the Muslim fate at the forefront of their thinking as their Balkan policies unfolded—although, notes Huntington, the American support was actually rather limited in practice. Still, the American partial exception poses a question, says Huntington: "Why during and after the war was the United States the only country to break the civilizational mold and become the single non-Muslim country promoting the interests of the Bosnian Muslims and working with Muslim countries on their behalf?"

The answer emerges clearly from our review of American foreign policy thinking in the post–Cold War period. The country was led to that anomalous Balkan policy by the particular brand of humanitarian interventionism that had emerged among its elites as the decade of the 1990s dawned. The end of the Cold War, in this view, had brought us to the End of History. America's epic victory elevated it to a new status never before seen in the world, a nation representing the culmination of human civic development. As Woodrow Wilson had presciently put it, we now stood for "liberals and friends of humanity in every nation . . . for the silent mass of mankind everywhere."

And yet the forces of history and culture did not bend to these humanitarian convictions, as events in Bosnia and Kosovo following the American actions there attest. In March 2004, NATO rushed a thousand troops to Kosovo to join the 19,000 already in place after ethnic violence erupted. Albanian Muslim gangs orchestrated what one commentator called "an anti-Serb rampage," killing twenty-eight and wounding nine hundred. According to newspaper accounts, the Muslims forced 3,500 Serbs from their homes, destroyed 280 houses, and torched thirty Christian Orthodox churches. NATO forces mobilized to evacuate Serbs from the danger zones, whereupon the Muslims promptly burned down their houses.

NATO took pains to protect the Serbs in Kosovo after 1999. But the disparity in numbers and the passions of Kosovar Muslims led inevitably to the slow ethnic cleansing of the remaining Serbs in the province. As Christopher Caldwell wrote in the *Financial Times,* NATO essentially bought peace "at the price of letting the Kosovo Serbs melt away." Since the 1999 bombing, some 230,000 Kosovo residents, mostly Serbs, had applied for refugee status in neighboring countries. In Pristina and Kosovo Polje, writes Caldwell, the Serbs are almost entirely gone, and there are only about 100,000 of their number remaining in the province. Albanian Kosovars want the rest out as soon as possible so they can realize their dream of independence and alignment with Albania.

Officially, NATO opposes the ethnic Albanians' independence movement and clings to the multiethnic vision that animated American and NATO policy from the beginning. But it seems clear that America's humanitarian intervention in the region has not really solved any of the festering problems there.

In Bosnia, radical Muslims have emerged to exploit the area as a staging area and recruitment ground for operations in the Middle East, including Iraq. Thus have America's humanitarian impulses toward Bosnia served to harm American interests elsewhere in this era of civilizational clash. An uneasy peace prevails among ethnic groups in Bosnia, but the stated aims of the Dayton Accords have not been achieved. The country remains an artificial entity whose two political units—the Serb republic and the Muslim-Croat federation—rarely cooperate or interact on anything. Hundreds of thousands of refugees have yet to return to their towns and hamlets of origin. Thus, the de facto partition created by Dayton continues precariously, without any permanent solution in sight. Meanwhile, Bosnia's "international administrator," placed in office under NATO auspices, feels free to trample on whatever democratic sensibilities linger in the region. In June 2004 he fired sixty governmental officials of the Serb republic, including the head of the Bosnian Serb parliament, because he didn't think they were cooperating sufficiently in the hunt for Bosnian Serb war criminals from the 1990s.

Thus do we see that the realities of history and culture continue to expose that powerful vision of American exceptionalism and humanitarian impulse that propelled the country into those entangled lands in the heady early days of the post–Cold War era. And yet by all appearances the vision dances still in the consciousness of America's foreign policy elites, enduring with all the moral force that was generated nearly a century and a half ago when America's Union troops marched to the strains of "Onward Christian Soldiers."

PART III

AN ERA BORN IN BLOOD

CHAPTER 9

The Neoconservatives

JUST WEEKS BEFORE AMERICA'S invasion of Iraq in spring 2003, the country's leading neoconservative journal, *The Weekly Standard,* published a cover article by the country's most unabashed advocate of American imperialism, Max Boot. Called "The End of Appeasement: Bush's Opportunity to Redeem America's Past Failures in the Middle East," it urged the United States to provide those Islamic lands with "effective imperial oversight." The coming liberation of Baghdad, Boot suggested, could be one of those "hinge moments of history," like the storming of the Bastille or the fall of the Berlin Wall—a pivotal point in time "when the powerful antibiotic known as democracy [would be] introduced into the diseased environment of the Middle East, and . . . transform the region for the better."

The Boot argument reflected the emergence of a foreign policy outlook that combined the Will to Power imperialism of Theodore Roosevelt with the humanitarian impulse of Woodrow Wilson. This proved to be a powerful political potion after the 9/11 terrorist attacks on America, and it stirred George W. Bush to send his military halfway around the world to plant his nation's flag into the heartland soil of Islam. He would do this while denying that his action, or the events that precipitated it, signified a clash of civilizations of the kind that Samuel Huntington had predicted. He would also deny any imperial intent.

Rather he would insist that his military initiative was aimed strictly at the scourge of terrorism, at those who pray to the "God of hate," as Thomas Friedman had put it. A corollary conviction was that these worshippers of hate could not thrive where societies embraced the principles of Western democratic capitalism. And so he would introduce those principles into Iraq and perhaps other Middle Eastern lands as well, his administration suggested, as the most effective way of thwarting the threat of Islamic fundamentalist attacks on the West.

Subsequent events surrounding the U.S. Iraqi occupation exposed both the naïveté and the folly of that outlook. And, as these events unfolded, it was not surprising that national attention would turn to the neoconservatives whose thought and advocacy had proved so influential in crafting the governmental rationale for the war. A pressing area of inquiry became the philosophical etymology of the neoconservative resolve to remake the Middle East in the image of American democratic capitalism. The story begins by all accounts in the late 1930s in the City College of New York cafeteria's Alcove No. 1. That's where a small group of non-communist socialists—Irving Kristol, Seymour Martin Lipset, Nathan Glazer, Daniel Bell, and Melvin Lasky, among others—gathered daily to engage in fervent undergraduate debates over the nature of the world—and the distinctions between their worldview and that of the communists across the way in Alcove No. 2.

They graduated to careers as academics, pamphleteers, essayists, and editors of small but influential journals, along the way drawing to their New York circle other like-minded intellectuals, notably Norman Podhoretz, Midge Decter, and Gertrude Himmelfarb. In the early Cold War years they emerged as full-throated liberals who supported civil rights legislation, the welfare state, and the need for labor unions. But they also demonstrated a strong aversion to communism and a willingness, unlike many liberals of the day, to battle the radical left. During the student upheavals of the 1960s, they were aghast at how craven the liberals of academia were in the face of this assault on liberalism. The 1972 capture of the Democratic Party by the counterculture forces of Senator George McGovern of South Dakota caused further disenchantment.

On domestic policy, the final breaking point came when liberalism embraced the widespread use of quotas in hiring, promotions, and academic admissions. The core of the neoconservative contingent was Jewish, and these people had a historical aversion to such policies, which had been employed in decades past to exclude them. As Mark Gerson put it in his penetrating and sympathetic history, *The Neoconservative Vision: From the Cold War to the Culture Wars,* "Jews felt the pain and suffered the consequences of quotas and consistently fought for the abolition of race, religion, and ethnicity as factors in admission and hiring practices."

On foreign policy, a watershed event was the 1968 Soviet invasion of Czechoslovakia, which galvanized a potent skepticism about prospects for accommodation with the Soviet Union and about President Richard Nixon's later policies of détente aimed at engaging Soviet leaders on a host of issues. The 1973 Yom Kippur War in the Middle East "completed their conversion to geopolitical realities," according to former Secretary of State Henry A. Kissinger. Writing in *Years of Renewal,* the third volume of his memoirs, he added: "They interpreted that war as a Soviet-Arab conspiracy against Israel and the industrial democracies and concluded that the challenge was best resisted in the name of opposition to détente."

Thus these frustrated liberals emerged from the upheavals of the late 1960s and early 1970s as full-fledged "new conservatives," although some remained reluctant to accept the appellation. They became fully credentialed in 1971 when William F. Buckley Jr.'s *National Review* welcomed them with the sprightly words, "C'mon in, the water's fine." As Mark Gerson described the transition, "It took a decade to do it, but most neoconservatives went from George McGovern (reluctantly) in 1972 to Ronald Reagan (enthusiastically) in 1980."

And the neoconservatives gained a significant measure of influence in the process of this conversion. That their ambitions went beyond the literary to the realm of real-world politics is reflected in an anecdote from journalist and author Richard J. Whalen about his brief tenure as a 1968 campaign official for presidential candidate Nixon. At Irving Kristol's request, Whalen had lunch with Kristol in New York to discuss the campaign. As a good Democrat, said Kristol, he was supporting Hubert Humphrey for president. But as a good political analyst, he was putting his money on Nixon— "literally," as Whalen explained in a memo to his boss, "he's a betting man." Now, to hedge his bets, he was offering his thoughts to the Nixon campaign on how it might handle the emotion-charged race issue for maximum political benefit.

GIVEN THE INFLUENCE of neoconservative thought in the time of George W. Bush, it's important to understand just what that body of thought is and how it has changed with shifting circumstances in the post–Cold War period. For a baseline analysis we turn to Mark Gerson, whose book seeks to enumerate and parse the fundamentals of the neoconservative creed. He breaks it down to four essential elements.

The infinite complexity of life: This complexity will always thwart man's ability to maintain order and inculcate goodness through social engineering or sweeping policy blueprints to remake society. Also, the neoconservatives believe with Edmund Burke that social institutions incorporate and reflect wisdom developed over long periods of time and thus are almost always more sound than prescriptions of the moment that run counter to established institutions.

The inherent evil in mankind: Human nature contains plenty of goodness, but evil is forever lurking also in the human spirit. With Reinhold Niebuhr, the neoconservatives believe there will always be children of darkness as well as children of light. What is more, good and evil don't always operate on equal terms; evil sometimes wins out. Thus the struggle against the children of darkness requires constant vigilance and courage.

Man as a social animal: The sound society requires a sense of community consecrated by shared values and mores operating in behalf of virtue. Moreover, communities can and should make claims on individual autonomy in the interest of virtue and stability. Finally, as Gerson puts it, "Politics and economics are functions of culture. Any system or set of ideas that purports to replace the workings of culture . . . is bound to fail."

Ideas and their consequences: Society must take account of the underlying ideas that give it shape and definition, including the ideas of complexity, the evil in human nature, and the importance of community. And there is a constant danger that the words giving meaning to society—words such as democracy, freedom, liberty, and virtue—will be expropriated by those who don't actually share those values. Those who do share such values must always be prepared to fight against this expropriation.

When placed alongside current neoconservative advocacy, Gerson's four elements of neocon philosophy cry out for exploration—which yields in turn four essential points about the intellectual explorations of these influential thinkers.

First, Gerson's description of the neoconservatives' bedrock principles and beliefs is remarkably consonant with the fundamental principles and beliefs of traditional conservatism, as propounded, for example, by the editors and writers of *National Review*. These include the Burkean conception of humanity's complexity and the distrust of social engineering to remake society; the concept that evil resides in human nature and that this nature is essentially immutable; the inexorable role of culture in human affairs; the importance of community, which sometimes must take precedence over the prerogatives of the individual; and the need to revere those ideals that give meaning to the human experience.

Second, contrary to the common misconception that the neocons adopted these attitudes as they emerged from their days as self-professed liberals, in fact they had embraced them as far back as the 1950s. Even as liberals embracing equal opportunity, robust taxation, civil liberties, and income distribution, they also consistently castigated the liberal tendency toward "moral equivalency," or the failure to make distinctions between the imperfections of democracy, say, and the evils of communism.

Similarly, the early anti-communist liberals faulted progressives for having an insufficient appreciation for the tragic sense of life, caused, they believed, by a naive faith in the inherent goodness of man. As Gerson puts it, "With individuals born good and corrupted by society, there were no limits [in the progressives' thinking] to the improvements that well-intentioned people can enact when they put their minds together." The conservative view, embraced by the neocon forerunners very early, rejects this Rousseauian notion and holds that essential human nature imposes serious limits on how much goodness can be enacted through governmental interventions.

Or consider Norman Podhoretz's reaction to the Beat Generation writers, including Allen Ginsberg and Jack Kerouac, who emerged in the 1950s to widespread enthusiasm throughout many liberal quarters. In a famous *Partisan Review* piece entitled "The Know-Nothing Bohemians," he attacked their assault on bourgeois morality as a dangerous descent into nihilism that eventually could do serious damage to the fabric of society.

Third, in recent years some of the country's most prominent neoconservatives have unceremoniously abandoned most of those bedrock principles and beliefs identified by Gerson. In place of the conservative hostility to meliorist or utopian visions and skepticism about bold governmental initiatives, many neocons have embraced a Brave New World in which American exceptionalism holds sway everywhere and peoples around the globe abandon their own cultures in favor of Western ideals. This conversion is almost as fascinating as the initial conversion from liberalism to neoconservatism—and is perhaps more significant.

Thus we come to the fourth observation: the neoconservatives have arrived at a point where they aren't really conservative at all. In fact, they were more conservative in temperament and outlook when they were liberals than they are today as so-called neoconservatives. These days the neocons' famous intellectual pugnacity is most often directed not at liberals but at conservatives. As William Kristol, son of Irving Kristol and editor of *The Weekly Standard,* told the *New York Times* when asked about an emerging split within conservatism over the Iraq War, "If we have to make common cause with the more hawkish liberals and fight the conservatives, that is fine with me." He added that readers of his magazine would discern that it had "more in common with the liberal hawks than with traditional conservatives." In other words, Kristol had cast his lot with the humanitarian interventionism of Woodrow Wilson over the conservative interventionism of the Cold War.

That raises a question: just what is the core philosophy of these peripatetic intellectuals who have covered so much ideological territory over the past six decades? The apparent answer: there really isn't one. Gerson, whose biography of neoconservative thought is largely hagiographical, writes, "There is not one political position that can be considered distinctly neoconservative. There are modes of thought, styles of reasoning, and ways of analyzing the social world, but no distinctive political positions."

AN EXPLORATION OF those modes of thought, styles of reasoning, and ways of analyzing the world yields a picture of the neoconservative temperament that has not received much attention during their years of prominence. A number of characteristics come into focus.

One is that they seem most happy directing sectarian hostility toward their ostensible allies while ignoring their ideological foes. As leftists in the 1930s, they defined themselves primarily by their hostility to communism. Later in the 1950s, as traditional liberals, they ostentatiously separated themselves from strains of liberalism that dismissed the significance of human nature and culture in civic affairs. Later still, as advocates of American imperialism after 9/11, they reserved their most pugnacious attacks for anti-imperialists of the right rather than the left.

Probably the most vivid example of this tendency occurred during the administration of Richard Nixon, who assumed office in January 1969 and immediately faced a precarious political predicament. America was buckling under its Cold War exertions, frustrated with the Vietnam quagmire, which had consumed forty thousand American lives in a conflict with no definable military objective. Domestically, the country was in upheaval, beset by the violent student demonstrations and frightened by recent urban riots. Overseas, the United States faced increasing strains in its Western alliances, a menacing Soviet Union, and an inevitable decline in American hegemony as both its economic and nuclear preeminence waned.

Nixon addressed these challenges with a series of elaborately conceived and deftly executed maneuvers. To extricate America from Vietnam while preserving national honor and containing the politically dangerous antiwar fervor as much as possible, he led one of the largest military retreats in the history of warfare—extracting half a million troops from a hostile military environment, thus exposing his soldiers in Vietnam while he himself was politically exposed at home. He initiated his famous overture to China, putting geopolitical pressure on the Soviets while acknowledging the inevitable transition from a bipolar to a multipolar world. And he fostered his policy of détente, designed to deal with the Soviets where feasible while recognizing that they remained both hostile and threatening.

Initially, according to Kissinger's recollection of his early days in the White House, the neoconservatives "disdained Nixon, passionately opposed the Vietnam War, objected to our military budgets as too Cold War–oriented, and pressed for a more conciliatory approach to the Soviet Union." In other words, they were still liberals. But once they abandoned liberalism and became Cold War hawks, they turned on Nixon with even greater vehemence. Having become conservatives during the tenure of a conservative president, they gave the man little credit for the immense political and global difficulties he faced. They paid little heed to the relentless pressures converging upon him from the left, their own political habitat until a short time earlier. "Their historical memory," writes Kissinger, describing his political wars with the neoconservatives, "did not include the battles they had refused to join or the domestic traumas to which they had so often contributed from the radical left." The Nixon approach was dismissed as "appeasement."

Not even Ronald Reagan was spared this neoconservative tendency to turn on their own. He strode into office in 1981 as a man who opposed Soviet communism and Nixon's old détente policies in equal measure. What's more, he actively courted the neoconservatives and echoed many of their foreign policy perceptions. Following his election, he publicly urged Americans to read Norman Podhoretz's recently published *The Present Danger,* which the president-elect pronounced a "critically important book." Once in office, Reagan sent American liberals into fits of rage and despair by calling the Soviet Union an "evil empire" and suggesting it would end up in "the dustbin of history." Neoconservatives loved those pronouncements, which for them contained "crucial ideas that could have magnificent consequences," as Mark Gerson puts it.

And it helped that when Reagan took office the country and the world had changed utterly from the days of Nixon and his successor, Gerald Ford. The Vietnam ordeal and its attendant domestic turmoil were over. The intervening presidency of Jimmy Carter had left the world more dangerous and the country more ready to confront those dangers. The Soviets had sent an invasion force into Afghanistan, aimed scores of highly accurate medium-range nuclear missiles at the heart of Europe, and fanned ongoing East-West tensions by fostering bloody regional conflicts in Angola and Central America. On top of that, Carter had proved hapless in the face of the incarceration of some fifty-three American citizens in Iran.

Carter attributed all this to intractable historical forces, but Reagan viewed it as the result of failed policies, and he "promised to lead us back to the true path of American greatness," as Podhoretz put it. He did it by restoring America's confidence, building up its military, demonstrating plenty of rhetorical pugnacity toward the Soviets, and eventually outmaneuvering the stodgy Kremlin bureaucrats. The man and the national mood came together with tremendous force, and Reagan's policies led directly to America's Cold War triumph.

And yet during his tenure many neoconservatives were never quite happy with his performance. As Gerson puts it, they "began the 1980s hoping that Reagan would be the president they had been waiting for, and left with mixed feelings." They perceived in his stewardship, among other lapses, "striking foreign policy weaknesses at crucial moments." Podhoretz expressed these concerns most starkly hardly more than a year into the Reagan presidency with a 1982 *New York Times Magazine* article entitled "The Neo-Conservative Anguish Over Reagan's Foreign Policy." The piece praised Reagan's military buildup as necessary but, alas, insufficient. Missing, Podhoretz wrote, was the kind of bold action that could change the direction of American policy toward the Soviet Union. "Yet it was precisely on this promise that his administration was failing to make good," he recalled later in a piece for *The Weekly Standard*.

Podhoretz was particularly incensed over the president's refusal to intervene with Western bankers bent on rolling over Polish loans then coming due. Podhoretz considered this an "enormous opportunity" to give teeth to Reagan's prediction that the Soviet empire would eventually collapse from within, and he expressed frustration that his president would slip to "this incredibly perverse combination of action and inaction."

It is worth pausing over these characteristically stark words, as well as the general neoconservative critique of Reagan. Here was a president committing himself utterly to the neoconservative goal of victory over the Soviet "evil empire," and the neoconservative impulse was to fret over whether he was missing an opportunity for a dramatic but ultimately empty gesture. For a president, it is important to select words, actions, and gestures carefully; for an intellectual no such tactical imperative obtains. Thus, the neoconservatives' approach to the Reagan presidency was different only in degree from their approach to the Nixon presidency during the tumultuous Vietnam period. In both instances, they became so preoccupied with small-bore disagreements with fellow conservatives that they found difficulty in coming to grips with the real lessons of foreign policy.

That brings us to the second intellectual trait often seen among the neoconservatives: a tendency to see the world in stark terms of good and evil, requiring absolute consistency of outlook and action. "Tactics bored them," writes Kissinger of the neoconservative opposition during the Nixon years. "They discerned no worthy goals for American foreign policy short of total victory." The result has been a generally unnuanced view of the global challenge, divorced from the political and global complexities that often force presidents to pursue their goals with flexibility, deftness, and patience. That's why the neoconservatives never acknowledged the powerful forces from the left that buffeted Nixon throughout his presidency. It's also why Reagan could say all the right things and nudge events generally in the right direction, but still generate much hand-wringing and hair-pulling when he didn't attack Western bankers with outstanding loans in Poland.

Another characteristic of neoconservatives is a tendency to place themselves at the center of the story, to view historical events as inseparable from their own history. "When the neoconservatives first appeared on the scene," writes Kissinger, "their defining experience was their own ideological conversion to the pursuit of the Cold War." Nothing illustrates this more vividly than their interpretation of Reagan's Cold War victory, for which they claim a fair amount of credit. This rankles Kissinger, who considers the neoconservative analysis self-serving, faulty, and dangerous. "According to this interpretation," he writes, "a group of accommodation-prone, European-influenced leaders was overcome by the knights-errant who suddenly appeared on the scene and prevailed in short order by proclaiming the distinction between good and evil and the revolutionary role of democratic principles."

But that's not what really happened. In fact, Reagan's policies were built upon the foundation established by Nixon and Ford. Like them, Reagan sought to contain the Soviets and deflate their influence while engaging them on matters ripe for discussion. But there were three differences between the two times. First, Reagan, unlike Nixon, had sufficient political support at home to build up the American military and force the Soviets into an arms race they could not win. Second, Reagan exploited that opportunity by wrapping his real-world maneuverings in the rhetoric of American idealism and democratic virtue. Nixon thought he could stir the national soul with his ultimate success. Reagan, a far better politician, understood that stirring the national soul was a precondition to success.

And, third, Reagan the eternal optimist expunged from the higher reaches of government the lingering vestiges of historical pessimism that had seeped into the Nixon-Ford presidencies, most notably in the thinking of the era's most powerful diplomatic figure, Henry Kissinger. He betrayed his geopolitical pessimism in a host of ways, most starkly in his 1970 remarks to Chief of Naval Operations Elmo R. Zumwalt Jr. America, said Kissinger, had passed its historic high mark "like so many earlier civilizations." Thus, he saw his job as wheedling from the Soviets "the best deal we can get, recognizing that the historical forces favor them." Sure, said Kissinger, history would pummel him for negotiating terms favorable to the Soviets, but the American people should blame themselves for lacking the stamina "to stay the course against the Russians who are 'Sparta to our Athens.'"

This pessimism betrayed a profound misreading of American politics, as subsequent events demonstrated. Frustrated by the street protests of the nihilist left and the persistent opposition from liberal isolationists in Congress, Kissinger missed the most significant political development of his time—the political backlash emerging from the right. Indeed, he contributed to the backlash with such foolish acts as persuading Ford to shun exiled Russian dissident Aleksandr Solzhenitsyn during a visit to Washington by that literary giant and exemplar of moral conviction. Kissinger and his boss worried about bruising Soviet sensibilities, but in the process they enflamed passions among conservatives who wondered whether the administration had any moral backbone at all.

No group expressed those passions more forcefully or eloquently than the neoconservatives, who perceptively zeroed in on Kissinger's defeatism and hammered away at what they considered the moral bankruptcy of his realpolitik thinking. But in the process they learned the wrong lesson, with profound implications for the post-9/11 era. Over time the increasingly influential neoconservatives trained their intellectual firepower on the very notion that foreign policy should be based on perceptions of geopolitical realism; they opted instead for morality in foreign policy. But the real lesson wasn't the moral bankruptcy of realpolitik in general. It was the analytical deficiency of Kissinger's particular realpolitik, based on flawed assumptions about the political power balance in America and the military and diplomatic power balance in the world.

Along the way they perpetrated what might be called the myth of the Reagan presidency—the notion that the fortieth president was a champion of foreign policy initiatives based on morality. William Kristol, writing in *The Weekly Standard,* recalls the title of the Reagan foreign policy plank at the 1976 Republican National Convention—"Morality in Foreign Policy"—and says of George W. Bush's foreign policy officials, "Now they are all Reaganites." This may be an accurate portrayal of the Bush team, but it is a misreading of Reagan, whose aim was to win the Cold War, not to spread democracy throughout the world, particularly when such efforts could complicate the crusade against Soviet communism.

Indeed, candidate Reagan in 1979 had plucked from relative obscurity a Georgetown University political scientist named Jeane Kirkpatrick—lifelong Democrat and an emerging neoconservative—based on a single article she had written for *Commentary* magazine. Called "Dictatorships and Double Standards," the article criticized the Carter administration for attempting to force democratic reforms on autocratic leaders who aligned themselves with the United States. Democracy, she argued, could not be established in such countries in the brief time span envisioned by the Carter officials, and thus such efforts were simply destined to destabilize those regimes and create more international headaches for the United States, as happened in Iran and Nicaragua. No idea, wrote Kirkpatrick, holds greater sway among educated Americans "than the idea that it is possible to democratize governments, anytime, anywhere, under any circumstances." Such democratic conversions, she argued, take "decades, if not centuries."

Those words earned Kirkpatrick not only an invitation into the Reagan campaign circle but eventually an ambassadorship to the United Nations. But Kirkpatrick was not alone among neoconservatives in railing against moralistic foreign policy initiatives. She was joined around the same time by the man often considered the father of neoconservatism, Irving Kristol.

In a 1978 essay entitled "The 'Human Rights' Muddle," Kristol called on America to be "less vaguely moralistic in its pronouncements," and attacked the tendency among State Department bureaucrats to inject human rights preachings into foreign policy. "The proper extent of political rights in any nation is not something our State Department can have a meaningful opinion about," he wrote. "It can only be determined by the people of that nation, who will draw on their own political and cultural backgrounds in arriving at a suitable disposition of this matter."

Two years later he dismissed as a "fundamental fallacy" the idea that all peoples everywhere are entitled to a liberal constitutional government. Before Woodrow Wilson took his country into World War I in behalf of all mankind, said Kristol, it wasn't generally perceived in America that all peoples everywhere could replicate Western constitutional democracy. But afterward, America fell under the sway of Wilson's "utopian enthusiasm," and American foreign policy found itself effectively disarmed whenever it dealt with regimes that were authoritarian in nature. Displaying both the eloquence and polemical sweep that came to be associated with neoconservative thought, Kristol concluded, "The world is heterogeneous and complex—and until we learn to cope with this complexity, and rid ourselves of a guilt complex engendered by our refusal to confront this very complexity, we shall never have a foreign policy worthy of the name."

These sentiments, expressed nearly a generation ago, raise some intriguing questions for our own time: How did the foreign policy thinking of the neoconservatives evolve from the cautionary conservatism of Irving Kristol in 1980 to the bold vision of conquest and democratic pietism represented by William Kristol's *Weekly Standard*? How did we go from Irving Kristol's eloquent skepticism toward Francis Fukuyama's End of History thesis to William Kristol's embrace of it, manifest in his agitations on behalf of American hegemony and the export of Western-style democracy throughout the world?

The answer once again is that these restless intellectuals have a tendency to make their way to whatever watering hole they can find to quench their need for a rhetorical argument of the moment. Thus we see Irving Kristol brilliantly excoriating the liberal tendency to inject morality and "the human rights muddle" into foreign affairs at a time when other neoconservatives are actively seeking to inject morality and human rights into America's relations with the Soviet Union. We have Kristol lecturing his readers on the reality that the world is "heterogeneous and complex" as his brethren are reducing East-West relations to simple precepts of governmental homogeneity. There is Irving Kristol in 1980 dismissing Woodrow Wilson's "utopian enthusiasm," and yet here is William Kristol in 2003 embracing precisely that enthusiasm in behalf of his fervent advocacy of American hegemony. In a 2004 *Weekly Standard* piece entitled "The Neoconservative Persuasion," the elder Kristol makes no attempt to explain this contradiction.

Gerson is correct. There is no distinctly neoconservative bedrock of postulates or assumptions that provide a consistency of advocacy. Indeed, the underlying principles shift to fit the advocacy of the moment. Consider Gerson's effort to identify the essential elements of neoconservative thought. One was that life is infinitely complex and thus the ability to change the world is limited. That went out the window with 9/11 and the emergence of the neoconservative call for American action to remake the Middle East in the image of Western democracy. What about the idea that politics and economics are functions of culture and any set of ideas that purports to replace the working of culture will fail? Same thing. Consider the notion that social institutions embody wisdom developed over long periods of time? That seems to apply to Western institutions but not to those of other civilizations (Eurocentrism, once again).

What accounts for this apparent evolution in neoconservative thinking? The answer isn't clear, but there is a clear demarcation between the older World War II generation and the succeeding generation that grew up during the Cold War. The figure at the center of this evolution seems to be Professor Leo Strauss of the University of Chicago, a scholar of prodigious intellectual attainment and leading twentieth-century philosopher of conservative thought. Critics of the neoconservative emergence have demonized Strauss as a sinister figure guiding his lingering protégés toward some kind of Nietzschean fascism. In fact, Strauss's preoccupation was the crisis of the modern West born of its abandonment of such absolutist concepts as natural right—the idea that goodness is discernible through human reason—and its descent into moral relativism. He saw the need for an influential elite that could guide national leaders and educate the masses on the virtuous course and the need for moral judgments based on good and evil.

This was a traditional neoconservative precept, and most neoconservatives stood proudly with Strauss in declaring Soviet communism to be evil. But for some of the younger neoconservatives, including some who had actually studied under Strauss (for example, William Kristol and Paul Wolfowitz, later a top U.S. defense strategist), this outlook developed into a belief in American exceptionalism so strong that it obscured other conservative tenets once embraced by the neocons. These included the infinite complexity of life, the Burkean skepticism toward grand schemes to remake society, and the recognition of culture as a powerful determinant in politics and economics.

Those essential conservative precepts were jettisoned with the emergence of the post–Cold War world because they stood in the way of the vision of what might be called the new neoconservatives. That vision was one of American hegemony fueled by Wilsonian idealism, and it emerged in its most stark and eloquent guise with the founding of *The Weekly Standard* in 1996. Almost from its beginning, this spirited journal embraced the Idea of Progress and the End of History notion that American democratic capitalism represented the culmination of human civic development. But unlike Francis Fukuyama, who believed the big battles were now behind us, the neoconservatives of *The Weekly Standard* saw epic struggles ahead to ensure that that culmination actually took root. And they added a powerful new concept: that America must do everything possible on a global scale to ensure that its post–Cold War hegemony would continue throughout the world and into the future as far as the eye could see.

Thus, the *Standard* quickly embraced America's chosen role in Bosnia and the humanitarian vision that fueled it. The magazine's only complaint, expressed in a May 1997 article by Robert Kagan, was that President Clinton's aversion to casualties precluded him from using his military power more boldly on the ground to impose upon the people of Bosnia the kind of solution favored by the neoconservatives. The area, complained Kagan, "remains riven by ethnic hatreds which seem to be hardening rather than eroding." Precisely how American military power could be used to lessen those ancient hatreds wasn't explained by Kagan.

As Clinton's bombing war over Kosovo approached, the *Standard* thoroughly embraced the humanitarian zeal and military righteousness of Secretary of State Albright, even to the point of publishing a piece by a *San Francisco Chronicle* writer named Stephen Schwartz that was both tendentiously biased and highly inaccurate. It accused the Serbs of "a pogrom, an orgy of killing, intended to . . . thrill the Serbs by once more venting their frustrations." The Albanian Muslims and the KLA guerrillas were absolved of any shred of responsibility for the hostile environment that existed in that sad province, while all Serb arguments were brushed aside as mere propaganda.

Probably the most stark example of the new neoconservative creed was the *Standard*'s posture toward China, which can only be described as consistent bellicosity. As Congress considered whether to extend Most Favored Nation trade status to China, the *Standard* railed against the "hat-in-hand toothlessness of American engagement with China." The problem with conferring favored trade status, the *Standard* suggested in an editorial written by David Tell, was that it would deprive America of leverage that could be used to lecture and even bully the Chinese over their domestic policies (precisely the kind of moralistic posturing that Irving Kristol had criticized so effectively just seventeen years earlier). The *Standard* pronounced Clinton's desire for dialogue with China to be "offensive" and the MFN proposal to be tantamount to "appeasement."

It is worth pausing over the word "appeasement," often seen in the pages of the *Standard*. It carries a lot of historical freight, given that for decades it has described the soft and accommodative policies of Britain's Neville Chamberlain toward Adolf Hitler in the 1930s. Thus it suggests that if we don't get tough with any particular regional power, we are going to have another Hitler on our hands. But not every regional power with national ambitions constitutes a threat to world peace (although it might to American hegemony), and in fact policies based on that assumption are likely to be more destabilizing to peace than such countries themselves. For *The Weekly Standard* in June 1998, the mere decision by President Clinton to visit China constituted "a profoundly unrealistic and Sinocentric approach to Asian policy." What was required instead, argued University of Pennsylvania professor Arthur Waldron with an apparent straight face, was an understanding of what kind of country Americans want China to be and then a collection of policies designed to ensure that that's precisely what it becomes.

This call for what was in essence distilled Western arrogance took on added dimension after the September 11 terrorist attacks on America. Within a month of the attacks, Max Boot took to the columns of the *Standard* to argue that the troubled lands of Islam "cry out for the sort of enlightened foreign administration once provided by self-confident Englishmen in jodhpurs and pith helmets." Noting that the colonial imperialism of the past was supposed to be "good for the natives," he suggested that while that phrase once made progressives "snort in derision" it may prove more acceptable now—"after the left's conversion . . . to the cause of 'humanitarian' intervention."

As for the role of Saddam Hussein in the terrorist attacks, Boot said he didn't know whether the man was involved and didn't care. "He has been involved in so many barbarities over the years . . . that he has already earned himself a death sentence a thousand times over," wrote Boot in advocating military action to depose the Iraqi dictator.

A month later Norman Podhoretz appeared in *The Weekly Standard* to argue that a policy of forcing the enemy to "unconditional surrender" was necessary to satisfy America's craving for "'a new birth' of the confidence we used to have in ourselves and in 'America the Beautiful.'" In typical neoconservative fashion, Podhoretz viewed the coming war in apocalyptic terms, with "America the Beautiful" on one side and most of the nations of Islam on the other. He demanded that America break off relations with Arab states that had demonstrated ambiguity in dealing with their own anti-Western elements and expressed outrage that the United States would continue to play footsie with these nations while holding Israel at arm's length for diplomatic reasons.

About the same time Frederick W. Kagan weighed in with a recommendation that America send troops not only to Afghanistan but also to Uzbekistan in order to ensure stability in the whole of Central Asia. He acknowledged that such an American presence could generate a "serious crisis" in the region and also in U.S.-Russian relations, but he suggested this could be mitigated by diplomatic entreaties to the Russians aimed at establishing a "strategic alliance" in the area benefiting the interests of both nations. Some months later a think tank writer named Reuel Marc Gerecht wrote a *Weekly Standard* piece entitled "Regime Change in Iran," positing the idea that an American invasion of Iraq could destabilize the Iranian government and lead to the toppling of the mullahs there. "And if history repeats itself," he wrote with expansive enthusiasm, "as goes Iran, so will go the Muslim world." He praised what he called George W. Bush's "liberation theology" and added: "One has to go back to Woodrow Wilson to find an American leader who so clearly directs his message far outside the West."

But by mid-2002 *The Weekly Standard* editors became concerned that perhaps Bush wasn't going to invade Iraq after all. That prompted Kristol and Robert Kagan to write an editorial entitled "Going Wobbly?" Employing the language that previous neoconservatives had directed at Presidents Nixon and Reagan, they wrote, "Time is not on the president's side. He has lost considerable momentum in the war against terror and weapons of mass destruction. More drift and indecision would be disastrous." The magazine beat the drums for quick military action in Iraq throughout the months leading up to the March invasion, culminating in the February 10 Max Boot article on "The End of Appeasement."

In the piece Boot traces what he characterizes as American fecklessness in the Middle East in the face of consistent provocation by the region's national leaders, including Egypt's Gamal Abdel Nasser in the 1950s and 1960s, the sheikhs of the Persian Gulf who took control of the region's oil wealth in the 1970s, the mullahs of Iran who humiliated America in 1979, and finally Iraq's Saddam Hussein. America should have imposed its dominance upon these rulers and their lands long since, argues Boot, but since it didn't it must now ignore the regional leaders' warnings that an American invasion would generate instability throughout the Middle East. Such "instability" would be a far sight better, he suggests, than the "stability" of recent decades. That's because it would bring America into the region in a big way.

Beyond Iraq loom other challenges—especially Syria and Iran, which have been waging undeclared war on the United States for 20 years, but also Saudi Arabia, which has abetted this war even as it has benefited from American protection. It is possible that a U.S. victory in Iraq will intimidate these regimes into better behavior. If not, the United States will have to take more vigorous steps to align our relationships with these countries with our interests and principles. . . . [T]he long record of U.S. futility in the Middle East now presents us with this defining task.

And thus we see the emergence of a foreign policy vision with no historical antecedents in the American experience. It is a vision of American world dominance perpetrated, maintained, and justified in the name of American ideals. Thus does liberal interventionism become the underpinning for the Crusader State. We have to go back to Theodore Roosevelt to find an American politician who embodied such a bold concept of American global expansiveness. But, as we have seen, Roosevelt's expansive dream didn't survive even his own presidency. The intractable global forces of ethnic identity, national ambition, and culture rose up to reveal the dangers and futility of such a course, and Roosevelt ultimately retreated to an approach more consonant with the kind of conservative interventionism that animated American policy in World War II and the Cold War.

Moreover, as a nationalist Roosevelt had nothing but contempt for Woodrow Wilson's dreamy notion that America could transplant its idealism and hallowed traditions of governance into the soil of other peoples around the world. The challenge of projecting American dominance into alien regions was a dangerous business that ultimately would rise or fall based on the country's success in projecting power. Sure, by spreading stability and commerce to regions of U.S. dominance, America would be helping the peoples of those regions. That is what was viewed as the "white man's burden." But the idea that Americans could make such people more like themselves struck Roosevelt as dangerous nonsense.

In embracing Roosevelt's Will to Power imperialism, by contrast, the new neoconservatives brushed aside both his lesson in global reality and his contempt for the humanitarian impulse of Woodrow Wilson. In doing so, they reveal their thought to be not so much the product of a particular set of precepts or perceptions about the world and humanity as it is the product of a particular intellectual temperament. It is a temperament that favors pugnacity, bold thinking, and grand, encompassing visions of the world and the future. It is a temperament that shuns complexity, tactical adjustment, and the role of patience in geopolitical maneuverings. It also is a temperament, as we shall see, that could prove highly dangerous in a post–Cold War era characterized by brutal and persistent cultural and civilizational clashes. Those kinds of clashes can be adjudicated only with great difficulty, but they can be severely aggravated without much difficulty at all.

CHAPTER 10

The World of Islam

WHEN OSWALD SPENGLER pondered the fate of the Aztec civilization at the hands of a band of Spanish conquistadors, he could barely contain his rage. Spengler, as we have seen, revered the Faustian vigor of the West and its cultural legacy—the soaring Gothic cathedrals, the Dutch masters' spatial triumphs, the relentless fugues of Bach, the probing tragedies of Shakespeare, the boundless quest for scientific knowledge. And he believed this Faustian energy would drive the West to eventual world dominion during its forthcoming "civilizational" phase. But none of that could obscure the fundamental reality of history—that it is the story of discrete and distinctive cultures that deserve to be viewed and appreciated on their own terms.

And so it was inevitable that he should decry the catastrophe that befell the highly developed and refined civilization of central Mexico at the beginning of the sixteenth century. It was, he wrote, the one example of a culture ended by violent death. "It was not starved, suppressed or thwarted, but murdered in the full glory of its unfolding, destroyed like a sunflower whose head is struck off by one passing." This was an empire, Spengler added, "with a comprehensive policy, a carefully ordered financial system and a highly developed legislation; with administrative ideas and economic traditions such as the ministers of Charles V could never have imagined; with a wealth of literature in several languages, an intellectually brilliant and polite society in great cities to which the West could not show one single parallel—all this was not bro-

174

ken down in some desperate war, but washed out by a handful of bandits in a few years, and so entirely that the relics of the population retained not even a memory of it all."

Spengler wasn't put off even by the Aztecs' rituals of human sacrifice and cannibalism, practices that would shock Western sensibilities in any era. Such was his reluctance to judge non-Western civilizations based on Western principles and practices.

Spengler's respect for the Aztecs' distinctive culture is worth pondering as America and the West confront their most serious civilizational threat since the Turks suffered their 1683 defeat at Vienna and began their long, inexorable retreat from Western lands. The September 11, 2001, attacks on American citizens upon their own soil were quickly labeled acts of war. But a war with whom? How do we define the enemy?

The enemy is Islam, particularly its Middle Eastern core. George W. Bush denies this, preferring to see the enemy as a collection of "evil doers" who have stepped out of their own cultural heritage to attack Americans. Wilsonian liberals applaud this interpretation because the notion of a civilizational clash assaults their wishful vision of global peace attained through the spread of Western liberal ideals. America's diversity cadres add their endorsement to protect their push for open borders. And Americans generally shrink from the ominous specter of America and the West slipping into a clash of civilizations with the world of Islam.

Yet that is precisely what has happened, and denial will not help America or the West position itself for victory in this clash, which is likely to last for generations. The historical and cultural ignorance that guided America in the Balkans led to unfortunate results far removed from what had been predicted by those policies' architects. But the stakes were low for America and hence the outcome of limited consequence. The stakes in the war with Islam are enormous, and policies guided by similar historical and cultural ignorance could lead to disaster.

The West cannot prevail unless it understands its enemy, the world of Islam. And it cannot understand the world of Islam without understanding—and appreciating—its cultural heritage and the etymology of its present-day sentiments, impulses, angers, and aims. So far, neither America's leaders nor most of its intellectuals have brought to the challenge the kind of historical and cultural understanding that the ongoing crisis demands. One consequence was the Iraq War and the planting of the American flag into the heartland soil of a rival civilization—probably the worst approach to a cultural clash that could be devised at such a stage of hostilities.

TO BEGIN OUR EFFORT to probe the Islamic heritage, with particular attention to the peoples of the Middle East and North Africa, we turn to Spengler, whose historical interpretation of what he called the Magian culture was original. Most scholars view Islam and the culture of the Islamic peoples as essentially the same. But Spengler's Magian culture actually began much earlier, probably around 300 B.C., with its prehistory lying within the ambit of the old Babylonian civilization. In its first stirrings of cultural expression, it gave birth to the architectural dome and the basilica; to an approach to ornamentation that overcame all figure representation; to astrology, alchemy, and developments in algebra; to mosaics and arabesques; and to religious sensibilities that later would become incorporated into Islam.

But this early culture found itself beset by what Spengler called "pseudomorphosis"—when an older culture superimposes itself so massively over a younger one that the weaker entity can't get its breath and fails to develop its own self-consciousness. This is what happened to the Magian culture, first through the veneer of conquest imposed by the Macedonians and later through the blood and iron of the Roman Empire. "The Arabian soul," writes Spengler, "was cheated of its maturity—like a young tree that is hindered and stunted in its growth by a fallen old giant of the forest."

This explains the force and power with which the Arabian culture, released finally from its classical fetters and united under the banner of Islam, flung itself upon the lands that it had regarded for centuries as legacy territory. "It is the sign," writes Spengler, "of a soul that feels itself in a hurry, that notes in fear the first symptoms of old age before it has had youth." The Magian surge was unparalleled in history and remains so: Syria captured in 634; Damascus and Ctesiphon in 637; Egypt and India by 641; Carthage in 647; Samarkand in 676; Spain in 710; and by 732 the Moors are nearly in position to threaten Paris. "Into these few years," writes Spengler, "was compressed the whole sum of saved-up passions, postponed hopes, reserved deeds, that in the slow maturing of other Cultures suffice to fill the history of centuries."

It was the advent of Islam that inspired those passions, hopes, and deeds. But the cultural outlines had been established through the previous centuries. As we have seen, Spengler viewed the essential Magian world concept to be one of limitedness—of being confined, as in a cave. But, says Spengler, it isn't merely the Arabs' sense of space that is cavernlike, but also their sense of time. To the Western mind, time is "a limitless flight of the ages that never lets a lost moment recur"; but to the Arab sensibility, time is more static—"a Beginning and an End of 'This Day,' which is irrevocably ordained and in which the human existence takes the place assigned to it from creation itself."

The cavern feeling postulates a surveyable history consisting in a beginning and an end to the world, which is also the beginning and end of mankind, and between these terms, "spellbound to the limits of the Cavern and the ordained period," there ensues the battle between darkness and light, good and evil, the House of Islam and the House of War. In the face of this battle, there is no spiritual "I," but only a spiritual "We" that has entered into the quickened body as a reflection of the divine light. The Arab word for this, says Spengler, is Islam—submission. "The Faustian prime-sacrament of Contrition," he writes, "presupposes the strong and free will that can overcome itself. But it is precisely the impossibility of an Ego as a free power in the face of the divine that constitutes 'Islam.'" The Islamic prime-sacrament is Grace, which knows no such thing as free will.

As Islam emerged within this culture, the consensus of the community became by definition infallible. As Muhammad put it, "My people can never agree in an error." But the concept of an infallible community consensus bequeathed by the word of God predates Islam. It is in fact "part of the stock of every Magian religion," says Spengler, and lies at the heart of two fundamental ideas—first, that the individual is meaningless outside this infallible consensus and, second, that government and religion remain inseparable. Those ideas were incorporated into Islam in the seventh century and remain to this day bedrock maxims of Islamic thought.

Thus these emerge as fundamental differences not just between Islam and Christianity but between the Magian and the Western consciousness. It would be impossible to overstate the significance of the fundamental worldviews giving rise to these differences. They lie at the heart of a thousand years of conflict between the world of Islam and the West. Many Westerners today tend to disregard these differences, to brush them aside as not particularly meaningful in the modern world. After all, the primacy of the individual and the separation of church and state are hallmarks of the Idea of Progress, which applies to all mankind. As soon as the Islamic world adjusts to modernity, this reasoning goes, it will shed its fealty to its outmoded ancient rubrics and join the West in the pursuit of progress.

Of course this outlook is based on the conceit and myth that there is a universal culture that can capture and shape lesser cultures around the world. But Islam is not a lesser culture. It is merely a different culture, and within those differences can be found the essence of its threat to the West. That's because within those differences also lies Islam's hostility to the West.

Probably no Muslim has personified this more starkly than an Egyptian named Sayyid Qutb, born in 1906 and hanged in a dingy prison cell sixty years later at the behest of Egypt's President Gamal Abdel Nasser. Qutb (pronounced KUH-tahb) is "The Philosopher of Islamic Terror," according to the *New York Times Magazine*, which emblazoned that headline over an article tracing his life and thought. An intellectual of multiple talents, he devoted his youth to writing poetry, novels, and literary criticism. In his early forties, he traveled to America on a scholarship to study Western education, and what he saw of American morals and particularly the free conduct of its women shocked him. Upon returning to Egypt he wrote a book denouncing what he viewed as Western paganism.

Also upon returning he resigned his civil service position with the ministry of public instruction and became the leading publicist for the Muslim Brothers, a network of fundamentalist theorists, conspirators, and terrorists that had emerged in Egypt to strike out against all forces—whether British imperialists or feckless Arab leaders—contributing to what these warriors considered the ongoing humiliation of the Islamic peoples. One of their primary targets was Nasser.

Nasser was a modernist, a socialist, a pan-Arabist, and a strong-armed ruler presiding over what was increasingly a police state. During his rule, tens of thousands of Egyptians were swept into his prison system without benefit of jurisprudence of any kind. Qutb and his fellow fundamentalists were Islamists bent on fostering a theocracy run strictly according to *sharia,* the Koranic legal code. It wasn't long before Nasser identified the Islamic Brothers as among his most threatening domestic enemies—and Qutb as among the Brotherhood's most effective theoreticians.

He threw Qutb in prison in 1954, released him briefly sometime later, then jailed him again for a decade. After another short reprieve, Qutb was returned to prison and killed in 1966. By then he had surreptitiously produced an extensive oeuvre of philosophical writing, mostly a vast commentary on the Koran under the title *In the Shade of the Qur'an.* It fills more than fifteen thick volumes that have been making their way into English translation.

Paul Berman, author of the *Times Magazine* piece (later part of a book entitled *Terror and Liberalism*), has read everything translated thus far, and he describes Qutb's writing as lyrical, encompassing, deep, and powerful—in short, "in its fashion, a masterwork." Qutb's focus is what might be called the crisis of the modern world, a world suffused with ennui, unhappiness, anxiety, self-indulgence, and moral decay. Qutb is not alone in exploring this modern crisis; particularly in the West, thinkers and philosophers have been preoccupied with it since Nietzsche declared the death of God as a consequence of the inexorable rise of rationalism and scientific thought. But Qutb brought to the subject a broader world perspective that also encompassed the Islamic world—and included a fierce indictment of the West.

As explained by Berman, Qutb, following conventional Islamic thinking, viewed the doctrines of Judaism as having been divinely revealed, particularly the admonition to worship only one God and the myriad laws handed down to Moses and other prophets to regulate and govern nearly every aspect of life and thus to bring it into oneness with the Almighty. Ultimately, though, he viewed Judaism as having dwindled into what he called "a system of rigid and lifeless ritual."

Then came another prophet, Jesus Christ (not a messiah, in Qutb's view, but an important prophet in human form), who offered some valuable reforms to Judaism and crystallized a message of spirituality and love. But his message ultimately got distorted and twisted because of two factors—first, the early squabbles between Jesus' followers and the Jews; and, later, by the persecutions unleashed upon his disciples by Rome and other authorities. During these difficult early centuries, writes Qutb, the Christians took a horribly wrong turn. They rejected the intricate laws handed down to the Jews to regulate all aspects of daily life and instead embraced the Greek idea of the separation of the spiritual and the secular. "The old code of Moses," writes Berman, "with its laws for diet, dress, marriage, sex, and everything else, had enfolded the divine and the worldly into a single concept, which was the worship of God. But Christianity divided these things into two." The result, in Qutb's view, was a "hideous schizophrenia."

In Qutb's analysis, God rectified this terrible turn of events by sending a new revelation to the prophet Muhammad, who set forth a comprehensive code aimed at bringing into harmony the sacred and the secular. But there was a new twist—a bold admonition for man to take control of the physical environment, which was viewed not as alien to the spiritual sensibility or merely a passage to the afterlife but rather as part of the unity of human existence. And Muslim scientists embraced this instruction, developing the inductive scientific method and unleashing a torrent of scholarship on the nature of physical reality. Thus did Islam "seize the leadership of mankind," as Berman puts it. Of particular significance, he adds, was that this scientific inquiry was conducted within the context of the Islamic concept of the unity of mankind, with the spiritual and the secular being absolutely intertwined.

Then came the Muslim tragedy —the assault from Western Crusaders, Mongols, and other invaders that halted the progress of Islam and thwarted its ability to exploit the scientific method developed under its auspices. That method and much of its fruits up to that point passed to the West, which beginning in the sixteenth century dominated world scientific inquiry. Thus did modern science pass into the domain of the West, and thus was the West able to exploit that domain to dominate the world.

But the West's scientific juggernaut presented a distorted picture of the world, says Qutb, because of that "hideous schizophrenia" in Western thinking that separated the sacred from the secular. "Everything that Islam knew to be one," writes Berman, "the Christian Church divided into two. And, under these terrible pressures, the European mind split finally asunder." That was the origin of the West's anxiety and misery. And because the West's scientific prowess allowed it to dominate the world, it had spread that same anxiety and misery everywhere, including the lands of Islam. Some two thousand years of ecclesiastical error on the part of Christians were now being injected into the Muslim world in a way that was "doubly painful," says Berman—"an alienation that was also a humiliation."

To Qutb, this wasn't merely a doctrinal dispute across cultures. It was a death struggle on which hinged the very existence of true Islam. True Islam, in this view, is a society based on *sharia,* which meant, as Qutb saw it, "the abolition of man-made laws." He called for a resurrected caliphate like the one Muhammad had fashioned, with religion and daily life melded into one, with freedom of conscience that means essentially freedom from false doctrines, freedom from that hideous schizophrenia that Qutb saw as cultural pollution from the West. "Sharia, in a word, was utopia for Sayyid

Qutb," writes Berman. "It was perfection. It was the natural order in the universe. It was freedom, justice, humanity and divinity in a single system." In was, in short, precisely what Spengler had identified as the fundamental worldview of the Magian culture.

Shortly before his final imprisonment and execution, Qutb was urged to flee to Iraq or Libya, but he refused. He said he didn't want to cheat his followers out of seeing the power of true martyrdom. And many of those followers went on to fashion and lead various groups of the Egyptian terrorist movement in the 1970s and beyond. "Qutb gave these people a reason to yearn for death," writes Berman. "Wisdom, piety, death and immortality are, in his vision of the world, the same. For a pious life is a life of struggle or jihad for Islam, and struggle means martyrdom." He adds that those ideas may strike many Westerners as "creepy," and in many ways they are. But they are ideas with a lot of allure for growing numbers of Muslims.

Indeed, those ideas serve as a foundation for the thinking of Osama bin Laden, who studied under Qutb's brother in Saudi Arabia before becoming the famous Islamist terrorist leader the world knows today—and who, according to former CIA operative Robert Baer, is the most popular figure in Saudi Arabia today.

WHY, WE MIGHT ASK from the remove of our Western perspective, would growing numbers of twenty-first-century Muslims consider Qutb's arcane interpretation of thousands of years of history and theology to be more alluring than the promise of Western democracy? The answer, once again, lies in the inevitable force of culture—more specifically, in cultural traits that go back well before the advent of Islam. An understanding of what this means in the Arab world, where Islam's anti-Western feeling is most intense, requires an exploration of the heritage of the nomadic Bedouins of the desert, who are viewed throughout the Middle East as representing the essence of the Arabian culture—"latterday heirs and witnesses to the ancient glory of the heroic age," as Raphael Patai puts it in his penetrating *The Arab Mind*.

The Bedouin social unit was, and remains, the kin-based wandering group of a small number of families all of whom normally can trace their lineage to a single ancestor. These groups naturally developed strong feelings of solidarity in the face of the harshness of the environment and the threat of competing groups. Over several millennia, the challenge of the desert was met through the development of a strong set of values and customs, enforced relentlessly through group sanctions. These values, including hospitality, generosity, courage, honor, and self-respect, generally form the bedrock of Arab values even today. Aside from the modesty of women, enjoined by Muhammad, all the major elements of the Arabian ethical system are pre-Islamic and Bedouin in origin.

Moreover, these values can be reduced to one overriding moral imperative: the preservation of self-respect. This is not so much a matter of the individual conscience or a man's private relationship with his God—the Western perspective on self-respect—as it is a matter of how one is regarded and treated by others in society. Thus the code of behavior that guides an Arab is fashioned to impress others with those attributes that will command respect. And the loss of respect, which equates to a loss of honor, is the stuff of personal crisis. "Honor is what makes life worthwhile," writes David Pryce-Jones in his *The Closed Circle: An Interpretation of the Arabs*. "Shame is a living death, not to be endured, requiring that it be avenged." The concept of saving face—or preventing the "blackening" of one's face, as it is expressed in Arabic—is so intense among Arabs as to be nearly incomprehensible among Westerners.

This sense of honor and dread of shame emerged from tribal sensibilities developed over centuries of Bedouin experience. In that society, honorable behavior traits became those that contributed to the cohesion and survival of the tribe. Thus, virility was equated with honor because it led to the birth of many sons. It was honorable to have pure Arab blood, to fight for the group against alien raiders, to remain dignified, and to preserve the whiteness of one's face.

This connection between honor and group spirit is reflected in the dual meaning of the Arabic word *asabiyya*—defined in its primary usage as "family spirit" or "kinship spirit." Ibn Khaldun, the great fourteenth-century Arab thinker, viewed *asabiyya* as the greatest adhesive in human society and the fundamental motivating force in history. But the word also has a secondary meaning— "a sense of honor." That's because kinship devotion emerged in the Arab tribal culture as the quintessential manifestation of a person's honor. As Raphael Patai points out, *asabiyya* emerged as a Bedouin tribal trait but later carried over into settled society in the form of family and lineage cohesion, which remains to this day a highly potent trait throughout traditional Arab society.

This shame/honor syndrome is fundamental to the relations between the sexes. "Shame and honor," writes Pryce-Jones, "closely define the roles of men and women and all transactions between them, validating and dramatizing them unforgettably and at all times." For the male, honor consists in traditional masculine traits such as bravery, virility, the fathering of many children, particularly sons. For the woman, honor consists in modesty, faithfulness, and the bearing of many children, again particularly sons. Immodesty or unfaithfulness in a woman brings shame not only to herself but to her entire paternal family—her father and her brothers.

Here is where the distinctiveness of Arab culture comes into sharp focus. For the shame of female transgressions must be redressed at all costs, even to the point of killing the offending family member. Legal sanctions now inhibit this extreme reaction to this recurring human drama, but, according to Pryce-Jones (writing in 1989), even today such reactions are "commonplace," and many a retributive brother happily accepts prison as merely the necessary price for doing what must be done. If the woman is married, her father and brothers leave the seducer to her husband, who exacts his own retribution on the offending male. But the woman's family members absolutely must punish her or the stain remains on them forever.

As Patai points out, the Arabic language contains two words denoting two separate concepts of honor. Honor in its nonsexual sense is called *sharaf,* usually applied to the general honor of men.

This concept is flexible; a man can conduct his life in such a way as to acquire *sharaf,* lose it, regain it, bolster it, diminish it. But the word for female honor is *ird,* and this concept is utterly inflexible. A woman is born with it, grows up with it, and is charged with protecting it at all costs. In a sense her physical virginity and her emotional *ird* are intertwined. "Both virginity and *'ird'* are intrinsically parts of the female person," writes Patai. "They cannot be augmented, they can only be lost, and their loss is irreparable." And the *sharaf* of the menfolk is entirely wrapped up in the *ird* of the women.

This has led inevitably to an intricate complex of customs designed to protect the female *ird* and thus the male *sharaf.* Female dress, female segregation, elaborate rituals of sexual control, female circumcision—all stem from the imperatives of protecting this dual honor. And over many centuries the sensibilities engendered by these imperatives have fostered a view of the inferiority of women—"a pre-Islamic concept confirmed by the Koran," Patai informs us. And through thousands of generations women themselves have contributed to the perpetuation of this outlook.

This is manifest in breast-feeding practices among Arab women. According to Patai, daughters are breast-fed for one to two years, sons for up to three years. Thus are boys pampered for a considerably longer time than girls and shown their greater worth at a very young age while daughters are shown their lesser worth. Thus also do mothers define their own worth as being wrapped up in the raising of sons more than in the raising of daughters. Such practices and customs are ribboned throughout Arab society, bolstering and perpetuating this view of the sexes.

These customs and sensibilities are deeply embedded in the Arab consciousness and incorporated into the civic structures of society. The honor concept, for example, is extended from the individual, the family, and the tribe to the nation as a whole. As Pryce-Jones puts it, nationalism "simply adds what might be called an outer ring" to the tribal customs and judgments of Middle Eastern society.

This is particularly true of what Pryce-Jones calls the "power-challenge dialectic," a residue from the tribal experience that both guides and constricts behavior at the national level. In tribal society, all males are theoretically equal and capable of exercising authority. Thus, to gain power a man must develop a following by demonstrating that he is heroic, ruthless, tough, cruel, understanding—in short, commanding. Since there are no formal means of selecting leaders, the informal realities unleash the power-challenge dialectic, in which challenge is the only way to get power and the accumulation of power invites challenge. As Pryce-Jones explains, the power-challenge dialectic has survived as a tribal legacy—perpetuating "absolute and despotic rule, preventing the evolution of those pluralist institutions that alone allow people to participate in the processes of the state and so to identify with it."

What's more, it has left intact another tribal legacy—the family as the basic building block of society. For power holder and challenger alike, the key to retaining or gaining power lies in the cohesion of the family or the clan. As Pierre Bourdieu, the French social anthropologist, has written, in the Arab world the family is the "alpha and omega of the whole system . . . the indissoluble atom of society which assigns and assures to each of its members his place, his function, his very reason for existence." This solidarity is the foundation of power in Arab society. Think of the House of Saud, the extended and growing royal family that perpetuates power in Saudi Arabia.

This family solidarity renders Arab society largely impervious to outside cultures and hostile to outside pressures. And the circle widens inevitably to meet the magnitude of any outside threat. One of the Middle East's most frequently quoted proverbs is: "My brothers and myself against my cousins; my brothers and my cousins and myself against the world." In this proverb is seen the essential Spenglerian view of the Magian culture—the sensibility of confined space and time, within which unfolds the battle between the forces of light and the forces of darkness, the House of Islam and the House of War.

Through this prism we see the origin over centuries of traits and customs of the Magian culture that many Westerners have come to regard as malleable. They are not malleable. They are etched in the cultural consciousness of peoples throughout the Middle East and North Africa and of Muslims in other parts of the world as well: tribal sensibilities; the emotional power of shame; the imperative of redressing any dishonoring events at all costs; the shame of female transgressions upon her male relatives; the elaborate prescriptions designed to protect male society from female dishonor; the inferiority of women; the power-challenge dialectic; the hostility to outsiders; the aversion to Western precepts of the primacy of the individual and separation of church and state.

These are not merely relics of the past that will be crushed by modernity but deeply ingrained cultural characteristics. Indeed, because of these traits and customs modernity poses a greater crisis in the world of Islam than it does in any other civilization—and hence unleashes greater frustrations. And, while Islam emerged from the Arabian or Magian culture, its expansion to other regions of the world served to spread also that same Magian world outlook, those same traits and customs, and ultimately those same frustrations. They may be less intense and less sweeping in other regions, but the post–Cold War passions of Middle Eastern Islam, and the anti-Western sentiments that flow from them, are evident throughout the Muslim world. What's more, as hostilities between the West and Middle Eastern Islam deepen, other Islamic lands become increasingly inflamed. As Sam Huntington puts it, "In civilizational conflicts, unlike ideological ones, kin stand by their kin."

This view finds expression also in a book that sold briskly some years ago in the Central Intelligence Agency's gift shop in Langley, Virginia. Called *Through Our Enemies' Eyes*, it was written anonymously by a senior CIA official (later identified as Michael Scheuer) and received pre-publication approval from the agency even though its central thesis contradicts the fundamental views of the Bush administration. "The president has continually gone out of his way to say this isn't a war against Islam," Scheuer told *National Journal* writer Mark Kukis in July 2003. "Well, it may be turning into a war by Islam against us."

The book's thesis is that al Qaeda represents a large and growing body of cultural sentiment within the world of Islam and that Osama bin Laden is revered as an iconic figure among millions of Muslims in much the same way that Thomas Jefferson or Abraham Lincoln are in America. What's more, he asserts that al Qaeda and bin Laden have been gaining power and influence since 9/11, largely because America's bold resolve to confront terrorism frontally within Islamic lands is both fomenting fundamentalism among Muslims and rendering America increasingly vulnerable to al Qaeda's strategic insurgencies. The author told Kukis that bin Laden has reason to be delighted that America has turned up in the Philippines, in Yemen, in the east coast of Africa, in the former Soviet republic of Georgia, and in the heart of the Middle East. "I think that's exactly the kind of thing he's looking for," said the author, "to have Americans engaged against Muslims in as many places as possible."

Kukis himself cites a recent United Nations report warning of a growing contingent of Muslim militants organized as a loose network of guerrilla forces throughout the Islamic world, some tied to al Qaeda, some merely inspired by it. He notes further that bin Laden's stature as a world leader continues to grow among Muslims. A recent world survey by the Pew Research Center for the People and the Press revealed a groundswell of support for bin Laden in most Muslim countries. In Jordan, for example, bin Laden was trusted more than Jordan's own King Abdullah. He held more support than Yasir Arafat in the Palestinian territories before that revered leader's death in 2004, and he enjoyed growing popularity in Indonesia, Morocco, and Pakistan. Robert Baer writes that, if a free and fair presidential election were somehow to be held in Saudi Arabia today, the landslide winner would be bin Laden.

Thus do we see the emergence of a clash of civilizations between Islam and the West. Long before the 9/11 attacks on America, Samuel Huntington saw clearly the emergence of this clash, spurred in large measure by major developments both within Islam and the West—a population surge among Muslims generating large numbers of unemployed and disaffected youths hungry for meaning in their lives; a growing Islamic self-consciousness and cultural confidence born of the population surge; the West's expanding resolve to universalize its values and flex its military and economic superiority; growing interaction between members of the two civilizations that heightened group identity and raised issues about the rights of members of one civilization in countries dominated by members of the other.

Huntington quotes extensively from scholars and thinkers in both the West and the world of Islam who perceived this growing hostility between the two cultures as the Cold War faded into memory. As early as 1991, for example, the British scholar Barry Buzan was noting this inter-civilizational friction, which he attributed in part to "the bitterness and humiliation of the invidious comparison between the accomplishments of Islam and Western civilizations." Bernard Lewis, professor emeritus at Princeton and a leading scholar of Islam, suggested in 1990 that the West faced "a mood and movement" within Islam that posed "no less than a clash of civilizations—that perhaps irrational but surely historic reaction of an ancient rival against our Judeo-Christian heritage, our secular present, and the worldwide expansion of both."

Similarly, Huntington quotes a leading Egyptian journalist, writing in 1994, as foreseeing "a growing clash between the Judeo-Christian Western ethic and the Islamic revival movement." A prominent Indian Muslim suggested in 1992 that it would be in "the sweep of the Islamic nations from the Maghreb to Pakistan that the struggle for a new world order will begin." Also quoted was Fatima Mernissi, whose book *Islam and Democracy* was hailed in the West as a courageous statement from a modern, liberal, female Muslim. But she castigated the West as a "militaristic" and "imperialistic" civilization that had "traumatized" other nations through "colonial terror" and projected a "power that crushes us, besieges our markets, and controls our merest resources, initiatives and potentialities."

Huntington went so far as to suggest that since the Iranian Revolution in 1979 the West and Islam had been engaged in an "inter-civilizational quasi war." It was merely a quasi war for three reasons: First, not all of Islam had been fighting all of the West. The West's enemy within Islam had generally been two fundamentalist states (Iran and Sudan), three nonfundamentalist states (Iraq, Libya, and Syria), and a wide range of Islamist organizations financed by other Muslim countries. Second, it had been fought by limited means—terrorism on one side against airpower, covert action, and economic sanctions on the other. And, third, the violence had been intermittent. And yet, said Huntington, a quasi war is still a war, and more Westerners had been killed in it than died in the real Gulf War of 1991.

"The underlying problem for the West," wrote Huntington by way of summing up, "is not Islamic fundamentalism. It is Islam, a different civilization whose people are convinced of the superiority of their culture and are obsessed with the inferiority of their power. The problem for Islam is not the CIA or the U.S. Department of Defense. It is the West, a different civilization whose people are convinced of the universality of their culture and believe that their superior, if declining, power imposes on them the obligation to extend that culture throughout the world."

Remember that Huntington was writing before 9/11. But even after 9/11 most Western thinkers recoiled at his stark interpretation. *National Journal* writer Sydney J. Freedberg Jr. interviewed forty "experts" for a long analysis in May 2003 on "The War Within Islam." Not one, he writes, endorsed Huntington's perception of a civilizational clash. Rather, he wrote, nearly all embraced the idea that the West had been drawn into an epic struggle within the world of Islam over how to grapple with the modern world. Thus, the challenge is to identify within Islam "the positive forces that the United States must strengthen."

And then there is Thomas Friedman's ongoing commentary suggesting that if we could just create enough jobs the entire Muslim hostility toward the West would disappear. Writing from Davos, Switzerland, on January 25, 2004, under the title of "War of Ideas, Part 6," he noted that many people had remarked to him,

"Wow, Islam, that's a really angry religion." Friedman wrote, "I disagree. I do agree, though, that there are a lot of young Muslims who are angry, because they live in some of the most repressive societies with the fewest opportunities for women and youth, and with some of the highest unemployment." His solution was for Europe to open its arms and borders to these Muslim youths and find jobs for them, then pursue trade policies with Muslim lands akin to the North American Free Trade Agreement fostered by America in the early 1990s. In short, globalization. It is worth noting that Friedman was writing from Davos because he was attending the World Economic Forum, hotbed of what Huntington calls the "Davos Culture," which promulgates a global vision of "universal civilization."

AND SO WE SEE that even after 9/11 the most important foreign policy debate facing America boils down once again to the fundamental standoff between the two Western interpretations of history—the Idea of Progress and the Cyclical/Cultural View. Those who derive their world outlook from the Progress Idea resist at all costs the notion that we are engaged in a clash of civilizations with Islam. They don't wish to view Islam in such a harsh light, as a civilization that wants to harm the West and its peoples. They also don't wish to relinquish their view that the spread of Western civic ideals will mean the spread also of prosperity, happiness, and peace. Thus, they embrace the notion that the West's quarrel is really just with elements within Islam that hold distorted views about their religion and the world—"evil doers" who must be dealt with appropriately or frustrated job seekers who can be brought along with economic development. In either instance, they don't really represent their culture.

But in embracing the Idea of Progress, these latter-day Wilsonians also embrace one of its major contradictions—the powerful strain of Eurocentrism that Spengler, Toynbee, Huntington, and others have railed against for decades. It is this Eurocentrism that adherents of the Cyclical/Cultural View see as so dangerous.

Rather than ameliorating the frustrations, angers, and hatreds of the world of Islam, according to this view, the Eurocentric piety exacerbates all three.

In the realms of history and diplomacy, culture certainly isn't everything. Economic factors, geographic factors, ideological factors can always come into play. But culture remains the single most potent factor in history and geopolitics, and with the end of the Cold War the forces of culture were unleashed with a vengeance upon the globe. This is the reality of the twenty-first century, and it is a reality that demands from the West a steady, careful, measured approach to diplomacy and war. Will the West, with all its power and influence, stimulate and aggravate these emerging cultural tensions around the world? Or will it seek an approach aimed at protecting its interests while calming as much as possible the cultural hostilities that are an integral part of our era?

In the unfolding relations between the West and Islam, those questions take on profound significance. The war with Islam is so complex, so dangerous, so multifarious that missteps could have dire consequences. In such a war, unprecedented in modern history, probably the most destabilizing approach would be a combination of Theodore Roosevelt's Will to Power imperialism and Woodrow Wilson's missionary idealism. And yet that is precisely the dual policy that emerged from the George W. Bush administration after 9/11. Whether America can extricate itself from the consequences of that dual policy remains one of the most important foreign policy questions facing the country today.

CHAPTER 11

War

HAVING WON REELECTION by one of the narrowest margins in U.S. history, George W. Bush began his second term by proclaiming his intent to fashion America into a Crusader State, whose mission over untold generations will be to foster the culmination of human civic development through the spread of freedom around the globe. "It is the policy of the United States," declared the president in one memorable line early in his second inaugural address, "to seek and support the growth of democratic movements and institutions in every nation and culture, with the ultimate goal of ending tyranny in our world."

The speech generated a wave of intense scrutiny and debate focused on precisely what the president was trying to say. But a careful reading of the speech reveals there wasn't much ambiguity in his intent or the grand policy he was promulgating. Among the elements of that policy:

Missionary democracy. Bush argued that the legacy of the American founders is not merely a national one but a global one. Hence, American civic arrangements are to be considered universal, not merely the brilliant flowering of a distinctive culture at a crucial point in its history. "From the day of our founding," said the president, "we have proclaimed that every man and woman on this earth has rights and dignity and matchless value, because they bear the image of the maker of heaven and earth." America's influence is not unlimited, said Bush, but it is considerable and will be used "confidently in freedom's cause."

Missionary diplomacy. The president seemed to place the nations of the world into three categories. First, there are the U.S. allies, whose friendship we honor and whose counsel we seek. "And," added the president in a veiled but unmistakable warning, "we depend on your help." Bush suggested that America's allies must join us in this missionary spread of freedom or their own freedom will be at risk. "Division among free nations is a primary goal of freedom's enemies," he said. "The concerted effort of free nations to promote democracy is a prelude to our enemies' defeat." Second, there are the countries whose standards of democracy don't measure up. They will be badgered diplomatically. "We will encourage reform in other governments by making clear that success in our relations will require the decent treatment of their own people." And finally there are those governments defined as tyrannies. The president hinted that America reserved the right to overturn such governments, as it did Saddam Hussein's regime, if such actions are deemed in America's interest. Addressing peoples within such countries, he said: "When you stand for your liberty, we will stand with you."

World freedom and U.S. security. The president drew a direct connection between America's mission of spreading democracy and its own defense. "The survival of liberty in our land," said the president, "increasingly depends on the success of liberty in other lands. The best hope for peace in our world is the expansion of freedom in all the world." And, hence, this sweeping vision of American universalism driving American foreign policy comes down to an actual struggle for survival. "America's vital interests and our deepest beliefs," declared the president, "are now one."

Bush's second inaugural address wasn't his first effort to wrap himself in the language of missionary zeal to embrace the concept of American exceptionalism. Nor would it be his last. But the inaugural speech represented the most avid and sweeping presidential embrace of the Idea of Progress since Woodrow Wilson. In making that sweeping embrace at a time when America had 135,000 troops in the heartland of Arabian Islam under the banner of global freedom, Bush accentuated the new course in foreign policy that he had set for America in the post–Cold War period—a potent formula of humanitarian imperialism.

The story of the emergence of Bush's humanitarian imperialism is the story of how the post–Cold War perceptions of Francis Fukuyama and Thomas Friedman, based on the Idea of Progress, prevailed over the competing perceptions of Samuel Huntington, based on historical cycles and the role of culture in the human story. Indeed, even after the 9/11 attacks, when one might have expected a certain currency for Huntington's prediction of civilizational hostility, his ideas failed to gain traction against the gathering notion that the West represented an End of History culmination that ultimately would be embraced by the rest of the world.

The younger George Bush arrived late at this party. As candidate and later as president in the early months of his tenure, he seemed bent on resisting the call for humanitarian foreign actions dedicated to "nation building" in far-flung corners of the globe.

Then came September 11, which transformed the world, America, and the Bush presidency in equal magnitude. The president became, in his own mind and those of his advisers, a "war president." But this was unlike any war ever fought before, and it required new thinking about how it should be waged and sanctified in the minds of his countrymen. These imperatives of a new kind of war requiring a new dialectic of justification opened the door for the emergence within the Bush presidency of the neoconservative temperament. It made its way from the halls of academe and the columns of polemical journals to the highest reaches of the U.S. government, placing faulty lessons in the hands and into the consciousness of a callow president without any discernible sense of either history or culture. Captivated by the Cold War mentality of his top advisers and intoxicated with the idea of spreading Western-style democracy throughout the lands of Arabia, Bush embraced a post-9/11 foreign policy destined from the beginning to lead his country toward calamity.

THE EMERGENCE OF BUSH'S war presidency after 9/11 involves three distinct foreign policy outlooks that surfaced from the earliest days of the Bush tenure. Each had a history, a political following, and a contingent of defenders within the administration. One group was the pragmatists, sometimes called realists, who could trace their political lineage in certain ways to former Secretary of State Henry Kissinger and who were represented within the administration by its secretary of state, Colin Powell, his deputy, Richard Armitage, and, to a lesser degree, by National Security Adviser Condoleezza Rice (later secretary of state). Another might be called the nationalists, who believed in the maintenance and exercise of unparalleled American power but had little use for Wilsonian notions about spreading democracy around the world; they were represented by Vice President Dick Cheney and Defense Secretary Donald Rumsfeld. And finally there were the neoconservatives, at times labeled "democratic imperialists," whose top administration official was Deputy Defense Secretary Paul Wolfowitz and whose most influential hanger-on was the ubiquitous intellectual gadabout Richard Perle.

The Bush presidency is first and foremost the story of how these strains of thought came together, clashed, debated, and eventually melded into a post-9/11 foreign policy synthesis altogether new in American history. It was all there in Bush's second inaugural address. To find presidential rhetoric with such sweeping humanitarian ambition, you have to go back to Woodrow Wilson; to find presidential rhetoric encompassing such visions of American exceptionalism, you have to go back to the early Theodore Roosevelt.

Colin Powell has been portrayed frequently in the media as the dove in the Bush administration. Then in the run-up to the Iraq War he was viewed as having switched feathers from dove to hawk. Both portrayals, according to James Mann in his excellent biography, *Rise of the Vulcans: The History of Bush's War Cabinet,* are incorrect. He was never a dove in the sense most often associated with that term (liberal isolationism), and he never adopted a stance similar to that of administration hawks such as Cheney or Wolfowitz. Throughout his career, he believed in the importance of American military power. And throughout that time, he opposed military interventions that could prove to be long, bloody, or costly. "Powell's underlying rationale was ultimately pragmatic, not pacifistic," writes Mann. "He was seeking to maintain and build the strength of the U.S. armed forces by avoiding another draining venture like the Vietnam War."

Indeed, Powell so thoroughly embraced the famous doctrine of his Reagan administration mentor, Defense Secretary Caspar Weinberger, that it ultimately became known as the Powell Doctrine. It posits the view that the United States should resort to major overseas combat missions only when five tests are met: that they involve vital U.S. interests; have clearly defined political and military objectives; are undergirded by a clear resolve for victory; have the support of the American people; and have emerged after other options had been exhausted. Powell later added a call for overwhelming military superiority in such instances. This doctrine led Powell to adopt cautionary stances toward the 1991 Gulf War and particularly the Balkan situation in the early 1990s.

But Powell supported the Iraq War from the beginning, although he favored U.N. diplomacy as a means of garnering international support and maintaining the Atlantic Alliance. Once it became clear that countries such as France and Germany would never offer support, he favored proceeding with as many allies as the administration could get. He saw the Iraq offensive as part of the war on terrorism, a necessity of preventing terrorist groups from getting the kinds of weapons that could kill tens of thousands of Americans at a time. But Powell was never given to sweeping visions of America's role in the world or flights of geopolitical grandeur. He saw himself as a problem solver and loyal executor of presidential aims.

The nationalists, Cheney and Rumsfeld, on the other hand, viewed themselves as big-picture men who had learned the lessons of foreign policy during their Cold War days working for President Gerald Ford. It was then that they had rejected the so-called pragmatism of Secretary of State Kissinger, which they equated with defeatism and a willingness to accept a decline in American power. They came to believe that such a decline was neither inevitable nor acceptable. Thus, they ended up embracing the foreign policy impulses of Ford's great Republican rival, Ronald Reagan, far more than those of their own boss.

As Ford's secretary of defense, Rumsfeld worked tirelessly against Kissinger's détente policies and sought to stiffen Ford's stance toward the Soviets. His hard-line views were adopted also by Cheney, so thoroughly a Rumsfeld protégé during their White House years that the Secret Service awarded the younger man the code name "Backseat." Like Rumsfeld, Cheney worked quietly within the administration to get his boss to pull away from the Kissinger views and edge closer to those of Reagan. When the Reagan forces angered Ford by forcing an anti-détente foreign policy plank onto the 1976 Republican platform, Cheney quietly urged his boss to forgo any battle to remove the language lest it jeopardize his chances to win the nomination. It was sound political advice but also reflected Cheney's true sentiments. Later, as a member of Congress, Cheney's votes reflected a consistent resolve to help reverse America's post-Vietnam military decline. Aligning himself with Reagan during the run-up to the 1980 presidential campaign, he voted against implementation of the Panama Canal treaties negotiated by President Jimmy Carter. And he consistently voted for new weapons systems and big increases in defense spending.

After September 11, Rumsfeld and Cheney emerged as hardliners. Their aim was to employ America's military might to take the offensive against terrorist forces throughout the world and thus protect American lives at home. "9/11 changed everything," Cheney would say in the months following the attack. Often he would add, "The era of optional war is over." America, he argued, was locked in a long struggle with hidden and stealthy forces bent on killing as many Americans as possible. It was a struggle that required "unconventional" and "asymmetrical" military responses. Nothing less could ensure that the president and his officials were fulfilling their primary constitutional responsibility to protect American lives.

Given that constitutional responsibility, the Rumsfeld-Cheney response seems quite natural from nationalist politicians who believed in the uses of American power around the globe. But there was a problem in the Rumsfeld-Cheney approach: it was based on the last war—the Cold War of the twentieth century. It didn't sufficiently account for the new realities of the new century. The nationalists never perceived a demarcation between the Cold War struggle and the post–Cold War era. This was to become particularly significant after September 11, when Rumsfeld and Cheney brought to the new crisis an outlook forged and shaped in the Cold War, when bold confrontation and the construction of an unparalleled military machine carried the day and ultimately destroyed the enemy.

But the Cold War was a clash of ideology and power against an inorganic communist entity superimposed upon the cultures of nations unfortunate enough to have been engulfed by it. In that sense it truly was an evil empire, as Reagan had said, because it thwarted the free cultural expression of peoples and nations. The war with Islam, on the other hand, is a clash of civilizations in which the free cultural expression of peoples alien to the West is contributing to the hostile environment that America is facing. Thus, the current clash poses an entirely different kind of threat. The twin forces of history and culture suggest that the approaches that worked in the earlier struggle aren't likely to work in the latter one. Yet those were the approaches embraced by Rumsfeld and Cheney. Thus, they became susceptible to the arguments of the neoconservatives.

The administration's leading neoconservative was Paul Wolfowitz, a product of that Straussian milieu at Cornell and the University of Chicago that despised the moral relativism of modern liberalism and embraced foreign policy thinking based on virtue and strong moral judgments about good and evil. In mid-1976, as an obscure defense bureaucrat in Washington, Wolfowitz invited to dinner an intern working for him that summer. He was Francis Fukuyama, also a product of the Straussian circle at Cornell and later of course the author of that famous essay heralding the emergence of Western liberal democracy as the culmination of human civic development. It wasn't surprising, given the two men's interest in world events, that one topic of conversation would be Henry Kissinger, then in his eighth year as America's premier foreign policy architect.

Wolfowitz offered a critique of Kissinger's most famous book up to that time, *A World Restored*, which praised the Austrian statesman Metternich for brilliantly crafting a sturdy European balance of power at the Congress of Vienna, following the chaos of the Napoleonic years. It was a good book, said Wolfowitz, but essentially off the mark. The hero of the Vienna Congress was not Metternich, the realist preoccupied with equilibriums of power, but rather Czar Alexander I of Russia, whose moral and religious sensibilities led him to tougher positions against Napoleon.* As Fukuyama reported later, "I remember him saying the thing that's wrong with Kissinger is that he does not understand the country he's living in, that this is a country that is dedicated to certain universalistic principles."

James Mann, in relating this anecdote in his *Rise of the Vulcans*, quotes Kissinger in *A World Restored* as expressing his disdain for foreign policy moralisms: "Moral claims involve a quest for absolutes, a denial of nuance, a rejection of history." That pretty much describes Paul Wolfowitz, Mann suggests, and adds: "More than any other single figure in the Republican foreign policy hierarchy, Wolfowitz viewed himself as Kissinger's opposite, his adversary in the realm of ideas."

But, as we have seen, that is essentially a faulty distinction that emerges from the wrong lesson learned by the neoconservatives about the Kissinger years. Kissinger's particular brand of realpolitik deserved rejection because it was based on faulty assumptions— that America was in decline, that Americans had lost their nerve, that the Soviets owned the future. Those perceptions were all false, and hence Kissinger's view of realpolitik wasn't realistic at all. It was a cluster of defeatist illusions. But the abandonment of realism in foreign policy in favor of moral fervor and universalist arro-

---

* The real hero of the Congress of Vienna, it could be argued, was neither Austria's Metternich nor Russia's Alexander but France's Talleyrand, who managed to pull a diplomatic victory out of a near ruinous military defeat. His cold eye of realism perceived that the West's dynastic age was giving way to a new dawn of nationalism, and thus was able to negotiate protections for his country that would be particularly beneficial in the coming era.

gance is equally tendentious. Kissinger's critique of morality-based foreign policy was and remains sound.

A crucial turning point in the history of the Bush presidency—and America—came when the nationalists embraced the faulty lesson of the neoconservatives regarding Kissinger's realpolitik. The key figure was Dick Cheney, who had forged close ties to various neoconservative figures and institutions over the years but had remained somewhat wary during the early months of the second Bush's administration. "It is important to note," writes *Newsweek,* "that at this early stage, the neocons did not have the enthusiastic backing of Vice President Cheney." All that changed with September 11: Dick Cheney quickly became the most powerful neoconservative in America.

He was well positioned to do so, for he had fostered the rise of various neoconservative figures during his years as defense secretary in the first Bush's administration. He discovered Wolfowitz in the early 1990s and oversaw his career, promoting him for Rumsfeld's deputy. Then he avidly embraced a coterie of Wolfowitz protégés who ended up in crucial positions on the Bush national security team: Stephen Hadley, deputy national security adviser in the White House (later promoted to the top job); Zalmay Khalilzad, principal Iraq expert on the National Security Council (later ambassador to Afghanistan); Douglas Feith, a Wolfowitz deputy at the Pentagon; I. Lewis (Scooter) Libby, Cheney's chief of staff and national security adviser; Eric Edelman, Libby's deputy; and William Luti, whose Office of Special Plans at the Pentagon served as a kind of alternative intelligence arm.

It wasn't difficult for Cheney to embrace these men and their Wilsonian vision of remaking the world under the auspices of American hegemony. He had been moving in that direction for some time. Indeed, it was under Cheney's auspices that some of these men had fashioned the 1992 Defense Planning Guidance document that proved highly controversial at the time and has lingered in controversy since. Written in its initial draft by Khalilzad, it essentially called for American hegemony into the future as far as the eye could see. It justified "military steps to prevent the development or use of weapons of mass destruction"—an allusion to preemptive war of the kind the United States ultimately waged in Iraq. It urged all actions necessary to prevent the emergence of any rival power, particularly among the "advanced industrial nations"—a reference to Japan and Germany but also to Europe generally (thus suggesting that our key allies would be our allies only so long as they accepted junior status). It suggested the United States might have to forge "ad hoc assemblies" of nations, supplanting permanent alliances, in pursuit of particular ends—foreshadowing George W. Bush's later "coalition of the willing."

In short, it posited the powerful notion that America didn't fight the Cold War to save Western Europe from the mortal threat of Soviet communism and then allow the Europeans themselves to seek their own destiny. It fought the Cold War to gain world dominance and to keep down other powers, including the very European entity we had saved. As noted in Chapter 6, the draft document was leaked to the press almost immediately upon being circulated around the Pentagon, and the reaction from America's allies abroad and George H. W. Bush's political opponents at home was swift and harsh. But Cheney was delighted with the draft. "You've discovered a new rationale for our role in the world," he told Khalilzad.

The draft had to be revised, and the revision, shepherded by Scooter Libby, was clever in the extreme. To outward appearances the new draft seemed toned down, but in fact it was merely more euphemistic. In place of language about blocking rivals, the new document talked about preserving America's "strategic depth," which to insiders meant its advantageous position in the world, its vast network of bases, weapons, and advanced military technology. It also referred to "shaping America's future security environment," which meant unilateral and preemptive actions aimed at maintaining a global power arrangement favorable to the United States. The new document omitted mention of "ad hoc assemblies," but suggested America must be ready to protect its vast overseas interests "with only limited additional help, or even alone, if necessary." In place of the word "preemption," it left open the prospect of "measured military action" to "contain or preclude a crisis."

In short, the new document was every bit as bold and sweeping as the earlier draft, only less candid. Cheney liked it so much that he ordered parts of it declassified. As Khalilzad told James Mann in an interview years later, "He took ownership of it." In January 1993, Cheney had it published under his own name, presented as America's "Defense Strategy for the 1990s." In fact, it was a blueprint for a new world order dominated then and forever by American military might.

And it was lying in plain view when September 11 forced the administration to craft a global strategy for the civilizational clash reflected in that dark day of American bloodshed. Many neoconservatives—most notably Wolfowitz and his alter ego outside official government circles, Richard Perle—had been agitating for years in favor of a military assault on Iraq, based on their supposition that Saddam was actively producing weapons of mass destruction. Now they received a respectful hearing. An Iraqi invasion as part of the war on terror fit nicely into that bold vision of American hegemony encompassed in the 1992 Defense Planning Guidance.

But sending an American expeditionary force into the world to conquer another country is tricky when it comes to justification, and the Defense Planning Guidance offered no particular guidance on that. It merely extolled the benefit to America of American hegemony. That wasn't salable—certainly not abroad but also not at home, where Americans weren't clamoring for global hegemony. They just wanted protection from attacks aimed at killing them as they went about their daily lives. What to do?

The answer came from neoconservatives throughout the government and in outside institutions such as *The Weekly Standard* and the American Enterprise Institute, a leading Washington think tank increasingly identified with the neoconservative outlook. First, there was the job of connecting Iraq and its leader Saddam Hussein to past and prospective terrorist attacks, either through links to international terrorist organizations or through the production of mass weapons that could fall into terrorist hands. Then there was the job of attaching to the cause an expression of idealism to give it a higher meaning. The neoconservatives came through on both counts, and their arguments formed the basis for Bush's war policy.

What happened next calls to mind David Halberstam's profile of Vietnam-era Secretary of Defense Robert S. McNamara in his famous book *The Best and the Brightest*. McNamara as portrayed by Halberstam had people shaking their heads in wonderment at his brilliance, his forcefulness, his supreme confidence, his uncanny ability to reduce complex problems to simple quantifications that brought them into sharp focus for quick disposition. The only problem was that the fundamental realities of the Vietnam challenge eluded him, and so he presided over a gathering disaster without seeing it coming. Writes Halberstam: "He was, there is no kinder or gentler word for it, a fool." As Bush's Iraq War approached and then unfolded, many of his top officials also took on the appearance of people who didn't quite grasp what they were dealing with.

Administration rhetoric justifying and explaining the war policy turned out to be riddled with inaccuracies and misperceptions. The war was justified primarily on the basis of the weapons of mass destruction that Saddam possessed and was building. No such weapons were ever found. Vice President Cheney insisted Saddam was linked to the al Qaeda network that perpetrated the September 11 attacks, but there was no evidence of consequence to that effect, and Director of Central Intelligence George Tenet felt obliged to correct Cheney privately on more than one occasion. Donald Rumsfeld suggested that "no terrorist state poses a greater or more immediate threat to the security of our people and the stability of the world than the regime of Saddam Hussein in Iraq." Subsequent events proved that statement to be false; the ongoing terrorist threat was much greater than any threat from the hapless Saddam Hussein and his military, severely attenuated by the 1991 Gulf War and subsequent U.N. sanctions.

Then there was the matter of what we expected to find in Iraq once the invasion was complete. "I really believe we will be greeted as liberators," said Cheney, demonstrating a lack of historical and cultural understanding of the region. When Army Chief of Staff Eric Shinseki, a four-star general, responded to a congressional query by suggesting a post-invasion occupation of Iraq would require a troop deployment of "something on the order of several hundred thousand," his civilian superiors at the Pentagon pounced on him. "Wildly off the mark," said Wolfowitz publicly. Rumsfeld harangued the general in meetings, saying he just didn't get it. Even before this, with a year left in Shinseki's term, Rumsfeld's office leaked the news that he would be dumped, leaving the staff chief hobbled as a lame duck for the remainder of his service.

Meanwhile, Wolfowitz explained to reporters that Shinseki's estimate was off the mark because there was no history of ethnic strife in Iraq, that other countries would step in to help during the transition to Iraqi democracy, and that the country's reconstruction would be a relatively bloodless venture financed largely by Iraqi oil revenues. He suggested that "a couple of divisions" would likely suffice. All those points turned out to be wrong or unrealistic—but none more revealing than Wolfowitz's troop estimate, which betrayed a fundamentally unsound perception of the military challenge at hand.

Similar folly surrounded the neoconservatives' adoption of the Iraqi-born former banker and convicted swindler Ahmen Chalabi as the man who should be installed by America as Iraq's post-Saddam leader. Cheney had met Chalabi through Perle, who had been touting the Iraqi exile leader for years as an ideal figure for the new Iraq. Chalabi's London-based government in exile, the Iraqi National Congress, had subsisted over the years on some $36 million in U.S. funding and had been feeding tidbits of intelligence on developments within Iraq to American government officials and journalists. Although the Bush CIA and State Department ultimately became skeptical of the man's character and veracity, Cheney, Wolfowitz, and Rumsfeld continued to view him as the man to lead the Iraqi liberation.

But after the American invasion, when Chalabi and some four hundred supporters were whisked into southern Iraq by U.S. forces to lead a march on Baghdad and help topple Saddam, the Iraqi people brushed him aside. "He was jeered more than cheered," one U.S. official told the *Washington Post*. "It was embarrassing." Chalabi nonetheless was installed as part of the twenty-five-member Iraqi Governing Council, but within a year he became embroiled in an investigation into corruption on the part of his Iraqi National Congress colleagues and possible espionage connections with Iran. Yet in the fall of 2003, before the investigation but after it had become clear that Chalabi had no following in Iraq, Cheney told Powell that the difficulties encountered in the occupation could have been largely avoided had Chalabi been put in charge, as the Pentagon had wanted.

As the occupation encountered growing difficulties never publicly anticipated by America's war leaders, those leaders continued to cling to unrealistic notions about what was really going on. For weeks Rumsfeld denied that the American military was facing a guerrilla insurgency in Iraq. That forced the new commander in the country, General John P. Abizaid, to contradict his civilian boss publicly, saying in July 2003 that the United States faced a "classical guerrilla-type" war that was growing in organization and sophistication.

The same month Wolfowitz toured Iraq and pronounced conditions there to be "much better than I thought they were before I came." He did acknowledge a "serious security challenge," but then, echoing Rumsfeld, he added: "I believe it's just a very small minority of Iraqis and some foreigners who are doing that"—words signifying that he had no idea what was in store for the U.S. military in that increasingly chaotic land. Indeed, before long it became clear that coalition troop levels were inadequate to any kind of effective pacification, that coalition forces could not control the country beyond a few fortified enclaves, that Iraq was on the edge of a bloody civil war, and that there was no credible strategy in Washington for dealing with the mess.

Perhaps most revealing of this escape from reality was Wolfowitz's reply to a query during congressional testimony in April 2004. Asked how many troops had died in Iraq since hostilities began some thirteen months earlier, Wolfowitz, the architect of the war, replied, "It's approximately 500, of which—I can get the exact numbers—approximately 350 are combat deaths." In fact, the correct number was 722, of whom 521 were combat deaths. His misstatement came on the heels of the bloodiest month of the war up to that time, with 125 troops killed and 900 wounded.

This litany of misstatements, misperceptions, faulty thinking, and off-the-mark predictions raises a question: how could so many highly intelligent people be so wrong? The only answer is that they stumbled into a classic case of ideological policy making—viewing the world through the prism of a rigid ideology and then placing the pieces together to fit that ideological picture. The guiding ideology was the latest incarnation of the neoconservative persuasion, which had embraced the idea that America can remake the world based on the modern liberal notion that human development has reached its zenith as represented essentially by us.

Had that ideological perception been correct, the war in Iraq would have proceeded along a far different course, and signs of stability would be discernible there as you read this. But of course that ideological perception was entirely wrong. The Bush administration was led astray by modern elements of thinking emanating from the Progress Idea—the notion of American exceptionalism, suggesting human development has reached a culmination stage with Western and particularly American governmental and economic structures; the perception that human nature can be molded and shaped to fit idealized visions of society; and the belief that culture doesn't matter much in the march of progress.

Had the administration brought a historical and cultural sensibility to the challenge of Saddam Hussein, its approach likely would have been different. Merely a sense of the essential Arab culture as outlined in the previous chapter certainly should have given pause to policy makers. And one would think that a more focused look at the history and culture of Iraq itself would have added to that sense of caution.

Iraq is not a nation in any strict sense of the word and never has been. It was forged out of chaos by Great Britain at the end of World War I, at the height of the British Empire. On March 11,

1917, the British army arrived in Baghdad, the capital of what was then called Mesopotamia, after defeating a Turkish army at Kut. General Stanley Maude greeted the populace with words that would echo in a slightly different accent some eight decades later: "Our armies do not come into your cities and lands as conquerors or enemies, but as liberators"—offering liberation from the Ottomans, who had dominated most of Arabia for centuries.

The idealism of liberation soon gave way to the imperatives of empire. The British wanted the Ottomans out of the entire Middle East. They wanted to set themselves up as the dominant force in the region so they could control the trade routes to India and exploit the emerging resource of oil. But it wasn't easy forging the unruly Bedouin tribes of Arabia into a coherent military entity capable of inflicting serious losses on the Turks. Then young T. E. Lawrence—the famous Lawrence of Arabia—arrived, recruited the sharif of Mecca's third son, Faisal, and organized a guerrilla force of speed, dexterity, and brutality. The tide turned; the Turks were out; the British and French were in.

Though the British had promised Faisal that he would be king of the Arabs in Damascus, that promise ran afoul of British-French designs in the region. So the British set up Faisal in Baghdad to rule over a state that had been arbitrarily pieced together from three Ottoman provinces—Mosul in the north, composed largely of Kurdish tribesmen; Baghdad in the center, dominated by the Sunni minority; and Basra in the south, populated mostly by the majority Shi'ites. They all hated each other, but they came to hate the British more. Soon angry Arabs were in open revolt, cutting down British soldiers almost at will with rifles and long scimitars.

Writing from Baghdad, Lawrence told readers of *The Sunday Times* that the public had been led "into a trap from which it will be hard to escape with dignity and honor." He added, "Things have been far worse than we have been told, our administration more bloody and inefficient than the public knows." Winston Churchill, who as colonial secretary presided over the Iraqi effort, called the place "an ungrateful volcano."

The British eventually prevailed, but at a fearsome price in brutality inflicted on the Iraqi people. Villages were bombed into oblivion, and artillery-equipped ground units rounded up insurgents, lined them against walls, and shot them en masse. The Iraqi death toll approached ten thousand, while some 2,300 British died. Through the ordeal, there was never any talk of spreading Edwardian democracy through the lands of Mesopotamia.

What's remarkable about this history is how closely it matches the American experience of the past two years and how adamantly the Bush team resisted any suggestion that there were lessons embedded in the British experience. Further lessons can be found in the culture, ethnic mix, and struggle for national identity that have characterized Iraq for centuries.

As Sandra Mackey explains in her book, *The Reckoning: Iraq and the Legacy of Saddam Hussein,* the country presents a mix not just of ethnic groups or religious doctrines or geographic sensibilities or cultural sensibilities—but all of these. They include a degree of urban sophistication between the two famous rivers and Bedouin tribalism in the countryside; Sunni religious doctrines in the central triangle and Shi'ite passions in the south; Arabs in the lowlands and Kurds in the mountains; and a vast array of other religions, sects, languages, and tribes. All this, writes Mackey, could be the description of a rich multicultural society. But it isn't. Instead, these multifarious distinct communities have spent the last eight decades fighting fiercely for the right to define a state that lacks any natural identity.

The most powerful mystique in the state is the Bedouin culture, a product of extensive migrations from Arabia between the seventeenth and late nineteenth centuries that poured Arab tribes into the Tigris-Euphrates valley and stamped the region with tribal impulses and habits of mind. All of the elements of Bedouin culture discussed in Chapter 10 came into play here, and thus these tribes "have fed much of the political disorder that has been a hallmark of the Iraqi state," as Mackey puts it. "The result," she adds, "is that nationalism, whether seen as good or bad, simply does not exist in the sense that an individual feels a strong primary loyalty to his country."

All the rulers of Iraq in modern times, beginning with the three kings who ruled for nearly four decades from the early 1920s and extending to the military dictators thereafter, have struggled to find a definition either in Arab nationalism or Iraqi nationalism—or, in Mackey's words, "Arabism or a contrived Iraqi nationalism built upon the history and symbols of ancient Mesopotamia." Neither could work because Mesopotamia has little meaning to present-day Iraqis, and Arabism, while resonant with Sunnis, is rejected by non-Arabs and most Shi'ite Iraqis.

And so the persistent hatreds that faced the British occupation in the 1920s continued to fester right up to the American occupation eighty years later. And the same distribution of power persisted throughout that time also. The Bedouin tribes that migrated there centuries ago, though eventually a majority in this land without nationhood, always found themselves to be outsiders. That's because the Sunni Ottomans who emerged as overlords, fearing the power of Persia on their eastern border and the Shi'ite tribesmen in their own countryside, turned to the one element in society they could trust—the Sunnis of the cities between the Tigris and Euphrates. They relied on these cities, particularly Baghdad, to hold the desert Arabs in check. Thus, the old Sunni families held all the major administrative positions, staffed the bureaucracy, and dominated the Sunni religious *ulama*, the establishment of clerical wise men. It was a closed world, and it was perpetuated in turn, in the name of stability, by the British, the kings, and the military dictators right up through Saddam Hussein.

SOME KIND OF FEDERALISM with elements of democracy might be possible someday in such a cultural environment, but it doesn't take an Islamic scholar to see that such an unprecedented and revolutionary turn of events couldn't possibly emerge spontaneously simply with the demise of the latest military dictator. Neither is extensive scholarship needed to see that the demise of that dictator would unleash sectarian and cultural passions that could only result in chaos, with any foreign elements on the premises standing athwart the search for cultural identity quickly becoming the enemy.

Further, it isn't likely that the Iraqi elections of January 2005, which brought forth a constituent assembly charged with the task of forming a government, will turn out to be the watershed event advertised by the Bush administration and other global optimists. It was indeed inspiring to see so many Iraqis braving mortal danger to cast ballots on election day. But, while the Bush team viewed this as an important battle in the ongoing war between freedom and tyranny (or good and evil), in reality it was merely one more manifestation of the continuous struggle to affect the distribution of power in a land without national identity. America, by fostering the elections, cast its lot with the Shia majority, which had been subjugated by the Sunni minority for centuries—under the Ottomans, the British, the kings, and a succession of dictators ending with Saddam Hussein.

The Sunnis won't relinquish their centuries-long control through America's call for democracy. And the Shia won't likely relinquish their own oft-stated dream of a government dominated by their higher clergy and inclined toward Shia Iran. This raw struggle for power won't end with elections. As retired U.S. Army Colonel Patrick Lang, an expert on the Arab world and former intelligence officer puts it, "We do not seem to be willing to accept the idea that war and politics in present-day Iraq are basically a contest among the lions for the spoils of the 'kill' that we Americans have left on the desert floor in Mesopotamia." And yet that is the ongoing reality of Iraq.

But it isn't simply the cultural expression and future identity of Iraq that is in play here. If indeed the West is locked in a civilizational war with Islam, as this book argues, then the implications are enormous as well as ominous. In such a war, the dual imperative is to do everything possible to protect American lives from the ravages of terrorism while avoiding actions, to the greatest extent possible, that are sure to enflame anti-Western passions in the world of Islam. There are two reasons behind the imperative to avoid fanning the flames of Islamist passion as much as possible.

First, higher levels of passion mean more jihadists directed against the United States, more tentacles in the current terrorist networks, and more networks. This in turn means a greater threat to American lives.

Second, as the civilizational war intensifies, stirring ever greater Islamist sentiment in the Middle East and elsewhere, the potential for destabilization throughout Islamic lands increases. The implications are particularly ominous as they relate to two countries—Saudi Arabia with its oil and Pakistan with its nuclear weapons. If either were to fall to Islamic fundamentalism, and both face serious threats in this regard, it would be a crushing blow to the economic or military security of the West. Either would require immediate and massive military action to secure the West's economic lifeline or its physical safety. And in such an eventuality there wouldn't be any gauzy talk about spreading democracy or American exceptionalism or protecting non-Americans from bad people. It would be a war of survival.

In taking his military into the heart of Islam and planting his country's flag into the soil of a foreign culture based on flimsy perceptions of a national threat, George W. Bush has brought his country and the world closer to that kind of Armageddon than it faced before. He did so on the basis of a world outlook and political idealism that are alluring, comforting, and widely embraced throughout American intellectual circles. They are also false and highly dangerous.

President Bush, who by all accounts never assembled his national security team for any extensive discussion of the benefits and dangers inherent in his looming decision, would have done well to have invited into the Oval Office an Iraqi expert or two for a chat on the implications of what he was about to do. Sandra Mackey would have served the purpose nicely. Writing before the Iraq invasion, she laid it out in all of its stark reality. At some point, she predicted, Saddam would fall. "Immediately after the boot is lifted from the neck of the Iraqis," she added, "a bloodbath is likely to ensue as each group pours out its anger at decades of despotism, enormous suffering under the sanctions, and real and perceived injustices of one group against the other." Even without blood, she said, there would be chaos and the need for enormous efforts at nation building. Failing that, the country would simply fragment into the component parts that never were fused into a real nation in the first place.

Could America avoid involvement in such a scenario, even if America didn't precipitate it? Mackey didn't think so. But she urged that American policy makers seek a real understanding of these swift currents of geography, history, ethnic identity, sectarianism, and tribalism lest the country find itself locked in a geopolitical disaster from which it couldn't extricate itself. It was sound advice, far better than what George Bush got from Cheney, Rumsfeld, Wolfowitz, Perle, and their neoconservative allies beating the drums of intellectual discourse in behalf of a war fought in the name of American exceptionalism.

PART IV

THE REAL WORLD

CHAPTER 12

Ghosts of Mithridates

I T WAS AROUND 88 B.C. when the king of Pontus—Mithridates VI, sometimes called Mithridates the Great—decided he had had enough of Roman influence in his region, of Roman meddling in his affairs, of Rome's arrogance and imperial pretensions. He vowed to destroy the Roman presence in the eastern lands that he considered his own to dominate. Waiting patiently until his western nemesis became embroiled in a bitter civil conflict on the Italian peninsula, he then struck with a force and vengeance characteristic of cultural wars.

Mithridates of Pontus is removed from us by a couple thousand years of time, but the locus of his kingdom is removed from present-day Iraq by only a couple hundred miles of distance. And the story of Rome and Mithridates is worth pondering today as the story of America and the world of Islam unfolds. Oswald Spengler, as we have seen, based his view of the world on insights derived through the study of historical analogy. And probably no analogy sheds more light on today's global forces than that between Rome of the first century B.C. and America of the twenty-first century A.D. Indeed, America stands today on a threshold of adventure remarkably parallel to where Rome stood at a similar point in its history.

Both Rome and America had found themselves locked in death struggles with enemy powers that threatened their way of life. For Rome it was the Punic Wars, for America the wars to save Europe, 1917–1989. Both were drawn into their struggles as protectors of threatened allies. Both fought their wars over generations and ultimately proved victorious, largely through superior economic strength, greater mastery over technology and a higher commitment to their fundamental values and democratic ways. Both then emerged as sole superpowers in unipolar worlds and found themselves drawn to the siren song of empire.

Imperialism is but one of the five American strains of foreign policy thinking identified and explored in Chapter 5. After 9/11 it was probably inevitable that this particular strain would emerge once again in the country's political discourse. In the months after the attack Americans seemed preoccupied with the question of whether they stood on the threshold of empire. The subject received cover treatment in one form or another in such diverse publications as *Time, Newsweek,* the *New York Times Magazine, Atlantic Monthly, National Journal, U.S. News & World Report, Foreign Affairs, The Weekly Standard,* and *Mother Jones.* "What word but empire describes the awesome thing that America has become?" asked Michael Ignatieff of Harvard's Kennedy School of Government in a provocative *New York Times Magazine* essay entitled "The American Empire (Get Used to It)."

Ignatieff noted that America is the only nation that maintains five global military commands encompassing more than a million armed personnel on four continents; roams every ocean with major naval forces; guarantees the survival of client states around the world; assumes custodianship of global trade and commerce; and declares its dreams and desires to be universal for all peoples everywhere. And yet such widespread dispersal of military power doesn't automatically lead to empire. That power could be used instead in behalf of humanitarian interventionism; or humanitarian interventionism mixed with strains of imperialism; or the kind of conservative interventionism described in Chapter 5. Ultimately it boils down to how America leverages its power. Thus we shall explore once again those various strains of foreign policy thinking in the cold light of 9/11 and the civilizational war with Islam now under way.

Empire. One thing we know from history is that imperial expansion always breeds the likes of Mithridates in the far-flung reaches of the imperial domain. Rome's actual Mithridates might be viewed in many ways as the Saddam Hussein of his time. He was a cagey and ruthless ruler, which he had to be to survive the intrigues and treacheries of court life in Asia Minor. His Syrian-Greek mother passed on to her son a strong intellect and cultural sensibility. It was said that he could converse in twenty-two languages. But his impulses and instincts, says one historian, were those of "a typical oriental barbarian." He became king at age eleven but fled almost immediately to avoid being killed by his mother, who coveted his throne. He lived in the wild as a hunter, "dressed in skins," as Will Durant describes it, and returned at age eighteen, strong enough now for matricide. Subsequently, to ensure his hold on power he killed his brother, three sons, and three daughters (or so the Roman historians tell us; we have no Pontic versions). He developed a practice of ingesting small amounts of various poisons every day to build up immunity and thwart any would-be stealthy assassins. He trusted no one and gave threat to everyone.

Mithridates harbored big plans for his kingdom, located in what is now Turkey, on the southeastern shores of what is now called the Black Sea (then called the Euxine), not far from what is now the Turkish-Iraqi border. With a mercenary army, he captured Cappadocia to the south, then conquered Armenia to the east, then stretched his sway around the eastern and northern shores of the Euxine Sea. But his ambitions were not slaked because to his west lay Bithynia, and Bithynia controlled the Hellespont, linking the Euxine to the Aegean and the Mediterranean—portal to vast and lucrative markets and a strategic leverage point in the region.

He could crush Bithynia in a week's time and take that economic and strategic prize except for one thing: Rome. Bithynia was a Roman client state and thus untouchable. When he had marched into Bithynia a few years before to insert himself into a dynastic dispute there, Rome had ordered him out. Reluctantly he bowed to this imperial power, but then the Roman proconsul in the region, one Manius Aquilius, encouraged the new Bithynian ruler to invade the Pontic lands. That was the last straw for this Eastern potentate. As Durant puts it, "Mithridates felt that his sole chance of survival lay in arousing the Hellenic East to revolt against its Italian overlords."

He expanded his army to nearly 300,000 men and took Bithynia. He built up a navy of four hundred ships and destroyed the Roman presence in the Euxine Sea. He "liberated" Greece from Roman dominion. Then he unleashed a pogrom on Roman and Italian citizens throughout the region, slaughtering more than eighty thousand and confiscating their property. As a demonstration of contempt, he poured molten gold down the throat of Manius Aquilius.

Of course this bloody development shocked Rome, which promptly set about to send an army to Asia Minor to crush Mithridates and his military. But then things began to go awry as foreign policy imperatives disturbed intractable domestic political fault lines. The two greatest generals of the day—rivals Gaius Marius and Lucius Cornelius Sulla—each wanted to command the expeditionary force. Worse, each represented a major faction in the ongoing political struggle of the day—Marius, the *populares*, who wanted political power distributed more widely throughout society; and Sulla, the *optimates*, who wanted power held firmly in the hands of the old patrician families.

As this persistent rivalry heated up and the factions became increasingly enraged, the tectonic plates under the surface of the Roman polity shifted dramatically. In the ensuing civil war, many precedents of the ancient republic were shattered: for the first time, a Roman army marched on Rome; for the first time, the six-month dictatorship allowed in the constitution to meet civic emergencies was usurped for an indefinite period; at one point, a victorious faction unleashed a "proscription" upon its political enemies, marking them for death. And slowly the Roman republic, more than four hundred years old and one of the greatest civic achievements in the history of mankind, ceased to be.

Nobody in our own time and country can envision America descending into such internal chaos and violence. But foreign adventures tend to have unintended consequences both at home and abroad. And two powerful lessons of history emerge from the saga of the Roman republic's inexorable push toward empire and dominance of the known world. First, the story reflects the dangers and inevitable bloodletting inherent in the imperial game. In his book *The Lexus and the Olive Tree,* Thomas Friedman calls America "the ultimate benign hegemon." But if there are lessons in history, certainly one teaches that there is no such thing as a benign hegemon. Hegemonic ambition inevitably inserts the hegemon into environments that turn out to be threatening, brutal, and savage. And then, if it wants to remain a hegemon, it can no longer be benign. We don't have to look to Roman history for this lesson; America's current Iraqi adventure serves nicely.

Second, the imperial impulse, even when unfurled in the name of democracy, can prove threatening to the democratic institutions of the imperial power itself. As Ignatieff puts it, "Why should a republic take on the risks of empire? Won't it run a chance of endangering its identity as a free people?" That's what happened in Rome, where the push toward empire unleashed upon the polity a flood of issues and conflicts that couldn't be contained by the structures of the republic. And so the republic was replaced by a string of emperors not far different from the kings that the Romans so proudly had deposed nearly five centuries earlier.

Democracy is intrinsically fragile. Many Americans view it as sturdy and durable because our own republic has lasted more than two centuries. But the Roman republic enjoyed nearly four centuries of civic solidity before slipping into its era of crisis. Benjamin Franklin expressed it more realistically when, at the end of the Constitutional Convention, he replied to an inquiry on what he and his colleagues had wrought: "A republic, madam, if you can keep it."

Keeping it will become much more difficult if America pursues the lure of imperial ambition and experiences the stresses and strains inevitably released by such bold pursuits. No, it is far better for America to focus its attention on protecting and preserving the fragile but hallowed civic system bequeathed to us by our Founders.

Humanitarian interventionism. The 9/11 attacks served to mute the call for the kinds of humanitarian actions seen in Somalia and Bosnia in the 1990s. When Americans are under threat of attack in their own homeland, it is difficult to make a case that American blood should be shed in behalf of starving Somalis or beleaguered Bosnian Muslims. *Time,* for example, no longer labeled as "heartless" those who opposed risking American lives in causes unrelated to American interests; neither did it any longer hail the use of military might in foreign humanitarian missions as "an estimable principle." Such moralistic expressions now had a hollow ring against the reality that Muslim fundamentalists were conjuring ways of killing American civilians as they pursued their daily lives.

Beyond that, Americans generally seemed to absorb the geopolitical lesson of Somalia and Bosnia—namely, that helping people doesn't always carry its own reward. The effort to help starving Somalis got eighteen American soldiers killed, another seventy-eight wounded, and one poor dead GI dragged through the streets of Mogadishu in a brutal display of anti-Western glee. America's Bosnian adventure helped create a Muslim staging area and recruitment ground for actions aimed at killing Americans in Iraq. Inevitably, it seeped into the American consciousness that this particular brand of humanitarian intervention didn't always work out as advertised. Gone were those heady days of the early 1990s when the American people heeded the media drumbeat celebrating the high national calling of salving the woes of tormented humanity in distant precincts of the globe. Gone also was the media drumbeat.

Kenneth H. Bacon, president of Washington-based Refugees International and former Pentagon spokesman, notes that the American media in 2003 and 2004 largely ignored a human "catastrophe" in Sudan, where government-backed militias conducted a systematic assault of murder and rape on African Sudanese in the country's western Darfur region. The media took note only after 200,000 refugees had fled to Chad, a million people had been driven from their homes, and hundreds of villages had been destroyed. By the time American news outlets began covering the story, 300,000 people in Darfur faced the threat of starvation and disease. Even less attention in the West was directed at the civil conflict in the Democratic Republic of Congo, which claimed four million lives over eight years.

Thus, the Wilsonian impulse to ameliorate the ills of the world through the use of military force, a significant political outlook in the early 1990s, had largely evaporated as a political influence by 2004. But the other strain of Wilsonian idealism—the notion that Western nations can manufacture democracies around the world in places with no democratic tradition—was going strong. This idea had been grafted onto the Will to Power imperialism that emerged from neoconservative circles following 9/11, giving this particular imperial doctrine a gloss of idealism.

This gloss wasn't apparent when the nationalists of the first Bush administration promulgated their doctrine of American hegemony at the dawn of the post–Cold War era. That 1992 Defense Planning Guidance put forth by Dick Cheney's Pentagon made no mention of ensuring peace and American security by spreading democracy around the world. The aim simply was to dominate geopolitics in such a way as to thwart the emergence of any rivals to American power anywhere on the globe, including Europe. The melding of this aim with the goal of spreading democracy came later, largely through the pages of *The Weekly Standard*. Then, following 9/11, a third element was added to the doctrine— national security. It was argued that American global dominance and the spread of democracy were crucial to the protection of American lives in an era of terrorism.

Thus was born the Bush foreign policy vision, put forth in a presidential speech at West Point in June 2002 and codified in a National Security Strategy document three months later. It included three key elements: (1) "preemption," or America's declared right to start a war to thwart a suspected attack; (2) an unchallengeable America, meaning no other power would be allowed to develop military strength equivalent to that of the United States; and (3) the spread of democratic values as a fundamental American mission and a hedge against global instability and American vulnerability.

We must pause here over this matter of spreading democracy

because it is complicated and easily distorted through simplification. As we have seen, some of the most articulate skepticism directed at this notion came from the neoconservative camp in the late 1970s and early 1980s—notably in the writings of Jeane Kirkpatrick and Irving Kristol (whose outlook later was brushed aside by the younger generation of neoconservatives). And we have noted Samuel Huntington's famous 1968 treatise on political development in the Third World, which argued that democracy is not an antidote to instability but rather, in unstable environments, more likely a spur to further instability. But none of these writers ever argued that only Western nations successfully could embrace democratic systems.

Kirkpatrick argued rather that it normally required "decades if not centuries" for people "to acquire the necessary disciplines and habits" to establish successful democratic regimes. Kristol enjoined his readers to recognize and accept that some authoritarian regimes were further along the road than others toward constitutional democracy—thus implying that many were likely to get there eventually. And Huntington, writing in 1993, hailed the strides toward democracy of such countries as Spain, Portugal, Greece, the Philippines, Korea, and Taiwan, as well as numerous states in Central and South America.

Three points deserve emphasis here: First, because the road to democracy is long and arduous, it offers no immediate panacea for global ills or threats that pose problems for the West or the world at any given time. Second, there is no reason to believe that democratization in non-Western lands will equate to Westernization; countries moving toward democracy can be expected to retain their own cultural sensibilities and impulses, their own habits of mind, their own ways of looking at the world. And any anti-Western sentiments lingering in those countries likely will become more intense when freed from the shackles of authoritarian rule. And, third, the one civilization in the world that remains inherently unreceptive to the precepts of Western democracy is Islam, particularly its Middle Eastern core, where the Bedouin culture retains its influence.

Thus, the recent neoconservative formulation melding the imperial impulse with the ideal of spreading democracy is an empty formulation. In practical terms, the push for democratic nation building doesn't pave the way for imperial dominance but rather hinders it, as the current American experience in Iraq so starkly demonstrates. In political terms, when the American people see just how hopeless and potentially dangerous this formulation can be, they will reject it.

And thus the call of humanitarian interventionism holds little salience in post-9/11 America. There is no support now for the dreamy Wilsonian notion of sending American troops into the world's chaotic regions to apply balm to the wounds of humanity. And the mission of spreading democracy to regions unaccustomed to such governmental structures, whether as a stand-alone national calling or in conjunction with the imperial impulse, will give way eventually to its own hollowness. America will have to find other strains of thinking to guide it through the difficult years ahead.

Isolationism. Neither the conservative isolationism of Robert Taft nor the liberal variety of George McGovern can emerge in today's world as a serious political force. Most Americans understand that 9/11 revealed a serious ongoing threat to America and its citizens and that to meet that threat the country must stand ready to exercise its power around the world. What this means in policy terms is another matter. There is no national consensus or even any kind of robust national debate on just how the country should address that global challenge. But there remains little doubt in the national consciousness that some kind of global role is necessary to protect the country from the ongoing threat of anti-Western terrorism born of Islamic fundamentalism.

A purely national response has not emerged conceptually on any serious level because it would transform the American polity too profoundly. To protect Americans strictly on the home front would require a curtailment of civil liberties, a restrictive approach to immigration, and a roundup of noncitizen Muslims far beyond what most Americans are willing to contemplate. It is possible that the civilizational war could intensify to such a pitch and threaten American citizens on such a scale that the country would find itself taking steps in those directions as part of a comprehensive policy. But that is not how most Americans view the crisis currently, and thus any response necessarily must entail global actions. The only question is what kinds of global actions can effectively address the threat.

Conservative interventionism. What's remarkable about America's foreign policy debate following 9/11 is how little focus was placed on the strain of thinking that guided America to victory in the Cold War. Recall that conservative interventionism valued realpolitik, balance-of-power diplomacy, and limited goals tied to America's self-interest and the protection of the West. During the nearly half century of this doctrine's ascendancy, from 1941 to 1989, America never dreamed of a unipolar world in which the United States dominated the globe. There was no hegemonic ambition, stated or unstated. The central aims were to protect Europe from Soviet ground forces poised for an invasion, to safeguard Western interests around the world, and to maintain global stability in key strategic locations.

Neither was there room in this framework for serious humanitarian interventionism of the kind that guided America into Somalia and the Balkans. The architects and stewards of conservative interventionism over those five decades insisted on keeping the national focus on the matter at hand—the ongoing struggle against aggressive Soviet communism. Ancillary desires and ambitions—whether curtailing starvation in Biafra or dominating the world—were brushed aside as distractions. The focus was on seeing the world as it really was, with power centers that had to be recognized as to their actual significance in the geopolitical realm. The aim was to maintain a balance among those power centers to ensure a stable world.

That's why Richard Nixon's 1971 overture to China was so brilliant. He could see that the bipolar confrontation of the first two decades of the Cold War, with America facing off against the Soviet Union, was giving way to a world with multiple power centers.

One of these clearly was going to be China. So he initiated a diplomacy designed to foster China's entry into this multipolar environment as a counterweight to the Soviets. Nixon knew that China would have to be dealt with on a host of delicate issues that could breed tensions with the West, including the fate of Taiwan and China's ultimate breadth of influence in East Asia. But he concluded that those issues would emerge anyway, and so it was best to accept the inevitable and seek to leverage it within a realistic and sophisticated diplomacy.

Compare that with the neoconservative attitude toward China, as evidenced in *The Weekly Standard,* which seeks to thwart Chinese ambitions in East Asia no matter what they might be and declares hostility toward China based on its internal political structures and insensitivity to "human rights." Nixon's approach opened avenues for dealing with China even when tensions ran high on sensitive issues between the two countries. The neoconservative approach would heighten prospects for dangerous escalations over such issues whenever they might arise.

That crystallizes the fundamental differences between the conservative interventionism of the twentieth century and the Bush doctrine of global dominance in the post-9/11 era. The former focuses on American and Western interests; the latter pursues a missionary aim of helping peoples around the world through the spread of democracy. The former believes in seeing the world as it truly is through the regimen of realpolitik, which in today's era would mean a recognition that the world is multipolar and multi-civilizational; the latter is beguiled by dreams of what an ideal world could be, particularly if it were dominated by the universalist culture represented by America. The former views the conflict unleashed by 9/11 as essentially a civilizational clash requiring Western solidarity; the latter views it as a clash between the exceptionalism of America and the "evil doers" who stand athwart progress. The former seeks a balance of forces among the civilizations of the world; the latter seeks to dominate the other civilizations of the world.

WHEN HISTORIANS OF the future probe the George W. Bush administration for clues on how it developed this bold, new vision of American hegemony, they may stumble across a political development that occurred without fanfare or even notice. But its consequence was immense. It was the alliance forged within the administration, after September 11, 2001, between the foreign policy nationalists and the neoconservatives.

That alliance ensured that the philosophical underpinning of the Bush administration's post-9/11 foreign policy would be Wilsonian idealism born of the latest inspiration of the Idea of Progress. As we have seen, the Bush nationalists, represented primarily by Vice President Dick Cheney and Defense Secretary Donald Rumsfeld, didn't care a fig for this gauzy internationalist vision. Their nonhumanitarian outlook had emerged during the Gerald Ford administration as a nationalist reaction to the Vietnam debacle, the anti-Americanism of the counterculture, and the defeatism of Secretary of State Henry Kissinger. Their driving aim back then—to get America's effort in the epic Cold War struggle back on track—eventually was subsumed under what became known as Reaganism—the fortieth president's blend of optimism, military resolve, and clear-eyed realism about the nature of the communist threat, all pulled together with large amounts of eloquent patriotism.

But after the Soviet collapse, these nationalists fell under the spell of American hegemony, as reflected in the 1992 Defense Planning Guidance produced in the Cheney Pentagon. It was this spell that led inevitably to the nationalists' alignment with the neoconservatives, who had emerged by the time of the second Bush administration as the country's leading promoters of America as missionary nation bent on inserting into other cultures of the world the American Creed—the country's bedrock of political ideals such as the protection of individual rights, separation of powers, free enterprise, the curtailment of religious intrusion into the daily lives of citizens, and equal protection before the law. Thus, they embraced Wilsonism with a zeal that exceeded even that of Wilson, for they viewed the Wilsonian impulse not just in terms of idealism and morality but as crucial to the protection of the American homeland and as the instrument of American world dominance. This viewpoint led directly to the invasion and occupation of Iraq.

It is interesting to speculate on what might have happened had the Bush administration's nationalists resisted the lure of hegemony and aligned themselves with the administration's pragmatists, represented primarily by Bush's Secretary of State Colin Powell and his deputy, Richard Armitage. These officials traced their philosophical etymology back to Nixon and Kissinger, but without any residues of defeatism that had undermined the latter's political standing during the Ford years. As conservative interventionists, they believed in American military strength as crucial to world stability and peace. But they also believed it should be exercised prudently and deftly to maintain a balance of geopolitical forces in a multipolar world. They desired first and foremost to avoid the kinds of quagmires that Powell saw up close as a young military officer in Vietnam. Thus the Powell Doctrine: never engage in military campaigns unless the martial and political forces are all aligned and then only when overwhelming strength is brought into play. In strategic terms, this means forging a deep understanding of the enemy.

The architects of the Bush invasion didn't understand the enemy. In a narrow sense, they didn't understand that their army would be greeted by the Iraqi people not as liberators but as alien aggressors. They didn't understand the troop strength they would need to occupy and pacify the country. They didn't understand the cost in blood and treasure the mission would exact. In a broader sense, they didn't understand that their country was engaged in a civilizational war and that the Iraqi invasion would open up a new front in that war that was neither necessary nor beneficial to the Western cause.

The pragmatists in the Bush administration had a clearer sense of these realities and dangers. They understood the enemy. What they lacked was the sense of national purpose needed in times of crisis such as the one America entered with the 9/11 attacks. Thus, the question emerges whether a melding of the nationalist and pragmatist impulses into a reprise of conservative interventionism could have positioned the country more effectively against the civilizational threat posed by radical Islam. We'll never know because the pragmatists became marginalized when the nationalists aligned themselves with the neoconservatives.

What we do know is that this powerful alignment set America upon a course toward empire, fueled by the idealism of democratic expansionism. Thus was born America as Crusader State. Thus also did some of the fundamental realities facing America in this era of civilizational tension get obscured.

ONE OF THESE REALITIES is that the West is in decline. It remains a mighty force, of course, largely because of American military and economic power, but no longer can it dictate the course of world events as in days of yore. There are other growing power centers in the world today, and most of them are tied to intense cultural sentiments that will have to be acknowledged and dealt with. Not even the primacy of American military power can ensure the supremacy of America or the West in a multipolar world driven by civilizational passions. Thus, America must develop a cold-eyed understanding of the world's civilizational forces before it can devise a strategy for imposing its will sufficiently to protect American citizens during the long cultural war with Islam.

Another reality is that we are indeed at war with Islam. No Islamic state government is overtly prosecuting this war, and none is publicly casting its lot with the terrorists. But the Islamist sentiment within Muslim lands is widespread, powerful, and rooted in cultural soil that has nurtured the sensibilities of Magian humanity for centuries—in fact, since before Muhammad. Whenever wars break out, there are people within the combatant states or civilizations who oppose the war, may even hate the very notion of what their leaders are imposing upon them. But ultimately they have to choose, and seldom do they choose to oppose their government or their civilization. So it is in the lands of Islam. Osama bin Laden seems to understand this reality quite well; America's leaders seem to believe, on the contrary, that the American Creed can win out over the force of Islamic culture. This is a dangerous outlook.

Third, a cultural war requires a cultural sensibility. The war with Islam is likely to last for a generation or more, against an enemy driven by a passion for its cultural heritage. In America, on the other hand, an ongoing push for multiculturalism is obscuring fundamental elements of the country's cultural tradition. If America relinquishes its heritage in this era of civilizational clash, the consequences could be serious. The ongoing challenge to the country's traditional culture could generate internal divisions and political battles that diminish American cohesiveness, enervate the body politic, and weaken the country's ability to prosecute the ongoing civilizational conflict. As Samuel Huntington points out, the challenge of our era calls for a multicultural sensibility in our foreign thinking and a monocultural outlook internally. This argues also for Western cohesiveness, for unity among the Western powers in the face of an external threat driven by a centuries-old hostility toward the West.

And finally, the American republic, the greatest civic achievement in the history of mankind, should not be taken for granted. In the face of Western decline and the threat of Islamist terrorism, it should be nurtured, fortified, and cherished. That argues for tradition over experimentation, for fealty to the country's traditional heritage and America's time-tested ways of governance, for restraint in foreign adventurism lest the swirling forces of a chaotic world engulf the hallowed American experiment.

CHAPTER 13

Conservative Interventionism

THE NATURE OF THE THREAT faced by America and the West in this era of civilizational clash can be illustrated through a look at the rolling military challenges faced by the country since the rise of Nazi Germany in the 1930s. The German military machine during that time was something to behold—modern, high-tech, encompassing both speed and power, capable of unleashing devastating "blitzkrieg" ground-and-air attacks. When America entered World War II in 1941, Franklin Roosevelt resolved to overwhelm this awesome military machine by unleashing America's even more awesome industrial capacity and building a "crushing superiority of equipment."

By war's end, America had turned out nearly 6,000 merchant ships, 1,556 naval vessels, 299,293 aircraft, 634,569 jeeps, 88,410 tanks, 11,000 chain saws, 2,383,311 trucks, 6.5 million rifles, and 40 billion bullets. It was, writes historian David M. Kennedy, a "stupendous Niagara of numbers." And it succeeded in overwhelming America's enemies.

But after the war America's new adversary, Soviet leader Joseph Stalin, set out to trump America's productive capacity with his own superiority of equipment and throw it against what remained of free Europe. Thus began the Cold War and America's resolve to stare down this new military threat. But, absent an actual hot war, America was not inclined to match the military production that Stalin could order up through his controlled economy. So in the 1950s, President Dwight Eisenhower forged a new policy of "mas-

232

sive retaliation"—meeting a Soviet ground attack on Europe with a nuclear missile attack on the Soviet Union.

That brought stability to the situation for a time, but eventually the Soviets matched America's capacity to inflict massive destruction through nuclear missile attacks, and the new era of mutual terror ensued. With America's retaliatory capacity now in question, the Soviets' conventional superiority came back into play, and America responded by exploiting exciting new technologies to develop stealth aircraft and precision-guided weaponry—smart bombs and rockets that could find their targets with devastating accuracy. These potent new weapons were first demonstrated in the Gulf War of 1991, gained greater sophistication by the Yugoslavia bombing campaign of 1999, and proved during the Iraq War of 2003 that nobody in the world could match America in conventional war-making capacity.

But now America faces the new threat of brutal terrorist campaigns waged against civilians at home and abroad, and neither America's unmatched nuclear capacity nor its precision conventional weaponry can provide effective military countermeasures. In place of technology and productive capacity, the new challenge calls for a precision understanding of the true nature of the challenge, including the cultural forces swirling around the globe, and a sophisticated melding of military and diplomatic efforts. The challenge can be broken down into a number of national imperatives of outlook and action:

Understand the enemy. The enemy is Islamic fundamentalism, a powerful wave of cultural and political sentiment tied to the population explosion under way within the lands of Islam. This wave of fundamentalism has spawned a vast network of fanatical operatives bent on disrupting the West, destroying its economy, and killing its people. These shadowy figures exploit Western freedoms to travel largely unimpeded across borders, create cells throughout Western lands for future missions, and carry out acts of terrorism. The threat to America and the West is immense and ongoing.

It is important to note that, while most Muslims are not terrorists, anti-Western sentiment is both intense and widespread within

Islam—reaching majority status in many Muslim countries. What's more, as the civilizational war becomes more intense and more Muslims get killed, more and more Muslims around the world will feel forced to make a choice between their own culture and the West. Few will choose the West. Thus, missionary democracy in the Middle East is not necessarily our friend, for it likely would foster fundamentalist and anti-American regimes in that strategically important region. The mission of spreading "freedom" throughout the region is more likely to bring harm to America.

Our friends are those within the Islamic lands who are seeking to destroy or contain Islamic fundamentalism—even including strongman dictators, corrupt royal families, military bureaucrats. To the extent that they are successful, they should be supported through quiet diplomacy and aid, as well as stealthy actions by an effective intelligence service. When they falter, they should be propped up or quietly replaced by others bent on the same mission of thwarting the triumph of radical Islam within their countries. The American military should be expanded, honed, and kept always at the ready—but reserved largely for one purpose, to prevent radical Islam from taking over any Islamic country from which terrorist missions can be launched against the West or its oil jugular.

The American war in Afghanistan serves as an object example. The fundamentalist Taliban regime that fostered the 9/11 attacks on American soil had to go, and America acted with dispatch and efficiency in replacing it and disrupting the al Qaeda networks that had been flourishing in remote reaches of that brutalized country. But the Bush administration was wise in eschewing any aim of conquering Afghanistan or occupying its countryside. History demonstrates clearly that such a mission would not have carried reasonable prospects for success.

It is equally important to understand that the enemy is not terrorism per se—only terrorism of global reach that is directed at the West. As Robert Dujarric of the Hudson Institute has written, Hamas, Islamic Jihad, and Hezbollah, however repugnant, are not enemies of the United States. Neither are the Filipino Muslim insurgents in that Pacific archipelago. Various terrorist movements within Kashmir reflect the complex civilizational war between India and Pakistan and needn't be listed among America's chief concerns. But if anti-Western fundamentalists were to pose a credible threat to take over Pakistan, with its nuclear capacity, then the United States would have to act to prevent it with lightning speed and brutal force. The same is true of Saudi Arabia with its lifeblood of oil. And neither mission, if necessary, should be complicated or weighted down with talk of spreading democracy.

In this context, it can be seen that Saddam Hussein was not a prime enemy of the United States in the war with Islam. First, his brand of Arab nationalism was incompatible with the cultural zealotry of Osama bin Laden. Second, since his interests weren't colored by Islamic fundamentalism but rather by real-world considerations of power and wealth, he conceivably could have been enlisted in the West's war against radical Islam. He wanted sanctions lifted and guaranteed markets for his oil; the United States needed guaranteed flows of oil and intelligence on al Qaeda; therein lay a potential exchange.

True, Saddam was brutal. But the scale of his brutality was commonplace in comparison to that of Joseph Stalin or Mao Zedong, two men among many questionable characters America has treated with in the past to further its national aims. And the magnitude of the fundamentalist Islamic threat suggests America can't fight this new enemy while remaining ascetically pure. Other nations that particularly merit diplomatic attention in the same way are Syria and Iran, both on the neoconservative list of nations to be declared enemies, then destabilized and remade as Western-style democracies.

Diplomacy within Islam. Since there are no Islamic governments today that are actively fostering terrorism against the United States, in the manner of Talibanic Afghanistan before the U.S. invasion, the United States has no reason to declare any of those governments as enemies. At the same time, America should make clear in unmistakable but quiet terms that it will not accept even a hint of governmental support for al Qaeda or other Islamic fundamentalist terrorist organizations, nor will it tolerate complacent inaction that allows attacks on Americans to be organized on their soil. The threat must be credible and ominous. Attached to it should be an implicit expression that America doesn't care how those countries conduct their affairs or organize their governments—so long as they neither pose nor tolerate threats to America and the West.

There should be no swagger attached to this diplomacy. That only exacerbates the civilizational war. Nor should there be the kind of sanctimony seen by the world when George Bush labeled Iran as "evil," thus practically declaring war on a leading state within another civilization. Words and actions should make clear that America harbors no designs on other lands within other civilizations, including the lands of Islam. The country's aim, substantial in itself, should be merely to protect American lives, parry all threats to Western economic health, and maintain world stability by fostering a balance of power among nations and civilizations.

A significant element of American diplomacy within Islam should be an extended effort to foster the emergence of Islamic core states. In an era of civilizational clash, the key to peace is the interaction among the core states of the various civilizations, which provide stability and enforcement of norms within particular civilizations and also negotiate in behalf of their civilizations when conflicts arise with outside cultures. Unfortunately, no single Islamic nation today possesses the economic power, military might, organizational effectiveness, and Islamic identity to ensure stability within that roiling civilization, to speak and negotiate in its behalf, or to enforce agreements.

Iran perhaps comes closest, but it is a Shi'ite nation whereas 90 percent of Muslims are Sunni. Turkey has all the requisites except that its secular identity militates against any Turkish role as leader of Islam. The 9/11 attacks should have led to a transformation in U.S. diplomacy toward both countries. Instead of labeling Iran part of an "axis of evil," the United States should seek to bring Iran into a position of respect among nations, much as Richard Nixon did with China in the 1970s. History has labeled Nixon's famous outreach as bold and creative, traits needed in U.S. relations with Iran today, particularly in the aftermath of the Iraq War. Iran holds one important key to stability in large portions of Iraq.

With 65 million people, a significant industrial base, large oil reserves, and unlimited natural gas, Iran is by far the most powerful state in the oil-rich Persian Gulf. Its people are not Arabs but Persians, tracing their heritage to a highly sophisticated ancient civilization that once included large sections of neighboring Iraq. Thus Iran has a natural and intense interest in what happens in Iraq, particularly to its Shi'ite population in the oil-laden south. Indeed, as Richard Whalen has written in his penetrating newsletter, Iran has infiltrated tens of thousands of agents and jihadists into southern Iraq as protection for the country's Shi'ite majority and eventual leverage in its behalf when power ultimately is distributed in that country.

Of course Iran is an Islamic theocracy, run largely by radical mullahs who despise America and the West. But of all the Islamic countries in the Middle East, it has the highest prospect for some kind of democratization. The 1979 Islamic revolution is spent and faces a growing challenge from moderates and modernizers, particularly among the young. It is only a matter of time before major change comes to Iran that will be more to the liking of America. But American involvement in the meantime, even mere exhortation in behalf of the modernizers, would only hamper their cause. And so America should stay out of that drama and develop a diplomacy toward Iran based on that country's position and power in the region, not on its governmental approaches at any given time.

Some neoconservatives favor a diplomacy of overt bellicosity and covert efforts to destabilize the mullahs' position. This would be a disaster. It would strengthen those in Iran who want to undermine the already beleaguered American invaders across the border in Iraq. It also would destroy any prospect that Iran could be enlisted to help restore stability to a part of the Persian Gulf rent by chaos in the wake of the American invasion.

A bold and creative U.S. president would opt instead for rapprochement with two specific aims in mind: First, Iran could help bring stability to Iraq as that country, under America's supervision,

moves inevitably toward a kind of three-way partition or confederation reflecting the three distinct provinces of Mesopotamia under
the Turks—a Kurdish-dominated northern region, a central Sunni
enclave, and a Shi'ite-dominated south. With Iran offering ties and
protection to the southern Shi'ites, prospects for stability there rise
considerably.

Second, Iran could serve as a kind of hedge against any potential interruption of Saudi oil supplies resulting from fundamentalist insurgencies. It isn't that Iran's oil supplies could ever supplant
the Saudis' huge reserves, but rather that Iran could serve as a kind
of protector and interlocutor not just for the southern Iraqis but
also for the Shi'ite populations stirring throughout the oil-rich and
heretofore Sunni-dominated mini-states of the Gulf. According to
Whalen, already there are signs of a Shi'ite "federation" arising
among these states under Iranian protection. With the corrupt
House of Saud beset by growing insurgencies, it is only prudent for
Washington to look for other power centers in the region that
could help out in the event of a Saudi crisis.

All of this is hugely complicated, however, by Iran's desire to become a nuclear power. Whalen argues that America may have to
accept Iran into the nuclear club as the price for an alliance that
could dramatically increase chances for stability in the region,
with long-term consequences for American economic stability. In
any event, the point here is that the civilizational war faced by
America demands imaginative and bold diplomacy unfettered by
past conventions and prejudices. American interests must prevail,
and, as Whalen puts it, "The future configuration of Iraq, the U.S.'s
attitude toward growing Iranian influence along the Gulf, and the
internal control of increasingly embattled Saudi Arabia are all tied
together." An effective American diplomacy would recognize all
that.

As for Turkey, America has encouraged that secular state to become more and more Westernized and has pressed Europe to ad-
mit it into the European Union. Both are faulty policies. President
Bush in June 2004 went so far as to stand on the banks of the
Bosporus in Istanbul and declare, "As a European power, Turkey

belongs in Europe." Turkey is not a European power. It is what Huntington calls a "torn country"—a nation belonging culturally to a particular civilization but whose leaders wish to redefine it as belonging to another. Since Ataturk in the 1920s, Turkish leaders have sought to push their Muslim nation into the West. It can never succeed. That has become increasingly clear in recent years as Islamic fundamentalism has gained force and Turkey's foreign policy has become increasingly Islamicized. As for entry into the EU, America should understand that Europe's cultural identity is at risk if it admits into its fold a Muslim country with sixty million inhabitants and chronically high unemployment.

A better diplomatic approach in this era of civilizational strife would be for America to stop encouraging Turkish Westernization and entry into Europe and push instead for Turkey to become a leading power of Islam, capable of maintaining some discipline within its civilization and speaking for it in dealing with the West. As Huntington puts it, "At some point, Turkey could be ready to give up its frustrating and humiliating role as a beggar pleading for membership in the West and to resume its much more impressive and elevated historical role as the principal Islamic interlocutor." For America and the West, a Turkey proudly taking on the mantle of Islamic leadership would be a more valuable force in the world than a Turkey struggling to claim an artificial Western identity and thus forfeiting any claim to speak on behalf of Islam.

Relations with Russia and China. Russia today poses no serious threat to America or Europe. Indeed, in an era of civilizational strife the West has more in common with the Orthodox core state than with any other country outside the West. As Patrick Buchanan has written, "Americans should recognize that in any 'clash of civilizations,' Russians will man the eastern and south-eastern fronts of the heartland of the West." Yet some American intellectuals want to pick a fight with Russia because of what they see as the twin evils of domestic and foreign nationalism.

Domestically, President Vladimir Putin's authoritarian regime has pushed aside Western-style pluralism in favor of "managed democracy"—economic freedoms in most realms of the society (an apparent exception being the oil sector) mixed with the muzzling of democratic institutions and restrictions on civil rights and press freedoms. In foreign policy, Russia aims to hold sway over a civilizational bloc of nearby nations that share its Orthodox heritage—particularly Belarus and Moldova, which are largely Orthodox and oriented toward Russia, and to a lesser extent Ukraine, which is split between a Western-oriented Catholic west and a Russian Orthodox east. Following Ukraine's fraudulent election in 2004, many American commentators and officials insisted on viewing the political drama there as a morality play pitting pristine Western-style democracy against corrupt oligarchs. In fact it is a clash of civilizations, and if the West attempts to resolve it through the triumph of the European-oriented west and the absorption of the Ukrainian landmass into the West, the region will become a major world flashpoint.

Unlike the Soviet Union with its global ambitions, Putin's Russia aspires merely to be a serious regional power with civilizational ambitions. As Russian Defense Minister Sergei Ivanov explained at a European conference, Russia considers its right to define its relationship with its closest neighbors to be an "imperative for security."

But even this modest ambition rankles many Americans. Republican Senator John McCain of Arizona consistently rails against Russia's domestic authoritarianism, which he calls a "creeping coup," and its resolve to maintain influence over its nearby neighbors who share its cultural heritage. *New York Times* columnist William Safire wrote, "As its role becomes global, NATO must not lose its original purpose: to contain the Russian bear." There is no hint that Safire saw the irony in that sentence: here is NATO, founded as a defensive alliance to save Europe from a menacing Soviet Union, now going "global" and pushing eastward into the historic Russian sphere of influence; and here is Russia, whose bellicosity necessitated the defensive NATO alliance, now struggling in the face of NATO expansion to retain credibility merely as a regional power with limited civilizational interests in its own neighborhood.

By all measures of analysis, the authoritarian system crafted by

Putin is precisely what the Russian people want. He won reelection in a 2004 landslide, prompting the *Wall Street Journal* to declare that "Mr. Putin is clearly in sync with the people." In a recent poll, only 22 percent expressed a preference for democracy, while 53 percent positively disliked it. In another survey, 52 percent of respondents said multiparty elections do more harm than good, while only 15 percent said they do more good. Asked in still another poll to choose between "freedom" and "order," 88 percent opted for order. In Russia, writes Richard Pipes, professor emeritus at Harvard, "democracy is widely viewed as a fraud."

Russia is a nation with a rich past and a cultural heritage that will guide Russians along their path through the modern era, which likely means they will choose stability over plurality in the immediate future. And, having lost their European empire and their status as world power, Russians also will insist upon the security that comes with dominance over the territories of their own region. America should accept these realities as not only inevitable but beneficial to the cause of world stability.

A strong and self-confident Russia acting as the core state of the Orthodox civilization can help monitor the southern Islamic lands of the Caucasus for Islamist military activity that could threaten the West as well as Russia itself. If military action is needed to thwart such activity, as in Afghanistan, Russia becomes a natural ally because of its interest in subduing fundamentalist militancy in nearby Muslim lands. Russia could be enlisted to help maintain order in the Balkans, a region that has been part of the Russian sphere of influence for centuries and where America has no geopolitical claim whatever. For years during the 1990s upheavals there America sought to keep Russia out because of its historical ties to the demonized Orthodox Serbs. Meanwhile, unfolding events in those tragic lands created something of a geopolitical monster in the form of a pipeline for weapons and warriors making their way from Muslim areas of Bosnia to Iraq to kill American soldiers. Thus, Russia's protective regard for the Serbs and America's new interest in monitoring Muslim activity in the region create a convergence of interests.

And Russia stands as a bulwark against a rising China to the east. Russia and China, after all, are natural adversaries, with a long shared border and festering territorial disputes going back centuries. America and Russia, on the other hand, are natural allies in the post–Cold War era, without any serious issues tearing them apart. That's why America should resist influential academics, journalists, and politicians who want to create artificial issues over Russia's system of government or its legitimate regional aims.

Unlike Russia, China poses a serious challenge to American diplomacy in the post–Cold War era. With dazzling rates of economic growth and expanding influence throughout its region, China has set for itself two fundamental foreign policy goals: first, to become the champion of Chinese culture, the civilizational core state to which all other Chinese diaspora communities would be drawn; and, second, to resume its historical role, relinquished two hundred years ago, as the hegemonic power in East Asia. Clearly, America can't maintain the role of global hegemon if China is to become the East Asian hegemon.

That perception, beginning in the mid-1990s, has fueled a body of sentiment within U.S. governmental and academic circles that America and China are on a collision course. George W. Bush assumed the presidency with a declaration that China was America's "strategic competitor." And when Defense Secretary Donald Rumsfeld, early in the Bush tenure, sought an expert to spearhead a report on U.S. defense strategy, he picked for the job a specialist named Andrew Marshall, well known for his earlier warnings about China's threat to U.S. strategic interests. After September 11, 2001, however, the Bush administration backed away from characterizing China as an adversary, and the Chinese responded with helpful diplomacy in support of America's effort to curtail North Korean nuclear weapons development.

There is no benefit to America in declaring China an adversary or carping about China's domestic political structures or practices. The economic and military rise of China in East Asia is inevitable. The only question is whether America can find a way to accommodate this emerging reality while retaining a measure of regional influence and avoiding war with a landmass nation with 1.2 billion people and millions more ethnic brethren throughout Asia. This is going to require deft diplomacy, an appreciation for the cultural underpinnings of the Sinic civilization, and strong alliances with Russia, Japan, India, and any other nation that serves as a counter-weight to Chinese power.

A policy of verbal or economic bellicosity in response to China's expansion of influence and power, as advocated by *The Weekly Standard*, is precisely the worst course that America could adopt at a time when it is struggling with Islamist terrorism. Policy makers should ignore warnings from pugnacious journalists and academics that China represents a direct threat to the American homeland or is bent on world dominance. China's true ambitions, far more modest than that, are challenge enough for America without raising false specters of geopolitical danger, which would only increase chances for war. The country that is flirting with global dominance in the world today is America, not China.

Unity of the West. Facing a civilizational war, Americans must think in terms of their own Western civilization, and that means solidarity with Europe. In no area of diplomacy did the George W. Bush administration choose a more ominous course than in its dealing with what Donald Rumsfeld dismissively called "Old Europe"—principally, France, Germany, and Russia. America must abandon that animosity and move to reverse this "progressive erosion of the Atlantic alliance," as Henry Kissinger has called it. The primary foreign policy goal should be Western unity.

With the onset of the Iraq War and European opposition, many Americans embraced a severe anti-European attitude. "To the list of polities destined to slip down the *Eurinal* of history," wrote Mark Steyn in the *Jewish World Review*, "we must add the European Union and France's Fifth Republic." Richard Perle argued that Europe's hesitation to embrace America's foreign policy suggests the continent has lost its "moral compass," while Thomas Friedman suggests that France "is becoming our enemy." After numerous conversations in America, Oxford University scholar Timothy Garton Ash concluded the stereotype is easily summarized: "Europeans are . . . weak, petulant, hypocritical, disunited, duplicitous, sometimes anti-Semitic, and often anti-American appeasers. In a word: 'Euroweenies.'"

The question persists as to whether America and Europe are now on separate tracks, so different in outlook and temperament that they aren't likely to act in tandem again anytime soon. This thesis was put forward with provocative astringency in 2003 by Robert Kagan, senior associate at the Carnegie Endowment for International Peace and a frequent contributor to *The Weekly Standard*. Kagan's little book, *Of Paradise and Power: America and Europe in the New World Order*, became an instant best-seller and stirred discussion on both sides of the Atlantic. "It is time to stop pretending that Europeans and Americans share a common view of the world," he writes, "or even that they occupy the same world."

America, he adds, occupies a Hobbesian world where the ultimate arbiter of events is power, while Europe languishes in a Kantian world of "perpetual peace" maintained by "laws and rules and transnational negotiation and cooperation." Europe thus has turned away from power while America has embraced it with a voracious enthusiasm. Actually, writes Kagan, Europe began to move beyond the embrace of power after the trauma of World War I, while World War II "all but destroyed European nations as global powers." By 1947, when Britain was forced out of the great power game and transferred to the United States responsibility for protecting Greece and Turkey from communism, it had become clear that Europe now was entirely dependent on America for its own security.

Still, the Cold War, with its massive threat to the Western heartland, ensured that American and European thinking remained in harmony. Kagan labels as "extraordinary" the "generosity" of America in linking its very survival to that of other nations while standing behind the relative protection of two oceans. This generosity almost seemed at times indistinguishable from idealism.

"Almost," adds Kagan, "but never entirely." Idealism, he writes, was never the sole source of this generosity and America's resolve to link its fate with that of its European allies. After all, going it alone would drive a wedge through the West and leave it vulnerable to the mortal threat of hostile Russian Bolshevism. Thus, any successful policy had to be "multilateral" in its inclusion of Western European interests. But the architects of this policy felt it necessary to go beyond this and publicly embrace a broader concept of multilateralism that included public respect for the United Nations Charter and other internationalist icons. In their hearts, though, they never really embraced this level of idealism, says Kagan. Dean Acheson, for example, considered the U.N. charter to be "impracticable" and the United Nations itself to be an example of a misguided Wilsonian "faith in the perfectibility of man and the advent of universal peace and law." For Acheson, support for the U.N. was nothing more than "an aid to diplomacy."

Writes Kagan: "This is important, because many aspects of American behavior during the Cold War that both Europeans and many Americans in retrospect find so admirable, and whose passing they so lament, represented concessions made in the cause of Western unity." Here we come to the crux of the issue of Western unity in the post–Cold War era and also the crux of Kagan's profound misjudgment in analyzing that issue. Kagan is saying here that American-European unity was necessary to save the Western heartland from communism and that the broader multilateral concessions were mere window dressing, a kind of facade of idealism to dress up the realpolitik that was driving policy. But what was really driving policy was America's connection to the West. America was a Western nation and thus had no choice but to come to the aid and protection of its own cultural heartland.

Now, however, with the Cold War fading into historical memory, Kagan sees no affinity between America and its ancestral homeland. Acheson and the other so-called Wise Men were wise in their skepticism toward the Wilsonian idealism associated with the U.N. Charter, but the cultural connection between Europe and America was something else entirely. And it is ongoing. In abandoning that, America would be abandoning its own cultural heritage. It would be going into the world fortified with the American Creed, meaning our devotion to our system of government, but not with the essential Western identity that breeds the deeper cultural cohesion needed in an era of civilizational clash.

It seems at times that that is precisely what Kagan and his neoconservative colleagues want. By focusing on the American Creed, to the exclusion of America's Western heritage, Kagan implicitly elevates America to a position of superiority among nations. America becomes a country with a purely civic national identity as opposed to the world's other tribally defined societies—in other words, an "exceptional" country whose identity is defined by hallowed principles of governance rather than crass ethnic or cultural histories. This can lead quite naturally to a kind of missionary zeal in foreign policy, to a geopolitical universalism, to the Crusader State. By declaring America's break with Europe, Kagan helps pave the way philosophically for the kind of foreign policy that is advocated in the pages of *The Weekly Standard,* often by himself.

This would be a dangerous course for America. Notwithstanding Kagan's penetrating perceptions about the divergence in outlook between America and Europe, it would be foolhardy for America to abandon its cultural heritage in devising its foreign policy. The Iraq War is an excellent case in point. The moderation advocated by France and Germany was based on three rationales: that there was insufficient evidence that the threat posed by Saddam was imminent; that the goal of building democracy was going to be infinitely more difficult, long, and bloody than anticipated; and that the resulting occupation would enflame anti-Western passions throughout Islam. The French and Germans were right on all three points.

America cannot abandon Europe in this era of civilizational strife, however frustrating and infuriating those nations might be. Yes, the ongoing Atlantic alliance will constrict American action in some ways, but the Iraq experience indicates that wouldn't be altogether bad. And America's ties to the West bring a natural moderation to America's foreign policy ambitions.

In perhaps its most egregious foreign policy misstep, the Bush administration has adopted a policy toward Europe described by one State Department official as "disaggregation"—meaning always playing some European countries off against others. This is a classic imperial strategy going back to Rome's *"divide et impera,"* or divide and rule. The aim is to keep Europe relatively helpless and dependent on the United States, lest it should become a competing world power center. As Philip Stephens, writing in the *Financial Times,* puts it, "Messrs Cheney and Rumsfeld see American hegemony better served by a fractured Europe from which they can select 'coalitions of the willing.'" In recent years this has been most starkly manifest in Washington's aggressive diplomatic campaign against Anglo-Franco-German plans for a more independent European military capability.

This is all wrong. America's policy toward Europe should be aimed at building up the EU in every way possible. A strong and independent Europe is a threat to America only if America is bent on world hegemony. And world hegemony should not be America's ambition. It should be simply to protect American interests, to protect Western interests, and to foster global stability to the fullest extent possible. Those aims can and should be pursued in the context of relations with Europe that are as cordial and sturdy as American diplomacy can effect. Great nations don't become adversaries to the countries of their heritage.

The homeland war. There are some six million to seven million Muslims living in America today, many of them noncitizens. The country ultimately will have to face the question of how much Muslim immigration it should foster in a time of cultural hostility. America cannot ignore immigration policy as one essential element of homeland security. It is naive to believe that the country can assimilate and protect itself from large numbers of Muslims entering the country as the civilizational war continues.

These are delicate and difficult issues. But throughout its history America has enacted various immigration policies that opened and closed the gates to particular population groups for various reasons. Certainly the fact that large proportions of Muslims around the world wish to kill Americans in large numbers, or see them killed, would argue for imposing entry restrictions that would have seemed indefensible before September 11, 2001.

By way of illustration, one need only look at life in France or even England, where Muslim populations are proportionately larger than in the United States and where elaborate internal security measures are undertaken to protect citizens from terrorism. In Paris, motorists are stopped at random, and police officials assuage the anger of non-Muslims by suggesting the intrusion is much more pronounced in the Arab ghettos. France struggles, meanwhile, with growing numbers of radical imams preaching hatred toward the West in mosques throughout the country. In England, the Labour government has increased funding for its MI5 internal security force by 50 percent to pay for one thousand new agents, many recruited from ethnic minorities who can infiltrate radical Islamic groups. As the *Washington Post's* Jim Hoagland has pointed out, the rising political stars in France, Britain, and Germany are interior ministers who run tough internal intelligence operations.

Those policies are driven by perceived threats emanating from Muslim population segments within. The brutal reality is that the larger the Muslim population, the greater the internal threat and the more difficult it is to monitor and prevent attacks. The *Washington Post* reports that hundreds of mosques throughout North America have been built or taken over by adherents of Wahhabism, the rigid and puritanical strain of Islam dominant in Saudi Arabia and stridently hostile to the West. Discrete investigations that began in Idaho, Michigan, New York, and northern Virginia have coalesced into a cluster of interrelated probes aimed at determining whether links among the groups suggest a network whose purpose is to foster and mount terrorist attacks against U.S. citizens.

Cultural tensions are on the rise as well. When the al-Islah Islamic Center in Hamtramck, Michigan, petitioned to broadcast its call to prayer over an outdoor loudspeaker five times a day, the result was a flare-up of cultural animosity. A librarian named Jackie Rutherford told the *New York Times* that she once considered herself free of prejudice. "But then I realized I had a problem with them putting Allah above everyone else. . . . I feel they've come to our country, infiltrated it, and they sit there looking at us, laughing, calling us fools." A Muslim secretary from a nearby mosque muses sadly that he has had to learn "how much they hate us."

America should seek to hold down such tensions as much as possible, and that means holding down Muslim population growth at a time when America and the West are locked in a civilizational war with global Islamist radicalism. If that seems politically untenable or reprehensible, consider the political sentiment that will emerge in the country after two or three more attacks on American soil, of the magnitude of 9/11 or larger. Such attacks are nearly inevitable, and so is the political demand that will arise in their wake to curtail the free entry of Muslims into the country.

AMERICA'S WAR AGAINST Islamist radicalism requires a broad policy that blends nationalism and pragmatism and remains free of unrealistic global ambitions that pull America into quagmires such as Iraq. America has neither the troop strength nor the will to carry out any reckless plan to take on nations such as Syria or Iran, to destabilize their regimes and remake them in some kind of Western image. It can't possibly succeed with an approach that includes hostility toward its cultural homeland, bellicosity toward Muslim governments struggling to contain Islamist sentiment, and arrogance toward the rest of the world.

What is required is an approach that is sustained, measured, defensive in nature, limited in ambition, and based on a sophisticated understanding of the cultural currents in play in the world. It must start with an appreciation that America and the West are at war with Islam and that this is a war like no other in history. It will last for decades. The enemy isn't a national one but a cultural one, consisting of cadres of religious and cultural zealots interspersed throughout the world, including the West, and willing to die for the sake of merely killing a few innocent Americans at a time. The enemy's primary aims are to drive a wedge through the West, to destabilize its economies and its governments, and to seize key Muslim countries, particularly Saudi Arabia and Pakistan.

And so the American response should be to unite the West, to maintain its economic and societal stability, and to prevent at all costs key Muslim countries from being engulfed by Islamist radicalism. The first challenge is a diplomatic one. The second demands internal security and intelligence capabilities far beyond anything the country now has. And the third will require a sophisticated blend of diplomacy, covert activity, and, perhaps, military action. America's success or failure in the face of this multiple challenge will depend on how deftly it brings to bear the precise tools that are needed to meet all the various threats as they arise in this ongoing clash of civilizations.

Disavowing the Crusader State

TOWARD THE END of his small but influential book on America's relations with Europe, Robert Kagan inserts a sentence that reveals the underlying philosophy that led him to conclude "the West" no longer has any need for unity or cultural coherence. It is a philosophy that was distilled with promotional brilliance back in 1989 and has animated foreign policy thinking in America ever since. "But the central point of Francis Fukuyama's famous essay, 'The End of History,'" writes Kagan, "was irrefutable: The centuries-long struggle among opposing conceptions of how mankind might govern itself had been definitively settled in favor of the Western liberal ideal."

Kagan's embrace of the Fukuyama thesis reflects once again the sturdy persistence of that false idea. It truly is the notion that will not die. It animated the humanitarian interventionism that emerged in the early post–Cold War years, taking America into Somalia on a mission unrelated to American interests. It drove the agitations of those who quickly sought to leverage the Somali adventure into American action in the Balkans. It served as the underlying rationale for America's entire Balkan adventure—to bring to those troubled lands what was hailed as Western-style multiethnic pluralism. Never mind that no Western country hailing such a vision had ever experienced the kinds of ethnic tensions that had roiled the Balkans for centuries or had a demographic map even remotely similar to the Balkan patchwork that perpetuated those ancient hatreds.

Even after September 11, 2001, when one might have expected renewed interest in Samuel Huntington's competing prediction of civilizational clash, the Fukuyama thesis prevailed. It led the Bush administration to view those epochal attacks as the work of an evil few rather than a product of animosities welling up from within an increasingly anti-Western culture. It convinced White House officials that the sentiment driving Muslims to kill Americans through suicide missions could be trumped by the spread of Western democracy in the lands of Islam. It fueled administration confidence that its mission to Iraq would be relatively painless not just because Saddam Hussein lacked a serious military force but because his people avidly would embrace Western democratic principles as soon as America carted them over.

All this turned out to be misguided and for largely the same reason in all instances—namely, the persistent power of culture. The 9/11 attacks should have been enough in themselves to call into question the End of History thesis and to turn thinking instead to the role of culture in driving world events. No developments since 9/11 have served to bolster the thesis that other cultures around the world are ready to embrace Western ideals as their own. And no events have demonstrated in any convincing way that cultural impulses will soon give way to Western universalism in the Middle East or elsewhere. One might think that the Iraq experience would put to the torch once and for all this hoary notion that Western progress applies to all mankind and that the peoples of the world are approaching a day when they all will look at the human experience through the same Western prism.

And yet the fundamental notion of Western universalism just marches on. Currently the neoconservative version is driving events, but a liberal version is waiting in the wings. Humanitarian interventionism of the kind that led us to Somalia stems from the same fundamental concept that we can mold and shape human behavior with the right policies, whether democratic institutions or transfers of wealth to rescue people from poverty. How did these notions become such a powerful American ideology in the post–Cold War era?

The answer lies in the fact that its roots stretch back some eight hundred years, to Roger Bacon's first stirrings of recognition of what became the scientific method. It turned out his perceptions also were the first stirrings of the great Idea of Progress that would develop over the centuries from a dimly perceived sense of cumulative knowledge to an ever expanding notion of man's ability to master his fate through the mastery of his environment. That notion has come down to our day fully loaded with its two contradictions and its mischievous corollary.

Unlike in earlier centuries, progress now is seen as leading to a point of culmination, to some kind of final ideal so fundamental and meaningful that it can justify an audacious label such as "the end of history." That is the first contradiction—that, whereas progress once was considered part of the human condition and hence ongoing so long as man survived on earth, it now has taken on a utopian quality, a conviction that progress is reaching or has reached a final historical end point.

The other contradiction stems from Western man's troubling perception that nearly all the progress since 1500 has been Western progress. This doesn't square with the notion of progress as applying to all mankind, and so the Western mind has conceived a codicil to the Idea of Progress: it will apply to all mankind as soon as the rest of humanity can be brought up to speed. And thus we get the universalist orthodoxy that has become so powerful in American thinking in recent decades.

And then there is, once again, the mischievous corollary—that progress actually can extend to human nature itself, can alter man's behavior based on governmental or other societal structures. Hence, democracy can trump culture in regions of the world without any tradition of democracy because the very democratic institutions themselves will alter people's thinking and behavior in those regions.

These are all deep-seated ideas that have reached the American consciousness after centuries of development in the incubator of

Western thought. Unfortunately, they happen to be largely wrong. The Idea of Progress does not offer an accurate prism through which to view or understand history. The reason most of the progress of the last five hundred years is Western progress is that the West has been in ascendancy during that time. It has dominated the world intellectually, scientifically, economically, and militarily. But not culturally. The West's profound scientific discoveries throughout its ascendancy may have been universal in that other civilizations and cultures could embrace them as they desired. But the West's values, its ideas and ideals, its governmental structures and religious sensibilities—that entire Faustian outlook venerated by Spengler—are not universal. They are distinctly Western, and they will not survive the West after its inevitable decline.

In the meantime, they should be nurtured, protected, defended, and cherished. That requires fostering an appreciation for the Western cultural heritage in the face of the assault that has been waged against it in America for the past generation or more. It requires fostering Western unity across the Atlantic and a shared understanding by Americans and Europeans of what it means to belong to the same civilization. It requires relinquishing the powerful but false idea that Western values represent a universal culture for all mankind and that global harmony will attend the spread of those values. Finally, it requires rejecting Francis Fukuyama's End of History notion that is driving America to its heady new role as Crusader State. America as Crusader State would no longer be the nation that our Founders created and that has thrived so brilliantly and wonderfully upon the earth for the past two hundred years.

NOTES

PAGE

Introduction: The Ozymandias Syndrome

ix   *I met a traveler:* Percy Bysshe Shelley, "Ozymandias," in Oscar Williams (ed.), *Immortal Poems of the English Language* (New York: Washington Square Press, 1952), p. 295.

ix   "the universalization": Francis Fukuyama, "The End of History?," *The National Interest*, Summer 1989 (Special Reprint).

x   "I don't believe": Irving Kristol, "Reply to Fukuyama," *The National Interest*, Summer 1989 (Special Reprint).

x   "consciously intended": Quoted in Samuel P. Huntington, "The Lonely Superpower," *Foreign Affairs*, March/April 1999, p. 35.

x   "vision of democracy": Condoleezza Rice, "Transforming the Middle East," *Washington Post*, August 7, 2003, p. A21.

x   "freedom can be the future": Dana Milbank and Mike Allen, "Bush Urges Commitment to Transform Mideast," *Washington Post*, November 7, 2003.

xi   "No single idea": Robert Nisbet, *History of the Idea of Progress* (New York: Basic, 1980), p. 4.

xii   "between public purpose": Arthur M. Schlesinger, Jr., *The Cycles of American History* (Boston: Houghton Mifflin, 1986), p. 27.

xiv   fifty foreign interventions: Andrew J. Bacevich, *American Empire: The Realities and Consequences of U.S. Diplomacy* (Cambridge: Harvard University Press, 2002), p. 142.

PAGE

Chapter 1: The Idea of Progress

4   "a golden age": J. B. Bury, *The Idea of Progress: An Inquiry into Its Growth and Origin* (New York: Dover, 1955; first published in England in 1920), p. 135.

4   Saint-Pierre observed: Ibid., pp. 137–38.

5   "the omnipotence of government": Ibid., p. 141.

5   "His principles": Ibid.

6   "until [he] had grasped": Quoted in Charles A. Beard, Introduction to 1955 edition of Bury, *The Idea of Progress*, ibid., p. xvi.

6   "a discovery as important": Ibid., p. xvii.

7   "thus leading toward": Nisbet, *History of the Idea of Progress*, p. 5.

8   "The old legend": Bury, *The Idea of Progress*, p. 8.

8   "The theories of Plato": Ibid., pp. 10–11.

8   "Is the idea of progress": Nisbet, *History of the Idea of Progress*, p. 10.

9   "It was this order": Bury, *The Idea of Progress*, p. 19.

9   "So long as the doctrine": Ibid., pp. 21–22.

10   "the spiritual perfection": Nisbet, *History of the Idea of Progress*, p. 47.

10   "What wonderful": Quoted in ibid., p. 55.

11   "announced the idea of Progress": Bury, *The Idea of Progress*, p. 25.

12   "the direct interrogation": Ibid., p. 62.

12   "the first philosopher": Ibid., p. 50.

12   "the endowment of human life": Quoted in ibid., p. 52.

13   Descartes' famous four rules: Nisbet, *History of the Idea of Progress*, p. 116.

13   "supra-human" inquiries: Bury, *The Idea of Progress*, p. 128.

14   "the indefinite malleability": Ibid., p. 65.

14   "This doctrine": Ibid., p. 167.

14   "combinations fatal": Quoted in Nisbet, *History of the Idea of Progress*, p. 244.

15   "If it is good to know": Nisbet, *History of the Idea of Progress*, p. 241.

15   "If you would have": Ibid.

16   "The general tendency of British thought": Bury, *The Idea of Progress*, p. 218.

16   "the sad but instructive monuments": Edmund Burke, *Reflections on the Revolution in France,* reprinted in John Louis Beatty and Oliver A. Johnson (eds.), *Heritage of Western Civilization* (Englewood Cliffs, New Jersey: Prentice Hall, 1958), pp. 506–17.

16   "biblical view": Russell Kirk, *The Roots of American Order* (La Salle, Illinois: Open Court, 1974), p. 29.

16   "Two thousand years later": Ibid., p. 101.

17   "ideal society": Nisbet, *History of the Idea of Progress*, p. 250.

17   "the ultimate result": Quoted in ibid., p. 278.

17   "in necessary, inexorable": Nisbet, *History of the Idea of Progress*, p. 266.

18   "Eurocentric": Ibid., p. 150.

19   "has grown and spread": Ibid., p. 317.

19   five fundamental premises: Ibid.

19   "Each of these premises": Ibid.

Chapter 2: Cycles of History

21   Spengler set out to write: H. Stuart Hughes, *Oswald Spengler: A Critical Estimate* (New York: Charles Scribner's Sons, 1952), p. 6.

22   "Never had a thick": W. Wolfradt, quoted in ibid., p. 89.

22   "Spengler year": Hughes, *Oswald Spengler,* p. 89.

23   disappointment of his early life: John Farrenkopf, *Prophet of Decline: Spengler on World History and Politics* (Baton Rouge: Louisiana State University Press, 2001), pp. 5–12.
23   "has been embarrassed to know": Hughes, *Oswald Spengler*, p. 1.
23   They included George Kennan: Farrenkopf, *Prophet of Decline*, p. 272.
24   "place in modern international theory": Ibid., p. 273.
24   "the essence and kernel": Oswald Spengler, *The Decline of the West*, abridged edition by Helmut Werner, prepared by Arthur Helps from the translation by Charles Francis Atkinson (New York: Modern Library, 1952), p. 6.
24   "'Mankind'": Ibid., p. 17.
24   "I see . . . the drama": Ibid.
25   "Ptolemaic system of history": Ibid., p. 13.
25   "separate worlds": Ibid., p. 14.
25   "Cultures are organisms": Ibid., pp. 71–72.
26   "To the world-city": Ibid., p. 25.
26   "So long as the culture": Hughes, *Oswald Spengler*, p. 72.
26   "Imperialism": Spengler, *The Decline of the West*, p. 28.
27   The Egyptian soul: Ibid., pp. 100–101.
27   Chinese prime symbol: Ibid., p. 102.
28   "The Doric column": Ibid., p. 97.
28   "the plurality of separate bodies": Ibid., p. 99.
28   "The free-standing nude statue": Hughes, *Oswald Spengler*, p. 78.
28   "persistent and unresolved struggles": Spengler, *The Decline of the West*, p. 299.
28   "is simply meaningless": Ibid., p. 301.
28   "In the Magian world": Ibid., p. 305.
29   "pure, imperceptible, unlimited space": Ibid., p. 61.
29   "the Faustian strove": Ibid., p. 130.
29   "In place of the sensuous": Ibid., p. 54.
29   "In it can be felt": Ibid., p. 106.
29   "will to spatial transcendence": Ibid., p. 118.
29   "decisive epochal turn": Ibid., p. 125.
29   "the depth-experience": Ibid.
30   "What relation": Ibid., p. 167.
30   "If, in fine": Ibid., p. 175.
30   "who belongs to herself": Quoted in ibid., p. 251.
31   "the last nation": Spengler, *The Decline of the West*, p. 105.
31   first Englishman: Arthur Herman, *The Idea of Decline in Western History* (New York: Free Press, 1997), p. 256.
31   "firefly flashes": Ibid.
32   "I am conscious": Arnold Toynbee, letter to Gilbert Murray, 1930, quoted in ibid., p. 256.

32   the West was in crisis: Herman, *The Idea of Decline in Western History*, p. 257.

32   "mechanical and material": Quoted in ibid., p. 259.

32   "deteriorate it": Quoted in ibid.

32   "One of these": Herman, *The Idea of Decline in Western History*, p. 261.

33   The older Toynbee: Ibid., pp. 261–64.

33   "was an exfoliation": Whittaker Chambers, "The Challenge," *Time*, March 17, 1947, reprinted in Terry Teachout (ed.), *Ghosts on the Roof: Selected Journalism of Whittaker Chambers, 1931–1959* (Washington, D.C.: Regnery Gateway, 1989), pp. 141–49.

34   Toynbee identifies twenty-one civilizations: Arnold J. Toynbee, *A Study of History*, abridgment of volumes I–VI by D. C. Somervell (New York and London: Oxford University Press, 1947), p. 48.

34   only five had survived: Ibid., p. 8.

34   born of adversity: Ibid., pp. 80–81.

34   "creative minority": Ibid., pp. 230–40.

35   "the creative minority ceases": Chambers, "The Challenge."

35   "a social element": Toynbee, *A Study of History*, p. 377.

35   "universal state": Ibid., p. 548.

35   "schism in the body social": Ibid., chapter heading, p. 371.

35   "schism in the soul": Ibid., chapter heading, p. 429.

35   "general confusion of tongues": Ibid., p. 467.

35   "syncretism of religion": Ibid., p. 473.

36   "one indiscriminate vulgarity": Chambers, "The Challenge."

36   There are the saviors: Toynbee, *A Study of History*, pp. 533–47.

36   "Under God": Chambers, "The Challenge."

36   "displays a greater dogmatism": Hughes, *Oswald Spengler*, p. 140.

37   "The Christian historian": Ibid., p. 141.

37   "he has come to represent": Ibid.

37   "the illusion of progress": Toynbee, *A Study of History*, p. 38.

37   "the misconception": Ibid., p. 37.

37   "While the economic": Ibid., p. 36.

Chapter 3: Globalization and the End of History

39   "How can modern life": Quoted in Thomas L. Friedman, *The Lexus and the Olive Tree: Understanding Globalization* (New York: Farrar, Straus & Giroux, 199), p. 197.

39   "By impressive examples": Barbara W. Tuchman, *The Guns of August* (New York: Bonanza, 1982; originally published by Macmillan, 1962), p. 10. All further quotations from Angell and Esher come from this book.

40   "actually right": Friedman, *The Lexus and the Olive Tree*, p. 197.

40   "the end point": Fukuyama, "The End of History?" All subsequent

Fukuyama quotations in this chapter come from the "End of History?" essay.

41 "the new era of globalization": Friedman, *The Lexus and the Olive Tree,* p. xv.

41 "the first indispensable book": Philip Seib, " 'Olive Tree' Provides Guide to Globalization," *Dallas Morning News,* July 25, 1999, p. 10J.

41 Francis Fukuyama: James Atlas, "What Is Fukuyama Saying? And to Whom Is He Saying It?," *New York Times Magazine,* October 22, 1989, p. 38.

42 "the most unreadable": Kristol, "Reply to Fukuyama." All Kristol quotations in this chapter come from his reply in *The National Interest.*

42 "without question the preeminent philosopher": Nisbet, *History of the Idea of Progress,* p. 276.

42 "In no philosopher": Ibid.

46 The response to all this: Atlas, "What Is Fukuyama Saying?"

46 "outselling everything": Ibid.

47 "pernicious nonsense": Quoted in ibid.

47 "At last, self-congratulation": Quoted in ibid.

47 "Hence conflict": Quoted in ibid.

47 "the predictability of history": Samuel P. Huntington, "No Exit: The Errors of Endism," *The National Interest,* Fall 1989 (Special Reprint).

48 "all the burgeoning global markets": Friedman, *The Lexus and the Olive Tree,* p. 28.

48 "everything that roots us": Ibid., p. 27.

49 "involves the inexorable integration": Ibid., p. 7.

49 "homogenizing": Ibid., p. 8.

49 "That lady": Ibid., p. 285.

49 Friedman background: Thomas L. Friedman, *From Beirut to Jerusalem* (New York: Farrar, Straus & Giroux, 1989), pp. 3–10.

50 "is enabling more and more people": Friedman, *The Lexus and the Olive Tree,* p. 41.

51 "Thanks to satellite dishes": Ibid., p. 54.

51 "any bloated": Ibid., p. 62.

51 "a consistent inability": Ibid.

52 "They offer": Ibid., p. 277.

52 "a high degree of motivation": Ibid., p. 328.

52 "The only defense": Ibid.

52 "The hidden hand": Ibid., p. 373.

53 "I'm not kidding": Ibid., p. 195.

53 "odd position": Ibid., p. 375.

53 "can threaten the stability": Ibid.

53 "tolerable hegemon": Quoted in ibid.

53 "Attention Kmart shoppers": Friedman, *The Lexus and the Olive Tree,* p. 378.

54   "a spiritual value": Ibid.
54   "A healthy global society": Ibid.
55   "It was never the Soviet Union": Quoted in ibid., p. 310.

Chapter 4: The Clash of Civilizations
PAGE

57   "The principal conflicts": Samuel P. Huntington, "The Clash of Civilizations?," *Foreign Affairs*, Summer 1993, p. 22.
58   "Neoconservatives assumed": Robert D. Kaplan, "Looking the World in the Eye," *The Atlantic Monthly*, December 2001, retrieved from www.theatlantic.com.
58   "linear . . . nature": Samuel P. Huntington, *The Clash of Civilizations and the Remaking of World Order* (New York: Simon & Schuster, 1996), p. 55.
59   "the most famous article": Fareed Zakaria, interview with the author, June 1999.
59   twenty-six languages: Kaplan, "Looking the World in the Eye."
59   twenty countries: Huntington, *The Clash of Civilizations*, p. 14.
59   twenty-four languages: Samuel P. Huntington, interview with the author, May 26, 1999.
59   "the most widely read book": Joel Migdal, interview with the author, June 18, 1999.
59   "Clashes of civilizations": Huntington, *The Clash of Civilizations*, p. 321.
59   "Dubious propositions": Jeane Kirkpatrick, "The Modernizing Imperative: Tradition and Change," *Foreign Affairs*, Fall 1993, p. 22.
59   "Misconceived": William Pfaff, "Inevitable Clashes Between Civilizations? Don't Believe It," *International Herald Tribune*, January 23, 1997, p. 8.
59   "threat to peace": Thomas R. DeGregori, "The New World Disorder; Flaws Undermine Controversial Thesis About Conflicts," *Houston Chronicle*, December 29, 1996, p. 22.
60   missed tenure: Huntington interview with the author.
60   He was born in 1927: Ibid. The background material here comes from the same interview unless otherwise noted.
61   Influenced by the thinking of Reinhold Niebuhr: Kaplan, "Looking the World in the Eye."
61   "substantive ideal": Samuel P. Huntington, "Conservatism As an Ideology," *The American Political Science Review*, June 1957, p. 454.
61   "The essence of conservatism": Ibid.
62   "This defense": Ibid.
62   "Conservatism does not ask": Ibid.
62   "a gray island": Huntington, *The Soldier and the State: The Theory and Politics of Civil-Military Relations* (Cambridge: Belknap Press of Harvard University Press, 1957), p. 465.
62   "Today America can learn": Ibid., p. 466.

63   inherently conservative: Ibid., p. 79.
63   "political decay": Samuel P. Huntington, *Political Order in Changing Societies* (New Haven: Yale University Press, 1968), term used in two chapter headings.
64   "The most important political distinction": Ibid., p. 1.
64   "one of the three or four": Zakaria interview with the author.
64   "The American political system": Quoted in Robert D. Putnam, "Samuel P. Huntington: An Appreciation," *Forum*, Fall 1986, p. 837.
65   "a sea of Mexican flags": Huntington, *The Clash of Civilizations*, p. 19.
65   "In the post–Cold War world": Ibid., p. 20.
65   "There can be no true friends": Ibid.
65   "The unfortunate truth": Ibid.
66   *The West is in decline:* Ibid., pp. 82–91.
66   "A central axis": Ibid., p. 29.
66   "Power is shifting": Ibid.
66   "Islamic resurgence": Ibid., p. 109.
67   "No other civilization": Ibid., pp. 53–54.
67   "The intracivilizational clash": Ibid., p. 54.
67   "the widespread and parochial conceit": Ibid., p. 55.
67   "the myopic view": Ibid.
67   "Ptolemaic approach to history": Ibid.
67   "parochialism and impertinence": Ibid.
67   "The West won the world": Ibid., p. 51.
68   "intellectual migrants": Ibid., p. 66.
68   "naïve arrogance": Ibid., p. 58.
68   "What, indeed, does it tell": Ibid.
68   "almost childish": Quoted in ibid., p. 78.
68   "In fundamental ways": Huntington, *The Clash of Civilizations*, p. 78.
69   "with the Cold War over": Friedman, *The Lexus and the Olive Tree*, p. xvii.
69   "The core states": Huntington, *The Clash of Civilizations*, p. 156.
69   "the interaction of Western arrogance": Ibid., p. 183.
69   "tempered and moderated": Ibid., p. 156.
70   "Where core states exist": Ibid., p. 157.
70   "The central issue": Ibid.
70   "concentrated and sustained onslaught": Ibid., p. 305.
70   "promoted racial, ethnic": Ibid.
70   "The contrast": Ibid., pp. 305–6.
71   "assiduously promoted": Ibid., p. 306.
71   "immigrants from other civilizations": Ibid., pp. 304–5.
71   "cleft country": Ibid., p. 305.
71   "The preservation": Ibid., p. 318.
72   Clinton's Balkans readings: Michael Dobbs, "Bosnia Crystallizes U.S. Post–Cold War Role; As Two Administrations Wavered, the Need for U.S. Leadership Became Clear," *Washington Post*, December 3, 1995, p. A1.

72 "the God of hate": Thomas L. Friedman, "Smoking or Non-Smoking?,"
    New York Times, September 14, 2001, p. A27.
73 "Some Westerners": Huntington, *The Clash of Civilizations,* p. 209.

Chapter 5: Isolation and Intervention

74 wounded or possibly even killed: Edward J. Renehan, Jr., *The Lion's
    Pride: Theodore Roosevelt and His Family in Peace and War* (New York and
    Oxford: Oxford University Press, 1998), p. 133.
74 "how glad I would be": Quoted in Kathleen Dalton, *Theodore Roosevelt:
    A Strenuous Life* (New York: Knopf, 2002), pp. 477–78.
76 "as unprotected as a jellyfish": Quoted in Patrick J. Buchanan, *A Repub-
    lic, Not an Empire: Reclaiming America's Destiny* (Washington, D.C.: Reg-
    nery, 1999), p. 146.
76 "I rather hope": Ibid., p. 149.
76 "I refuse to speak": Robert K. Massie, *Dreadnought: Britain, Germany, and
    the Coming of the Great War* (New York: Random House, 1991), p. 239.
76 "We want no wars of conquest": Quoted in Buchanan, *A Republic, Not
    an Empire,* p. 152.
76 "as soft as a chocolate éclair": Quoted in ibid., p. 155.
77 "The guns of Dewey": Quoted in ibid., p. 158.
77 *Take up the White Man's burden:* Quoted in ibid., p. 162.
77 "rather poor poetry": Quoted in ibid.
77 "The fruits of imperialism": Quoted in ibid., p. 159.
77 "We cannot maintain": Quoted in ibid., p. 160.
78 "It is in vain": Quoted in ibid., p. 167.
78 Open Door Notes: Bacevich, *American Empire,* pp. 25–26.
78 "provided the benefits of empire": Ibid., p. 243.
78 "a transitional internationalist": Dalton, *Theodore Roosevelt,* pp.
    242–43.
79 "We stole it fair and square": Quoted in Michael Barone, Grant Ujifusa,
    and Douglas Matthews, *The Almanac of American Politics 1980* (New
    York: Dutton, 1979), p. 52.
79 brutal guerrilla war: Dalton, *Theodore Roosevelt,* pp. 227–28.
79 "We have debauched America's honor": Quoted in ibid., p. 228.
79 "impetuous imperialist": Dalton, *Theodore Roosevelt,* p. 282.
80 "Should a friend disagree with him": Richard M. Watt, *The Kings De-
    part: The Tragedy of Germany: Versailles and the German Revolution* (New
    York: Simon & Schuster, 1968), p. 16.
80 "objectionable personal characteristics": Ibid.
81 "I hope and believe": Quoted in August Heckscher, *Woodrow Wilson*
    (New York: Charles Scribner's Sons, 1991), p. 425.
81 "it was a vague concept": Heckscher, *Woodrow Wilson,* p. 377.
81 "Fair treatment": Ibid., p. 531.

82   "What we demand": Quoted in Watt, *The Kings Depart*, p. 29.
82   "Almost everywhere the 'Fourteen Points'": Watt, *The Kings Depart*, p. 29.
82   "self-determination": Ibid., p. 30.
83   He manipulated neutrality: Buchanan, *A Republic, Not an Empire*, pp. 188–89.
83   "were unmoved by some gauzy vision": Ibid., p. 179.
83   "I must think of": Henry Cabot Lodge, speech delivered in Washington, D.C., August 12, 1919, retrieved from www.firstworldwar.com.
84   "merchants of death": Robert W. Merry, *Taking On the World: Joseph and Stewart Alsop—Guardians of the American Century* (New York: Viking, 1996), p. 57.
84   "We should be prepared": Quoted in James T. Patterson, *Mr. Republican: A Biography of Robert A. Taft* (Boston: Houghton Mifflin, 1972), p. 198.
85   "War is a vain policy": Ibid.
85   "If the English Channel": Ibid., p. 243.
85   86 percent of Americans: Buchanan, *A Republic, Not an Empire*, p. 269.
85   "among the most dishonest": Ibid., p. 270.
85   "global openness": Bacevich, *American Empire*, p. 3.
86   Groton curriculum: Merry, *Taking On the World*, p. 32.
86   abandoned his support: Steve Neal, *Happy Days Are Here Again: The 1932 Democratic Convention, the Emergence of FDR—and How America Was Changed Forever* (New York: Morrow, 2004), pp. 61–62.
87   "I am almost literally": Quoted in Merry, *Taking On the World*, p. 77.
87   "to twist the law": Robert Shogan, *Hard Bargain: How FDR Twisted Churchill's Arm, Evaded the Law, and Changed the Role of the American Presidency* (New York: Scribner, 1995), p. 17.
87   On February 22, 1947: Merry, *Taking On the World*, p. 171.
89   "toward the eternal damnation": Quoted in Stewart Alsop, "Eternal Damnation," *Newsweek*, January 29, 1973, p. 78.
89   "there will be no more": "McGovern Acceptance: 'Choose Life, Not Death,'" *CQ Weekly Report*, July 15, 1972, pp. 1781–82.
89   incinerated 200,000: Merry, *Taking On the World*, p. 513.
91   "The single name": Watt, *The Kings Depart*, p. 13.
91   "The [Wilson] dreams": Ibid., p. 12.

Chapter 6: The Triumph of Wilsonism

97   "precedent": Bruce W. Nelan, "Confronting the Thugs," *Time*, December 14, 1992, p. 26.
99   Powell listed several: Powell, *My American Journey*, p. 425.
100   "a classic assertion": Bacevich, *American Empire*, p. 70.
100   "not contemplating any such action": Powell, *My American Journey*, p. 463.
100   "this will not stand": Ibid., p. 466.

100 "go wobbly": Quoted in Dan Quayle, *Standing Firm: A Vice-Presidential Memoir* (New York: HarperCollins, 1994), p. 212.

101 Only ten Democratic senators: Robert W. Merry, "Pat Buchanan's Push for 'America First,'" *CQ Weekly Report,* November 23, 1991, p. 3498.

101 "He'll have easy access": Quoted in Powell, *My American Journey,* p. 463.

101 "We've got to make": Ibid., p. 464.

102 "Americans don't want": Quoted in Robert W. Merry, "The Imperative of Oil in the Persian Gulf," *CQ Weekly Report,* December 8, 1990, p. 4122.

102 A September poll: cited in Ibid.

102 the voice of Patrick Buchanan: Buchanan, *A Republic, Not an Empire,* pp. 327–28.

103 "The present international scene": Quoted in Bacevich, *American Empire,* p. 76.

103 the "Wolfowitz indiscretion": Ibid., pp. 43–46. Though I used Bacevich as a main source on this episode, he erred in suggesting Wolfowitz actually wrote the policy paper. For fine points, I relied on James Mann, "Larger than Iraq: The True Rationale? It's a Decade Old," *Washington Post,* March 7, 2004, p. B2.

104 "We don't have a dog": Quoted in Bacevich, *American Empire,* p. 68.

104 "a horrific war": Ibid., p. 67.

105 "There is no agreement": Nelan, "Confronting the Thugs."

106 "Clinton's first foreign challenge": *Time,* cover headline, December 21, 1992.

106 "The startling new way": Nelan, "Today Somalia . . . Tomorrow, Why Not Bosnia? The Success of Bush's Mission Could Put Pressure on Clinton to Intervene Elsewhere," *Time,* December 21, 1992.

106 Ostensibly, this mission: Bacevich, *American Empire,* p. 143.

106 "We waded ashore": Charles Krauthammer, "The Immaculate Intervention," *Time,* July 26, 2003, p. 78.

107 Mogadishu debacle: Mark Bowden, *Black Hawk Down: A Story of Modern War* (New York: Penguin, 2000), pp. 331–46.

107 Les Aspin: Bacevich, *American Empire,* p. 146.

108 "when the bombing starts": Quoted in Vin Weber, "Bosnia: Strange Alliances," *National Review,* June 7, 1993, p. 22.

108 "What is viable?": Quoted in ibid.

109 "dares the West": Tom Post, with Joel Brand and Margaret Garrard Warner, "Bosnia Waits for Clinton: A Serb Killing Dares the West to Intervene," *Newsweek,* January 18, 1993, p. 22.

109 "A LESSON IN SHAME": *Time,* headline, August 2, 1993, p. 38.

109 "the West will be tormented": James O. Jackson, "A Lesson in Shame," *Time,* August 2, 1993.

109 newspaper attacked General Colin Powell: Powell, pp. 558–59. All quo-

tations from the Powell speech, the *Times* editorial, and the Powell reply come from this rendition.

110 "Our status": Mark Whitaker, "Getting Tough—At Last," *Newsweek*, May 10, 1993, p. 22.

110 "moral imperative": Bruce W. Nelan, "Reluctant Warrior: Clinton Threatens to Take On the Serbs, but a Wary America Fears a Balkan Quagmire," *Time*, May 17, 1993, p. 26.

110 "A Star Is Born": Fred Barnes, headline over "White House Watch" column, *The New Republic*, May 24, 1993.

110 "let the weenies": Editorial, "Bosnia Boils Over," *National Review*, May 10, 1993, p. 10.

110 "childish": Unsigned "Comment," "Slouching Towards Bosnia," *The New Yorker*, November 8, 1993, p. 8.

111 fully 52 percent opposed: Nelan, "Confronting the Thugs" (poll results interspersed throughout the article).

111 60 percent of respondents opposed: Poll box, *Newsweek*, May 10, 1993, p. 25.

112 "by the nature of": Huntington, *The Soldier and the State*, p. 151.

112 "It is a common observation": Ibid., p. 152.

112 "choose peace": Quoted in ibid., p. 151.

113 "leads to a pacifist strain": Kaplan, "Looking the World in the Eye."

113 "universalization": Fukuyama, "The End of History?"

PAGE   Chapter 7: Balkan Ghosts

114 It was a drizzly spring day: Rebecca West, *Black Lamb and Grey Falcon: A Journey Through Yugoslavia* (New York: Penguin, 1982; first published in the United States by Viking, 1941), pp. 315–16.

115 "none of the men without fezes": Ibid. The rest of this episode is taken from pp. 315–18.

115 "The Turks ruined": Quoted in Robert D. Kaplan, *Balkan Ghosts: A Journey Through History* (New York: St. Martin's, 1993), p. 32.

116 "the Tito-built": Kaplan, *Balkan Ghosts*, p. 40.

116 "Not until I traveled": Ibid., p. 41.

117 Stefan Nemanja: Tim Judah, *The Serbs: History, Myth and the Destruction of Yugoslavia* (New Haven: Yale University Press, 1997), pp. 9, 18–20.

117 Stefan could sign his name: Kaplan, *Balkan Ghosts*, p. 31.

117 "sense of anatomy": Ibid., p. 32.

118 most powerful and most civilized: Ibid., p. 31; Judah, *The Serbs*, p. 25.

118 Lazar as imperial leader: Judah, *The Serbs*, pp. 27–28.

118 "As against their Moslem lords": R. G. D. Laffan, *The Serbs: The Guardians of the Gate* (New York: Dorset, 1989; first published in Great Britain in 1917), p. 22.

118 "Janizaries": West, *Black Lamb and Grey Falcon*, p. 302.

118   harems: Laffan, *The Serbs*, p. 22.
118   three-way choice: Ibid., pp. 22–23.
119   "Bogomils": West, *Black Lamb and Grey Falcon*, pp. 299–301.
119   "The Bosnian Moslems": Ibid., p. 303.
119   "safe-boxes of art and magic": Kaplan, *Balkan Ghosts*, p. 35.
119   "Homeric grandeur": Aleksa Djilas, "Imagining Kosovo: A Biased New Account Fans Western Confusion," *Foreign Affairs*, September/October 1998, p. 124.
120   Lazar chose: Judah, *The Serbs*, pp. 34–37.
120   *All was holy:* Quoted in Kaplan, *Balkan Ghosts*, p. 37.
120   "As the living death": Kaplan, *Balkan Ghosts*, p. 38.
120   "Every [Serbian] peasant soldier": Quoted in ibid., p. 38.
120   Vienna and laid siege: Bernard Lewis, *What Went Wrong? The Clash Between Islam and Modernity in the Middle East* (New York: Perennial, 2003; first published by Oxford University Press, 2002), pp. 11, 16.
120   *Krajina:* Judah, *The Serbs*, pp. 13–16.
120   In 1690: Djilas, "Imagining Kosovo."
121   "no mean thing": Kaplan, *Balkan Ghosts*, p. 25.
122   "burning, indestructible devotion": West, *Black Lamb and Grey Falcon*, pp. 52–53.
122   "idiotically stable": Ibid.
122   "Fear of the East": Kaplan, *Balkan Ghosts*, p. 24.
122   Ivankovac: Judah, *The Serbs*, p. 51.
122   sold into slavery: Ibid., p. 53.
122   1867, and Serbia: Ibid., p. 56.
122   Austro-Hungarian Dual Monarchy: Ibid., p. 59.
123   population in Croatia: Ibid., p. 92.
123   a powerful blow in 1908: Ibid.
124   "full powers": Ibid., p. 98. The World War I history is taken from this book.
124   in October 1918: Ibid., p. 106.
125   "The Yugoslavia that tottered": Ibid., p. 109.
125   Stjepan Radic: Ibid.
125   "one of the most extraordinary feats": West, *Black Lamb and Grey Falcon*, p. 2.
126   three friends: Ibid., pp. 41–43.
126   "quite simply a traitor": Ibid., p. 42.
126   "They greet us": Ibid., p. 43.
127   "Bosnian Muslim anger": Judah, *The Serbs*, p. 112.
127   "In primitive ferocity": Kaplan, *Balkan Ghosts*, p. 5.
127   who pegs the number at sixty thousand: Ibid.
127   Dragnich credits the 700,000 figure: Alex N. Dragnich, *Serbs and Croats: The Struggle in Yugoslavia* (San Diego: Harvest/Harcourt Brace, 1992), p. 103.

127 two credible post–Cold War studies: Judah, *The Serbs*, p. 134.
127 "The Croatian fascists": Kaplan, *Balkan Ghosts*, p. 5.
128 World War I veteran named Draza Mihailovic: Judah, *The Serbs*, pp. 117–24.
128 Tito, half Croat and half Slovene: Ibid., pp. 136–41.
129 "There can be no change": Ibid., p. 140.

Chapter 8: Balkan Tragedy

130 "By the way": Warren Zimmermann, *Origins of a Catastrophe: Yugoslavia and Its Destroyers—America's Last Ambassador Tells What Happened and Why* (New York: Times Books, 1996), p. 8.
130 "This is a story with villains": Ibid., p. vii.
131 "the most successful multiethnic experiment": Ibid., p. 244.
131 "a cancer": Ibid., p. 50.
131 "the arrow that killed Yugoslavia": Ibid., p. 212.
131 "What we witnessed": Ibid., p. 121.
131 "Most of all": Ibid., p. 244.
132 "crippling dependence": William W. Hagen, "The Balkans' Lethal Nationalisms," *Foreign Affairs*, July/August 1999, p. 52. All subsequent Hagen quotations are from this article.
134 Kosovo background: Judah, *The Serbs*, pp. 131, 150.
135 "the Albanian *intifada*": Kaplan, *Balkan Ghosts*, p. 42.
135 "numerous violent incidents": Quoted in Huntington, *The Clash of Civilizations*, p. 261.
135 "They'll never": Quoted in Kaplan, *Balkan Ghosts*, p. 39.
135 "As the crowd roared": Ibid.
135 Muslims who were subjected to abuse: Judah, *The Serbs*, p. 305.
136 Zimmermann . . . declined to attend: Zimmermann, *Origins of a Catastrophe*, p. 19.
136 "truth test": Ibid., p. 80.
136 "one of the few admirable figures": Ibid., p. 43.
137 "Western democratic country": Ibid., p. 45.
137 shock therapy policies: Ibid., pp. 48–49.
137 "the incompatibility of Islam": Quoted in Criton M. Zoakos, "Bosnia, a New World Order and the Shining City," *Polyconomics* newsletter, June 3, 1994.
137 "should be in the hands": Quoted in Huntington, *The Clash of Civilizations*, p. 269.
137 "dreamy": Zimmermann, *Origins of a Catastrophe*, p. 39.
137 population statistics: Dragnich, *Serbs and Croats*, pp. 194–95.
138 arms embargo: Zimmermann, *Origins of a Catastrophe*, p. 155.
138 economic sanctions: Ibid., p. 214.
138 "a coward's war": Judah, *The Serbs*, p. 230.

138   70 percent of the region: Ibid., p. 239.
138   "catastrophe": Ibid., p. 232.
139   crash course: Bacevich, *American Empire*, p. 165.
139   "That was all the time it took": Judah, *The Serbs*, p. 2.
140   Dayton Accords: Ibid., p. 302; Zimmermann, *Origins of a Catastrophe*, pp. 232–33.
140   American policy in the Balkans: Djilas, "Imagining Kosovo," p. 124.
141   a peaceful partition: John J. Mearsheimer and Robert A. Pape, "The Answer: A Partition Plan for Bosnia," *The New Republic*, June 14, 1993, p. 22.
141   "militant, nationalist": Chris Hedges, "Kosovo's Next Masters?," *Foreign Affairs*, May/June 1999, p. 24.
142   What followed was a civil war: Michael Mandelbaum, "A Perfect Failure: NATO's War Against Yugoslavia," *Foreign Affairs*, September/October 1999, p. 2.
142   "the indispensable nation": Quoted in Huntington, "The Lonely Superpower," p. 35.
142   "in a relatively short period": Madeleine Albright, with Bill Woodward, *Madam Secretary: A Memoir* (New York: Miramax, 2003), p. 408.
142   "schoolyard bully": Quoted in Mandelbaum, "A Perfect Failure."
142   bombing of Kosovo: Mandelbaum, "A Perfect Failure."
143   "went the extra mile": Quoted in ibid.
144   In the end America accepted: Mandelbaum, "A Perfect Failure."
144   Further, Mandelbaum argues: Ibid.
145   "objects indispensable": Quoted in ibid.
146   "The war in Yugoslavia": Mandelbaum, "A Perfect Failure."
146   policies of Muslim nationalism: Huntington, *The Clash of Civilizations*, pp. 269–70. This section on Muslim, Orthodox, and Western actions in the Balkans is taken entirely from this book, pp. 269–88.
148   "partial exception": Ibid., pp. 289–91.
148   In March 2004: Nicholas Wood, "NATO Expanding Kosovo Forces to Combat Violence," *New York Times*, March 19, 2004.
148   "an anti-Serb rampage": Christopher Caldwell, "NATO's Kosovo Dream Is Dead," *Financial Times*, March 27/March 28, p. 7. The numbers are all taken from this column.
149   "at the price": Ibid.
149   In Bosnia, radical Muslims: Ilan Berman and Borut Grgic, "A Wider Framework for Security in the Balkans," *Financial Times*, May 17, 2004, p. 13.
149   rarely cooperate: Daniel Williams, "60 Bosnian Serb Officials Fired over War Suspect," *Washington Post*, July 1, 2004, p. A14.
149   fired sixty governmental officials: Ibid.

PAGE   Chapter 9: The Neoconservatives

153 "effective imperial oversight": Max Boot, "The End of Appeasement: Bush's Opportunity to Redeem America's Past Failures in the Middle East," *The Weekly Standard,* February 10, 2003, p. 21.

154 Alcove No. 1: Peter Steinfels, *The Neoconservatives: The Men Who Are Changing America's Politics* (New York: Simon & Schuster, 1979), pp. 81–82.

154 full-throated liberals: Mark Gerson, *The Neoconservative Vision: From the Cold War to the Culture Wars* (Lanham, Maryland: Madison, 1996), p. 20.

154 battle the radical left: Ibid., p. 66.

155 "Jews felt the pain": Ibid., p. 149.

155 "completed their conversion": Henry A. Kissinger, *Years of Renewal* (New York: Simon & Schuster, 1999), p. 106.

155 "C'mon in": Steinfels, *The Neoconservatives,* p. 48.

155 "It took a decade": Gerson, *The Neoconservative Vision,* p. 191.

156 "he's a betting man": Richard Whalen, *Catch the Falling Flag* (Boston: Houghton Mifflin, 1972), p. 159.

156 four essential elements: Gerson, *The Neoconservative Vision,* pp. 16–19.

157 "moral equivalency": Ibid., p. 34.

158 "With individuals born good": Ibid., p. 47.

158 Norman Podhoretz's reaction: Ibid., p. 76.

158 "If we have to make common cause": Quoted in Buchanan, "Going Back to Where They Came From," newspaper column distributed by Creators Syndicate, Inc., April 26, 2004, retrieved from World Net Daily (wnd.com).

159 "There is not one political position": Gerson, *The Neoconservative Vision,* p. 15.

159 administration of Richard Nixon: Kissinger, *Years of Renewal,* pp. 105–12. Much of the analysis of Nixon's presidency comes from the Kissinger memoir cited above, as do all of the Kissinger quotations in this passage.

161 "critically important book": Quoted in Norman Podhoretz, "The Riddle of Ronald Reagan," *The Weekly Standard,* November 9, 1998, p. 22.

161 "crucial ideas": Gerson, *The Neoconservative Vision,* p. 250.

161 "promised to lead us back": Podhoretz, "The Riddle of Ronald Reagan."

161 "began the 1980s": Gerson, *The Neoconservative Vision,* p. 250.

162 "The Neo-Conservative Anguish": Podhoretz, "The Riddle of Ronald Reagan."

162 "enormous opportunity": Ibid.

163 "Tactics bored them": Kissinger, *Years of Renewal,* p. 107.

163 "When the neoconservatives": Ibid.

164 "like so many earlier civilizations": Elmo R. Zumwalt, Jr., *On Watch* (New York: Quadrangle/New York Times, 1976), p. 319.

164 shun exiled Russian dissident Aleksandr Solzhenitsyn: James Mann, *Rise of the Vulcans: The History of Bush's War Cabinet* (New York: Viking, 2004), pp. 64–65.

165 "Now they are all Reaganites": William Kristol, "Morality in Foreign Policy," *The Weekly Standard,* February 10, 2003, p. 7.

165 "Dictatorships and Double Standards": Kirkpatrick, "Dictatorships and Double Standards," reprinted in Mark Gerson (ed.), *The Essential Neoconservative Reader* (New York: Addison-Wesley, 1996), pp. 169–70.

166 "The 'Human Rights' Muddle": Irving Kristol, *Reflections of a Neoconservative: Looking Back, Looking Ahead* (New York: Basic, 1983), p. 269 (originally published in *Wall Street Journal,* 1978).

166 "fundamental fallacy": Ibid., pp. 263–65 (originally published in *Wall Street Journal,* 1980).

168 Professor Leo Strauss: Mann, *Rise of the Vulcans,* pp. 25–29.

169 "remains riven with ethnic hatreds": Robert Kagan, "Cohen and Clinton in Bosnia: A Senseless Bore," *The Weekly Standard,* May 5, 1997, p. 24.

169 "a pogrom": Stephen Schwartz, "Milosevic Murders Again," *The Weekly Standard,* March 23, 1998, p. 27.

169 "hat-in-hand toothlessness": David Tell, for the Editors, "No to Appeasement," *The Weekly Standard,* June 23, 1997, p. 7.

170 "a profoundly unrealistic": Arthur Waldron, "Wishful Thinking on China," *The Weekly Standard,* June 29, 1998, p. 25: "What is required is a realistic sense of China's potentialities, a definition of where we want China to go, and a balanced set of measures, both carrots and sticks, to move things along."

170 "cry out for the sort": Max Boot, "The Case for American Empire: The Most Realistic Response to Terrorism Is for the United States Unambiguously to Embrace Its Imperial Role," *The Weekly Standard,* October 15, 2001, p. 27.

171 "unconditional surrender": Norman Podhoretz, "Syria Yes, Israel No?: Our Anti-Terror Coalition Doesn't Distinguish Friend from Foe," *The Weekly Standard,* November 12, 2001, p. 30.

171 "serious crisis": Frederick W. Kagan, "Afghanistan—and Beyond: A Long-term U.S. Strategy for Central Asia," *The Weekly Standard,* October 22, 2001, p. 14.

171 "And if history repeats itself": Reuel Marc Gerecht, "Regime Change in Iran?: Applying George W. Bush's 'Liberation Theology' to the Mullahs," *The Weekly Standard,* August 5, 2002, p. 30.

172 "Time is not": William Kristol and Robert Kagan, "Going Wobbly?," *The Weekly Standard,* June 3, 2002, p. 11.

172 Beyond Iraq loom: Max Boot, "The End of Appeasement."

PAGE   Chapter 10: The World of Islam

174   "It was not starved": Spengler, *The Decline of the West,* pp. 239–40.

176   "pseudomorphosis": Ibid., p. 268.

176   "The Arabian soul": Ibid., p. 113.

176   "It is the sign": Ibid.

177   "Into these few years": Ibid., p. 114.

177   "a limitless flight": Ibid., pp. 301–2.

177   "The Faustian prime-sacrament": Ibid, p. 303.

177   "My people": Quoted in Spengler, ibid., p. 305.

178   "part of the stock": Spengler, *The Decline of the West,* p. 305.

178   an Egyptian named Sayyid Qutb: Paul Berman, "The Philosopher of Islamic Terror," *New York Times Magazine,* March 23, 2003, p. 25. All further references to Qutb, with the cited exceptions below, come from this excellent article, later part of a book entitled *Terror and Liberalism* (New York: W. W. Norton, 2003).

178   he traveled to America: David Pryce-Jones, *The Closed Circle: An Interpretation of the Arabs* (New York: Harper & Row, 1989), p. 226.

179   Nasser's police state: Ibid., p. 252.

182   most popular figure: Robert Baer, "The Fall of the House of Saud," *The Atlantic Monthly,* May 2003, p. 53.

182   "latterday heirs": Raphael Patai, *The Arab Mind* (New York: Charles Scribner's Sons, 1973; updated edition, 1983), p. 73.

183   values and customs: Ibid., pp. 84–96.

183   preservation of self-respect: Ibid., p. 100.

183   "Honor is what makes": Pryce-Jones, *The Closed Circle,* p. 35.

184   *asabiyya:* Patai, *The Arab Mind,* pp. 93–94.

184   greatest adhesive: Quoted in ibid., p. 93.

184   "Shame and honor": Pryce-Jones, *The Closed Circle,* p. 36.

184   "commonplace": Ibid., p. 37.

184   *sharaf* and *ird:* Patai, *The Arab Mind,* pp. 120–25.

185   "a pre-Islamic concept": Ibid., p. 125.

185   This is manifest in breast-feeding practices: Ibid., pp. 30–32.

185   "simply adds": Pryce-Jones, *The Closed Circle,* p. 31.

185   "power-challenge dialectic": Ibid., p. 25.

186   "absolute and despotic rule": Ibid., p. 26.

186   "alpha and omega": Quoted in ibid., p. 27.

186   "My brothers and myself": Patai, *The Arab Mind,* p. 21.

187   "In civilizational conflicts": Huntington, *The Clash of Civilizations,* p. 217.

187   "The president has continually": Mark Kukis, "Bin Laden's Growing Appeal," *National Journal,* July 5, 2003, p. 2188.

188   Robert Baer writes: Baer, "The Fall of the House of Saud."

189   Huntington quotes extensively: Huntington, *The Clash of Civilizations,* pp. 212–14.

190 "intercivilizational quasi war": Ibid., pp. 216–17.
190 "The underlying problem": Ibid., pp. 217–18.
190 forty "experts": Sydney J. Freedberg, Jr., "The War Within Islam," *National Journal*, May 10, 2003, p. 1444.
191 "Wow, Islam": Thomas L. Friedman, "War of Ideas, Part 6," *New York Times*, January 25, 2004, p. 15.
191 "Davos Culture": Huntington, *The Clash of Civilizations*, p. 57.

Chapter 11: War

193 "It is the policy of the United States": George W. Bush, second inaugural address, reprinted in *CQ Weekly*, January 24, 2005.
196 "democratic imperialists": Stephen Fidler and Gerard Baker, "America's Democratic Imperialists: How the Neo-conservatives Rose from Humility to Empire in Two Years," *Financial Times*, March 6, 2003, p. 11.
197 "Powell's underlying rationale": Mann, *The Rise of the Vulcans*, p. 350.
197 the Powell Doctrine: Ibid., p. 119.
198 "Backseat": Ibid., p. 59.
198 Cheney's conservatism: Ibid., pp. 72–73, 97.
198 "9/11 changed everything": Mark Hosenball, Michael Isikoff, and Evan Thomas, "Cheney's Long Path to War," *Newsweek*, November 17, 2003, p. 36.
198 "The era of optional war is over": Kenneth T. Walsh, "The Man Behind the President," *U.S. News & World Report*, October 13, 2003, p. 25.
198 "unconventional": Ibid.
200 Wolfowitz offered a critique of Kissinger's: Mann, *The Rise of the Vulcans*, pp. 75–76.
200 The real hero: Will Durant and Ariel Durant, *The Age of Napoleon* (New York: Simon & Schuster, 1975), pp. 732–33.
200 "I remember him saying": Mann, *The Rise of the Vulcans*, p. 76.
201 "It is important to note": Hosenball et al., "Cheney's Long Path to War."
201 rise of various neoconservative figures: Richard J. Whalen, "Republicans: Cheney the Radical," *The Big Picture* (private newsletter), December 1, 2003, p. 9.
201 1992 Defense Planning Guidance: Mann, "Larger than Iraq," p. B2. All subsequent quotations on this episode come from this article.
204 "He was": David Halberstam, *The Best and the Brightest* (New York: Random House, 1972), p. 306.
204 The war was justified: Carl M. Cannon, "What Bush Said," *National Journal*, July 26, 2003, p. 3.
204 George Tenet felt obliged to correct Cheney: Douglas Jehl, "C.I.A. Chief Says He's Corrected Cheney Privately," *New York Times*, March 10, 2004, p. 1.

204 "no terrorist state": Unsigned column item, "Face the Music," *The New Republic,* March 9, 2004, p. 10.

204 "I really believe": Hosenball et al., "Cheney's Long Path to War."

205 "Wildly off the mark": Albert R. Hunt, "What Might Have Been," *Wall Street Journal,* December 4, 2003, p. A17.

205 "a couple of divisions": Ibid.

205 Cheney had met Chalabi: Whalen, "Republicans."

205 Chalabi and some four hundred supporters: Robin Wright, "Standing of Former Key U.S. Ally in Iraq Falls to New Low," *Washington Post,* May 21, 2004, p. A20; David E. Sanger, "A Seat of Honor Lost to Open Political Warfare," *New York Times,* May 21, 2004, p. 1.

206 "He was jeered": Quoted in Wright, "Standing of Former Key U.S. Ally Falls."

206 embroiled in an investigation: Jane Mayer, "The Manipulator," *The New Yorker,* June 7, 2004, p. 58.

206 Cheney told Powell: Walsh, "The Man Behind the President."

206 "classical guerrilla-type": Vernon Loeb, "'Guerrilla' War Acknowledged," *Washington Post,* July 17, 2003, p. 1.

206 "much better": Eric Schmitt, "Wolfowitz Sees Challenges, and Vindication, in Iraq," *New York Times,* July 22, 2003, p. A8.

207 "It's approximately 500": Yochi J. Dreazen and Greg Jaffe, "Fallujah Pullback May Be in Sight as Marines Work Toward Accord," *Wall Street Journal,* April 30, 2004, p. A13.

208 "Our armies do not come": John Kifner, "Britain Tried First. Iraq Was No Picnic Then," *New York Times Week in Review,* July 20, 2003, p. 1. My account of the British in Iraq is taken from this article.

209 The Iraqi death toll: Sandra Mackey, *The Reckoning: Iraq and the Legacy of Saddam Hussein* (New York: Norton, 2002), p. 110.

209 As Sandra Mackey explains: Ibid., pp. 59–60.

209 "have fed much": Ibid., p. 66.

209 "The result": Ibid., p. 69.

210 "Arabism": Ibid., p. 32.

210 Thus, the old Sunni families: Ibid., p. 94.

211 "We do not seem to be willing": Patrick Lang, "A Primer on Iraqi 'Politics,'" *The Big Picture* (private newsletter), January 25, 2005.

212 "Immediately after the boot": Makey, *The Reckoning,* pp. 28–29.

Chapter 12: Ghosts of Mithridates

217 It was around 88 B.C.: Will Durant, *Caesar and Christ* (New York: Simon & Schuster, 1944), pp. 516–19.

218 "What word": Michael Ignatieff, "The American Empire (Get Used to It)," *New York Times Magazine,* January 5, 2003, p. 22.

219 "a typical oriental barbarian": Philip Van Ness Myers, *Rome: Its Rise and Fall* (Boston: Ginn & Company, 1902), p. 247.

219 "dressed in skins" and the following account: Durant, *Caesar and Christ*, pp. 517–18.

221 "the ultimate benign hegemon": Friedman, *The Lexus and the Olive Tree*, p. 375.

221 "Why should a republic": Ignatieff, "The American Empire."

221 "A republic, madam": Quoted in Walter Isaacson, *Benjamin Franklin: An American Life* (New York: Simon & Schuster, 2003), p. 459.

222 "catastrophe": Kenneth H. Bacon, "Hiding Death in Darfur," manuscript shared with the author, later published in the *Columbia Journalism Review*.

223 three key elements: Mann, *The Rise of the Vulcans*, pp. 328–31.

224 "decades if not centuries": Kirkpatrick, "Dictatorships and Double Standards," reprinted in Gerson (ed.), *The Essential Neoconservative Reader*, pp. 163–89.

224 And Huntington, writing in 1993: Huntington, "Challenges Facing Democracy: What Cost Freedom?," *ASAP*, June 1993.

Chapter 13: Conservative Interventionism

232 "crushing superiority of equipment": Quoted in David M. Kennedy, *Freedom from Fear: The American People in Depression and War, 1929–1945* (New York and Oxford: Oxford University Press, 1999), p. 618.

232 "stupendous Niagara of numbers": Ibid., p. 655.

234 not enemies of the United States: Robert Dujarric, "America Needs Arab Help to Beat al-Qaeda," *Financial Times*, November 10, 2003, p. 13.

237 agents and jihadists: Richard Whalen, "Iraq: De Facto Breakup Accelerates; U.S. Secretly Seeks Iran's Aid," *The Big Picture* (private newsletter), April 20, 2004, p. 6.

238 Shi'ite "federation": Richard Whalen, "Iraq's Future—and Iran's," *The Big Picture* (private newsletter), June 7, 2004, p. 5.

238 nuclear club: Ibid., p. 7.

238 "The future configuration": Ibid.

238 "As a European power": Bush speech in Istanbul, June 29, 2004, www.whitehouse.gov.

239 "torn country": Huntington, *The Clash of Civilizations*, pp. 148–49.

239 "At some point": Ibid., p. 178.

239 "Americans should recognize": Buchanan, *The Death of the West: How Dying Populations and Immigrant Invasions Imperil Our Country and Civilization* (New York: Thomas Dunne Books/St. Martin's, 2002), p. 106.

239 "managed democracy": Andrew Higgins, "Democracy Deferred: Re-

form in Russia: Free Market, Yes; Free Politics, Maybe," *Wall Street Journal*, May 24, 2004, p. 1.

240 serious regional power: Janusz Bugajski, "Russia's New Europe," *The National Interest*, Winter 2003–2004, p. 84.

240 "imperative for security": Quoted in William Safire, "Putin's 'Creeping Coup,'" *New York Times*, February 9, 2004, p. A27.

240 "creeping coup": Ibid.

240 "As its role becomes global": Safire, "Putin's 'Creeping Coup.'"

241 "Mr. Putin is clearly in sync": Higgins, "Democracy Deferred."

241 Russian polls: Richard Pipes, "Flight from Freedom: What Russians Think and Want," *Foreign Affairs*, May/June 2004, p. 9.

241 "democracy is widely viewed as a fraud": Ibid.

241 pipeline for weapons and warriors: Private conversation with a CIA operative.

242 China's goals: Huntington, *The Clash of Civilizations*, p. 168.

242 "strategic competitor": Quoted in James Harding and Peter Spiegel, "US National Security: 'Bush Has Been Forced to Moderate His Rhetoric, but He Has Yet to Come to Grips with a Clear Policy on China,'" *Financial Times*, October 17, 2003, p. 13.

242 Andrew Marshall: Ibid.

243 "Old Europe": Quoted in James Kitfield, "Damage Control: Still Reeling from the Rift over Iraq, the Western Alliance Is Trying to Patch Things Up," *National Journal*, July 19, 2003, p. 2336.

243 "progressive erosion": Henry A. Kissinger, "Repairing the Atlantic Alliance," *Washington Post*, April 14, 2003, p. A17.

243 "To the list of polities": Quoted in Timothy Garton Ash, "Anti-Europeanism in America," *Hoover Digest*, 2003, No. 2, p. 141.

243 "moral compass": Ibid.

243 "is becoming our enemy": Thomas L. Friedman, "Our War with France," *New York Times*, September 18, 2003, p. A27.

243 "Europeans are": Ash, "Anti-Europeanism in America."

244 "It is time to stop pretending": Robert Kagan, *Of Paradise and Power: America and Europe in the New World Order* (New York: Knopf, 2003), p. 3.

244 "perpetual peace": Ibid.

244 "all but destroyed": Ibid., p. 16.

244 "extraordinary": Ibid., pp. 77–78.

244 "Almost": Ibid.

245 "faith in the perfectibility of man": Quoted in ibid., p. 79.

245 "This is important": Kagan, *Of Paradise and Power*, p. 79.

246 three rationales: Paul Starobin, "The French Were Right," *National Journal*, November 8, 2003, p. 3406.

246 "disaggregation": Timothy Garton Ash, "Are You with Us? Are We Against You?," *New York Times*, May 30, 2003, p. A29.

247   "Messrs Cheney and Rumsfeld": Philip Stephens, "Europe's Defence Plans Are Worth Fighting For," *Financial Times*, October 17, 2003, p. 15.

247   six million to seven million Muslims: Jim Hoagland, "In Europe, the Enemy Within," *Washington Post*, February 26, 2004, p. A21. Europeans and Muslims information is from this article.

248   hundreds of mosques: Susan Schmidt, "Spreading Saudi Fundamentalism in U.S.: Network of Wahhabi Mosques, Schools, Web Sites Probed by FBI," *Washington Post*, October 2, 2003, p. 1.

248   "But then I realized": John Leland, "Tensions in a Michigan City over Muslims' Call to Prayer," *New York Times*, May 5, 2004, p. A16.

Conclusion: Disavowing the Crusader State

PAGE

251   "But the central point": Robert Kagan, *Of Paradise and Power*, p. 81.

BIBLIOGRAPHY

Books

Albright, Madeleine, with Bill Woodward. *Madam Secretary: A Memoir*. New York: Miramax, 2003.

Bacevich, Andrew J. *American Empire: The Realities and Consequences of U.S. Diplomacy*. Cambridge: Harvard University Press, 2002.

Baer, Robert. *Sleeping with the Devil: How Washington Sold Our Soul for Saudi Crude*. New York: Crown, 2003.

Barone, Michael, Grant Ujifusa, and Douglas Matthews. *The Almanac of American Politics 1980*. New York: Dutton, 1979.

Beatty, John Louis, and Oliver A. Johnson (eds.). *Heritage of Western Civilization*. Englewood Cliffs, New Jersey: Prentice Hall, 1958.

Blackman, Ann. *Seasons of Her Life: A Biography of Madeleine Korbel Albright*. New York: Scribner, 1998.

Bowden, Mark. *Black Hawk Down: A Story of Modern War*. New York: Penguin, 2000.

Braudel, Fernand. *On History* (translated by Sarah Matthews). Chicago: University of Chicago Press, 1980.

Buchanan, Patrick J. *A Republic, Not an Empire: Reclaiming America's Destiny*. Washington: Regnery, 1999.

———. *The Death of the West: How Dying Populations and Immigrant Invasions Imperil Our Country and Civilization*. New York: Thomas Dunne Books/St. Martin's, 2002.

Burnham, James. *The Suicide of the West: An Essay on the Meaning and Destiny of Liberalism*. New York: John Day, 1964.

Bury, J. B. *The Idea of Progress: An Inquiry into Its Growth and Origin*. New York: Dover, 1955; first published in England in 1920.

Chambers, Whittaker. *Ghosts on the Roof: Selected Journalism of Whittaker Chambers, 1931–1959* (edited by Terry Teachout). Washington, D.C.: Regnery Gateway, 1989.

Coon, Carlton S. *Caravan: The Story of the Middle East*. New York: Holt, 1951.

Dalton, Kathleen. *Theodore Roosevelt: A Strenuous Life*. New York: Knopf, 2002.

Diggins, John P. *Up from Communism: Conservative Odysseys in American Intellectual History*. New York: Harper & Row, 1975.

Dragnich, Alex N. *Serbs and Croats: The Struggle in Yugoslavia*. San Diego: Harvest/Harcourt Brace, 1992.

Durant, Will. *Caesar and Christ*. New York: Simon & Schuster, 1944.

Durant, Will and Ariel. *The Age of Napoleon*. New York: Simon & Schuster, 1975.

Farrenkopf, John. *Prophet of Decline: Spengler on World History and Politics*. Baton Rouge: Louisiana State University Press, 2001.

Friedman, Thomas L. *From Beirut to Jerusalem*. New York: Farrar, Straus & Giroux, 1989.

———. *The Lexus and the Olive Tree: Understanding Globalization*. New York: Farrar, Straus & Giroux, 1999.

Fukuyama, Francis. *The End of History and the Last Man*. New York: Free Press, 1992.

Gerson, Mark. *The Neoconservative Vision: From the Cold War to the Culture Wars*. Lanham, Maryland: Madison, 1996.

Gerson, Mark (ed.). *The Essential Neoconservative Reader*. New York: Addison-Wesley, 1996.

Gilfond, Henry. *Black Hand at Sarajevo: The Conspiracy That Plunged the World into War*. Indianapolis: Bobbs-Merrill, 1975.

Glass, Charles. *Tribes with Flags: A Dangerous Passage Through the Chaos of the Middle East*. New York: Atlantic Monthly Press, 1990.

Halberstam, David. *The Best and the Brightest*. New York: Random House, 1972.

Heckscher, August. *Woodrow Wilson*. New York: Charles Scribner's Sons, 1991.

Herman, Arthur. *The Idea of Decline in Western History*. New York: Free Press, 1997.

Hughes, H. Stuart. *Oswald Spengler: A Critical Estimate*. New York: Charles Scribner's Sons, 1952.

Huntington, Samuel P. *The Soldier and the State: The Theory and Politics of Civil-Military Relations*. Cambridge: Belknap Press of Harvard University Press, 1957.

———. *Political Order in Changing Societies*. New Haven: Yale University Press, 1968.

———. *The Clash of Civilizations and the Remaking of World Order*. New York: Simon & Schuster, 1996.

———. *Who Are We? The Challenges to America's National Identity*. New York: Simon & Schuster, 2004.

Isaacson, Walter. *Benjamin Franklin: An American Life*. New York: Simon & Schuster, 2003.

Judah, Tim. *The Serbs: History, Myth and the Destruction of Yugoslavia*. New Haven: Yale University Press, 1997.

Kagan, Robert. *Of Paradise and Power: America and Europe in the New World Order*. New York: Knopf, 2003.

Kaplan, Robert D. *Balkan Ghosts: A Journey Through History.* New York: St. Martin's, 1993.

Kempe, Frederick. *Divorcing the Dictator: America's Bungled Affair with Noriega.* New York: G. P. Putnam's Sons, 1990.

Kennedy, David M. *Freedom from Fear: The American People in Depression and War, 1929–1945.* New York and Oxford: Oxford University Press, 1999.

Kirk, Russell. *The Roots of American Order.* La Salle, Illinois: Open Court, 1974.

Kissinger, Henry A. *A World Restored: The Politics of Conservatism in a Revolutionary Age.* New York: Universal Library/Grosset & Dunlap, 1964.

———. *Years of Renewal.* New York: Simon & Schuster, 1999.

Kristol, Irving. *Reflections of a Neoconservative: Looking Back, Looking Ahead.* New York: Basic, 1983.

Laffan, R. G. D. *The Serbs: The Guardians of the Gate.* New York: Dorset, 1989; first published in Great Britain in 1917.

Lewis, Bernard. *What Went Wrong? The Clash Between Islam and Modernity in the Middle East.* New York: Perennial, 2003; first published by Oxford University Press, 2002.

Mackey, Sandra. *The Reckoning: Iraq and the Legacy of Saddam Hussein.* New York: Norton, 2002.

Mann, James. *Rise of the Vulcans: The History of Bush's War Cabinet.* New York: Viking, 2004.

Massie, Robert K. *Dreadnought: Britain, Germany, and the Coming of the Great War.* New York: Random House, 1991.

Merry, Robert W. *Taking On the World: Joseph and Stewart Alsop—Guardians of the American Century.* New York: Viking, 1996.

Myers, Philip Van Ness. *Rome: Its Rise and Fall.* Boston: Ginn & Company, 1902.

Neal, Steve. *Happy Days Are Here Again: The 1932 Democratic Convention, the Emergence of FDR—and How America Was Changed Forever.* New York: Morrow, 2004.

Nisbet, Robert. *History of the Idea of Progress.* New York: Basic, 1980.

Nye, Joseph S., Jr. *The Paradox of American Power: Why the World's Only Superpower Can't Go It Alone.* Oxford: Oxford University Press, 2002.

Patai, Raphael. *The Arab Mind.* New York: Charles Scribner's Sons, 1973; updated edition, 1983.

Patterson, James T. *Mr. Republican: A Biography of Robert A. Taft.* Boston: Houghton Mifflin, 1972.

Plutarch. *Plutarch's Lives, Vol. I.* New York: Modern Library, 2001.

Powell, Colin, with Joseph E. Persico. *My American Journey.* New York: Random House, 1995.

Pryce-Jones, David. *The Closed Circle: An Interpretation of the Arabs.* New York: Harper & Row, 1989.

Quayle, Dan. *Standing Firm: A Vice-Presidential Memoir.* New York: HarperCollins, 1994.

Renehan, Edward J., Jr. *The Lion's Pride: Theodore Roosevelt and His Family in Peace and War.* New York and Oxford: Oxford University Press, 1998.

Schevill, Ferdinand. *A History of the Balkans.* New York: Dorset, 1991.

Schlesinger, Arthur M., Jr. *The Cycles of American History.* New York: Houghton Mifflin, 1986.

Shepherd, William R. *Shepherd's Historical Atlas.* 9th edition. New York: Barnes & Noble, 1964.

Shogan, Robert. *Hard Bargain: How FDR Twisted Churchill's Arm, Evaded the Law, and Changed the Role of the American Presidency.* New York: Scribner, 1995.

Spengler, Oswald. *The Decline of the West.* (Abridged edition by Helmut Werner; English abridged edition prepared by Arthur Helps from the translation by Charles Francis Atkinson.) New York: Modern Library, 1965.

Steinfels, Peter. *The Neoconservatives: The Men Who Are Changing America's Politics.* New York: Simon & Schuster, 1979.

Toynbee, Arnold J. *A Study of History.* (Abridgment of Volumes I–VI by D. C. Somervell.) New York and London: Oxford University Press, 1947.

Tuchman, Barbara W. *The Guns of August.* New York: Bonanza, 1982; originally published by Macmillan, 1962.

Watt, Richard M. *The Kings Depart: The Tragedy of Germany: Versailles and the German Revolution.* New York: Simon & Schuster, 1968.

West, Rebecca. *Black Lamb and Grey Falcon: A Journey Through Yugoslavia.* New York: Penguin, 1982; first published in the United States by Viking, 1941.

Whalen, Richard J. *Catch the Falling Flag.* Boston: Houghton Mifflin, 1972.

White, William S. *The Taft Story.* New York: Harper & Brothers, 1954.

Williams, Oscar (ed.). *Immortal Poems of the English Language.* New York: Washington Square Press, 1952.

Winik, Jay. *On the Brink: The Dramatic Behind-the-Scenes Saga of the Reagan Era and the Men and Women Who Won the Cold War.* New York: Simon & Schuster, 1996.

Zimmermann, Warren. *Origins of a Catastrophe: Yugoslavia and Its Destroyers—America's Last Ambassador Tells What Happened and Why.* New York: Times Books, 1996.

Zumwalt, Elmo R., Jr. *On Watch.* New York: Quadrangle/New York Times, 1976.

Magazine and Journal Articles

Alsop, Stewart. "Eternal Damnation." *Newsweek,* January 29, 1973.

Ash, Timothy Garton. "Anti-Europeanism in America." *Hoover Digest,* 2003, No. 2, p. 141.

Atlas, James. "What Is Fukuyama Saying? And to Whom Is He Saying It?" *New York Times Magazine,* October 22, 1989.

Bacon, Kenneth H. "Hiding Death in Darfur." Manuscript.

Baer, Robert. "The Fall of the House of Saud." *The Atlantic Monthly*, May 2003.

Barnes, Fred. "A Star Is Born." *The New Republic*, May 24, 1993.

Berman, Paul. "The Philosopher of Islamic Terror." *New York Times Magazine*, March 23, 2003.

Boot, Max. "The Case for American Empire: The Most Realistic Response to Terrorism Is for the United States Unambiguously to Embrace Its Imperial Role." *The Weekly Standard*, October 15, 2001.

———. "The End of Appeasement: Bush's Opportunity to Redeem America's Past Failures in the Middle East." *The Weekly Standard*, February 10, 2003.

"Bosnia Boils Over." *National Review*, May 10, 1993.

Bugajski, Janusz. "Russia's New Europe." *The National Interest*, Winter 2003–2004, p. 84.

Cannon, Carl. "What Bush Said." *National Journal*, July 26, 2003.

Ceaser, James W. "O, My America: The Clash of Huntingtons." *The Weekly Standard*, May 3, 2004.

Djilas, Aleksa. "Imagining Kosovo: A Biased New Account Fans Western Confusion." *Foreign Affairs*, September/October 1998.

"Face the Music." *The New Republic*, March 9, 2004.

Freedberg, Sydney J., Jr. "The War Within Islam." *National Journal*, May 10, 2003.

Fukuyama, Francis. "The End of History?" *The National Interest*, Summer 1989.

Gerecht, Reuel Marc. "Regime Change in Iran: Applying George W. Bush's 'Liberation Theology' to the Mullahs." *The Weekly Standard*, August 5, 2002.

Hagen, William W. "The Balkans' Lethal Nationalisms." *Foreign Affairs*, July/August 1999.

Hedges, Chris. "Kosovo's Next Masters?" *Foreign Affairs*, May/June 1999.

Hosenball, Mark, Michael Isikoff, and Evan Thomas. "Cheney's Long Path to War." *Newsweek*, November 17, 2003.

Huntington, Samuel P. "Conservatism As an Ideology." *The American Political Science Review*, June 1957.

———. "No Exit: The Errors of Endism." *The National Interest*, Fall 1989 (Special Reprint).

———. "Challenges Facing Democracy: What Cost Freedom?" *ASAP*, June 1993.

———. "The Clash of Civilizations?" *Foreign Affairs*, Summer 1993.

———. "The Lonely Superpower." *Foreign Affairs*, March/April 1999.

Ignatieff, Michael. "The American Empire (Get Used to It)." *New York Times Magazine*, January 5, 2003.

Jackson, James O. "A Lesson in Shame." *Time*, August 2, 1993.

Kagan, Frederick W. "Afghanistan—and Beyond: A Long-term U.S. Strategy for Central Asia." *The Weekly Standard,* October 22, 2001.

Kagan, Robert. "Cohen and Clinton in Bosnia: A Senseless Bore." *The Weekly Standard,* May 5, 1997.

Kaplan, Robert D. "Looking the World in the Eye." *The Atlantic Monthly,* December 2001.

Kirkpatrick, Jeane. "The Modernizing Imperative: Tradition and Change." *Foreign Affairs,* Fall 1993.

Kissinger, Henry A. "Between the Old Left and the New Right." *Foreign Affairs,* May/June 1999.

Kitfield, James. "Damage Control: Still Reeling from the Rift over Iraq, the Western Alliance Is Trying to Patch Things Up." *National Journal,* July 19, 2003, p. 2336.

Krauthammer, Charles. "The Immaculate Intervention." *Time,* July 26, 2003.

Kristol, Irving. "Reply to Fukuyama." *The National Interest,* Summer 1989 (Special Reprint).

Kristol, William. "Morality in Foreign Policy." *The Weekly Standard,* February 10, 2003.

Kristol, William, and Robert Kagan. "Going Wobbly?" *The Weekly Standard,* June 3, 2002.

Kukis, Mark. "Bin Laden's Growing Appeal." *National Journal,* July 5, 2003.

Leo, John. "Ignoring Radical Racialism." *U.S. News & World Report,* September 15, 2003.

Mandelbaum, Michael. "A Perfect Failure: NATO's War Against Yugoslavia." *Foreign Affairs,* September/October 1999.

Mayer, Jane. "The Manipulator." *The New Yorker,* June 7, 2004.

"McGovern Acceptance: 'Choose Life, Not Death.'" *CQ Weekly Report,* July 15, 1972.

Mearsheimer, John J., and Robert A. Pape. "The Answer: A Partition Plan for Bosnia." *The New Republic,* June 14, 1993.

Menand, Louis. "Patriot Games: The New Nativism of Samuel P. Huntington." *The New Yorker,* May 17, 2004.

Merry, Robert W. "The Imperative of Oil in the Persian Gulf." *CQ Weekly Report,* December 8, 1990.

———. "Pat Buchanan's Push for 'America First.'" *CQ Weekly Report,* November 23, 1991.

Nelan, Bruce W. "Confronting the Thugs." *Time,* December 14, 1992.

———. "Today Somalia . . . Tomorrow, Why Not Bosnia? The Success of Bush's Mission Could Put Pressure on Clinton to Intervene Elsewhere." *Time,* December 21, 1992.

———. "Reluctant Warrior: Clinton Threatens to Take On the Serbs, but a Wary America Fears a Balkan Quagmire." *Time,* May 17, 1993.

Pipes, Richard. "Flight from Freedom: What Russians Think and Want." *Foreign Affairs,* May/June 2004, p. 9.

Podhoretz, Norman. "The Riddle of Ronald Reagan." *The Weekly Standard,* November 9, 1998.

———. "Syria Yes, Israel No?: Our Anti-Terror Coalition Doesn't Distinguish Friend from Foe." *The Weekly Standard,* November 12, 2001.

Post, Tom, with Joel Brand and Margaret Garrard Warner. "Bosnia Waits for Clinton: A Serb Killing Dares the West to Intervene." *Newsweek,* January 18, 1993.

Putnam, Robert D. "Samuel P. Huntington: An Appreciation." *Forum,* Fall 1986.

Schwartz, Stephen. "Milosevic Murders Again." *The Weekly Standard,* March 23, 1998.

"Slouching Towards Bosnia." *The New Yorker,* November 8, 1993.

Starobin, Paul. "The French Were Right." *National Journal,* November 8, 2003, p. 3406.

Tell, David. "No to Appeasement." *The Weekly Standard,* June 23, 1997.

Waldron, Arthur. "Wishful Thinking on China." *The Weekly Standard,* June 29, 1998.

Walsh, Kenneth T.. "The Man Behind the President." *U.S. News & World Report,* October 13, 2003.

Weber, Vin. "Bosnia: Strange Alliances." *National Review,* June 7, 1993.

Whalen, Richard J. "Republicans: Cheney the Radical." *The Big Picture* (private newsletter), December 1, 2003.

———. "Iraq: De Facto Breakup Accelerates; U.S. Secretly Seeks Iran's Aid." *The Big Picture* (private newsletter), April 20, 2004.

———. "Iraq's Future—and Iran's." *The Big Picture* (private newsletter), June 7, 2004.

Whitaker, Mark. "Getting Tough—At Last." *Newsweek,* May 10, 1993.

Wolfe, Alan. "Native Son: Samuel Huntington Defends the Homeland." *Foreign Affairs,* May/June 2004.

Zoakos, Criton M. "Bosnia, a New World Order and the Shining City." *Polyconomics* (newsletter), June 3, 1994.

Newspaper Articles

Ash, Timothy Garton. "Are You with Us? Are We Against You?" *New York Times,* May 30, 2003, p. A29.

Berman, Ilan, and Borut Grgic. "A Wider Framework for Security in the Balkans." *Financial Times,* May 17, 2004.

Brooks, David. "The Americano Dream." *New York Times,* February 24, 2004.

Buchanan, Patrick J. "Going Back to Where They Came From." Creators Syndicate, Inc., April 26, 2004, posted on World Net Daily (wnd.com).

Caldwell, Christopher. "NATO's Kosovo Dream Is Dead." *Financial Times,* March 27/March 28.

DeGregori, Thomas R. "The New World Disorder; Flaws Undermine Controversial Thesis About Conflicts." *Houston Chronicle,* December 29, 1996.

Dobbs, Michael. "Bosnia Crystallizes U.S. Post–Cold War Role; As Two Administrations Wavered, the Need for U.S. Leadership Became Clear." *Washington Post,* December 3, 1995.

Dreazen, Yochi J., and Greg Jaffe. "Fallujah Pullback May Be in Sight as Marines Work Toward Accord." *Wall Street Journal,* April 30, 2004.

Dujarric, Robert. "America Needs Arab Help to Beat al-Qaeda." *Financial Times,* November 10, 2003, p. 13.

Fidler, Stephen, and Gerard Baker. "America's Democratic Imperialists: How the Neo-conservatives Rose from Humility to Empire in Two Years." *Financial Times,* March 6, 2003.

Friedman, Thomas L. "Smoking or Non-Smoking?" *New York Times,* September 14, 2001, p. A27.

———. "Our War with France." *New York Times,* September 18, 2003, p. A27.

———. "War of Ideas, Part 6." *New York Times,* January 25, 2004, p. A15.

Harding, James, and Peter Spiegel. "US National Security: 'Bush Has Been Forced to Moderate His Rhetoric, but He Has Yet to Come to Grips with a Clear Policy on China.'" *Financial Times,* October 17, 2003, p. 13.

Higgins, Andrew. "Democracy Deferred: Reform in Russia: Free Market, Yes; Free Politics, Maybe." *Wall Street Journal,* May 24, 2004, p. 1.

Hoagland, Jim. "In Europe, the Enemy Within." *Washington Post,* February 26, 2004, p. A21.

Hunt, Albert R. "What Might Have Been." *Wall Street Journal,* December 4, 2003.

Jehl, Douglas. "C.I.A. Chief Says He's Corrected Cheney Privately." *New York Times,* March 10, 2004.

Kifner, John. "Britain Tried First. Iraq Was No Picnic Then." *New York Times Week in Review,* July 20, 2003.

Kissinger, Henry A. "Repairing the Atlantic Alliance." *Washington Post,* April 14, 2003, p. A17.

Leland, John. "Tensions in a Michigan City over Muslims' Call to Prayer." *New York Times,* May 5, 2004, p. A16.

Loeb, Vernon. "'Guerrilla' War Acknowledged." *Washington Post,* July 17, 2003.

Mann, James. "Larger than Iraq: The True Rationale? It's a Decade Old." *Washington Post,* March 7, 2004.

Milbank, Dana, and Mike Allen. "Bush Urges Commitment to Transform Mideast." *Washington Post,* November 7, 2003, p. A1.

Pfaff, William. "Inevitable Clashes Between Civilizations? Don't Believe It." *International Herald Tribune,* January 23, 1997.

Rice, Condoleezza. "Transforming the Middle East." *Washington Post,* August 7, 2003, p. A21.

Safire, William. "Putin's 'Creeping Coup.'" *New York Times,* February 9, 2004, p. A27.

Sanger, David. "A Seat of Honor Lost to Open Political Warfare." *New York Times,* May 21, 2004.

Schmidt, Susan. "Spreading Saudi Fundamentalism in U.S.: Network of Wahhabi Mosques, Schools, Web Sites Probed by FBI." *Washington Post,* October 2, 2003, p. 1.

Schmitt, Eric. "Wolfowitz Sees Challenges, and Vindication, in Iraq." *New York Times,* July 22, 2003.

Seib, Philip. " 'Olive Tree' Provides Guide to Globalization." *Dallas Morning News,* July 25, 1999.

Stephens, Philip. "Europe's Defence Plans Are Worth Fighting For." *Financial Times,* October 17, 2003, p. 15.

Williams, Daniel. "60 Bosnian Serb Officials Fired over War Suspect." *Washington Post,* July 1, 2004.

Wood, Nicholas. "NATO Expanding Kosovo Forces to Combat Violence." *New York Times,* March 19, 2004.

Wright, Robin. "Standing of Former Key U.S. Ally in Iraq Falls to New Low." *Washington Post,* May 21, 2004.

Web Sites

Bush, George W. Speech to the National Endowment for Democracy, November 6, 2003, www.whitehouse.gov.

Bush, George W. Speech in Istanbul, June 29, 2004, www.whitehouse.gov.

Lodge, Henry Cabot. Speech in Washington, D.C., August 12, 1919, www.firstworldwar.com.

ACKNOWLEDGMENTS

This is a book about ideas. Thus it falls into a category that is known in my business, not always respectfully, as a clip job, meaning it makes no pretense to originality of reporting or scholarship. My aim rather has been to explore major ideas of Western thought and recent geopolitical discourse in such a way as to show how they have fostered public policy debates in the post–Cold War era and how those debates in turn have driven events.

Ideas have consequences, as Richard M. Weaver famously declared, and I begin this passage of respect and appreciation by noting the thinkers whose work is explored in this volume, including those whose ideas I embrace as well as those whose thinking I reject, those of our distant cultural heritage as well as those of our contemporary world. They are all part of the Western yearning for knowledge—the Faustian drive to push into the outer realms of the universe, to use Spengler's construction—and together they breed what I must describe as a significant measure of humility—a product of my lifelong reverence for the West, the civilization bequeathed to us from our forebears.

As for those who contributed more directly to this volume, I must begin my expression of appreciation with Jack Merry, my brother, who read the manuscript in numerous iterations and offered invaluable guidance and counsel. His contribution actually began thirty-three years ago, as I was returning from military service in Germany and he was studying German history in graduate school. That's when he introduced me to Oswald Spengler, thus offering a powerful new prism through which to explore the essence of history. Robert E. Merry, my father, no longer possesses the eyesight that guided his painstaking critique of my previous book in manuscript form, but he listened attentively to every chapter and offered pungent insights throughout the process.

My editor at Simon & Schuster, Alice Mayhew, quickly grasped what I was trying to say with this volume and just as quickly identified ways to help me say it more effectively. Her colleague, Roger Labrie, provided valuable service by combing the manuscript for the kinds of lapses that can impede the reader's smooth journey through the pages. The editing process at Simon & Schuster was a pleasure throughout.

Neal B. Freeman and Alan Ehrenhalt read chapters as they emerged from the computer, deflecting me from faulty passages and steering me toward manifest improvements. Al Silverman helped get me started by offering his always generous assistance on the early chapters and the book proposal. And Philippa ("Flip") Brophy of Sterling Lord Literistic Inc. served wonderfully as agent for this project, demonstrating both an appreciation for the work's underlying concept and a resolve to see it placed in the right hands. While the ministrations of those noted here proved invaluable, they of course bear no responsibility for any faults embedded in the final product.

Bonnie Forrest, my assistant at Congressional Quarterly Inc., provided unstinting support in ways too numerous to enumerate. Internal support also came from the always cheerful Nell Benton and her CQ research team.

Among those whose encouragement helped fuel this project were Andrew Corty, my boss at Times Publishing Co. of St. Petersburg, Florida, and our new chairman, Paul Tash. Both personify the sterling corporate culture I have been privileged to be associated with for some eighteen years. Also supportive was David M. Smick, founder and publisher of *The International Economy,* in which portions of this work originally appeared.

Closer to home, words can't adequately convey my appreciation of Susan Pennington Merry, my wife and closest friend, who warms my consciousness daily with her wholesome love of life and her delight in the simple treasures of existence. As always, I received unwavering good cheer from the three Merry children, Rob, Johanna, and Stephanie, and from son-in-law John Derlega.

Finally, with sadness I recall the support and encouragement I received on this project from Steve Neal, in keeping with the support and encouragement he extended to me on every project of any kind since 1971. No one I ever knew had a wider knowledge of politics and history or a greater spirit of generosity in sharing his knowledge. Shortly after Alice Mayhew told me in her office one rainy January day that she would be bidding on my proposal, I returned to the wet pavements of Sixth Avenue below, ducked into a cab, pulled out my cell phone and dialed from memory the number of the man with whom I most wanted to share the news. I don't dial Steve's number anymore, but it will be forever etched in my consciousness, along with a multitude of recollections from our thirty-three-year friendship.

INDEX

ABOUT THE AUTHOR

ROBERT W. MERRY is president and publisher of Congressional Quarterly. Formerly a reporter for the *Wall Street Journal*, where he covered national politics, Congress, and the White House, he is the author of the award-winning *Taking On the World: Joseph and Stewart Alsop—Guardians of the American Century*. He lives in McLean, Virginia.

Printed in the United States
By Bookmasters